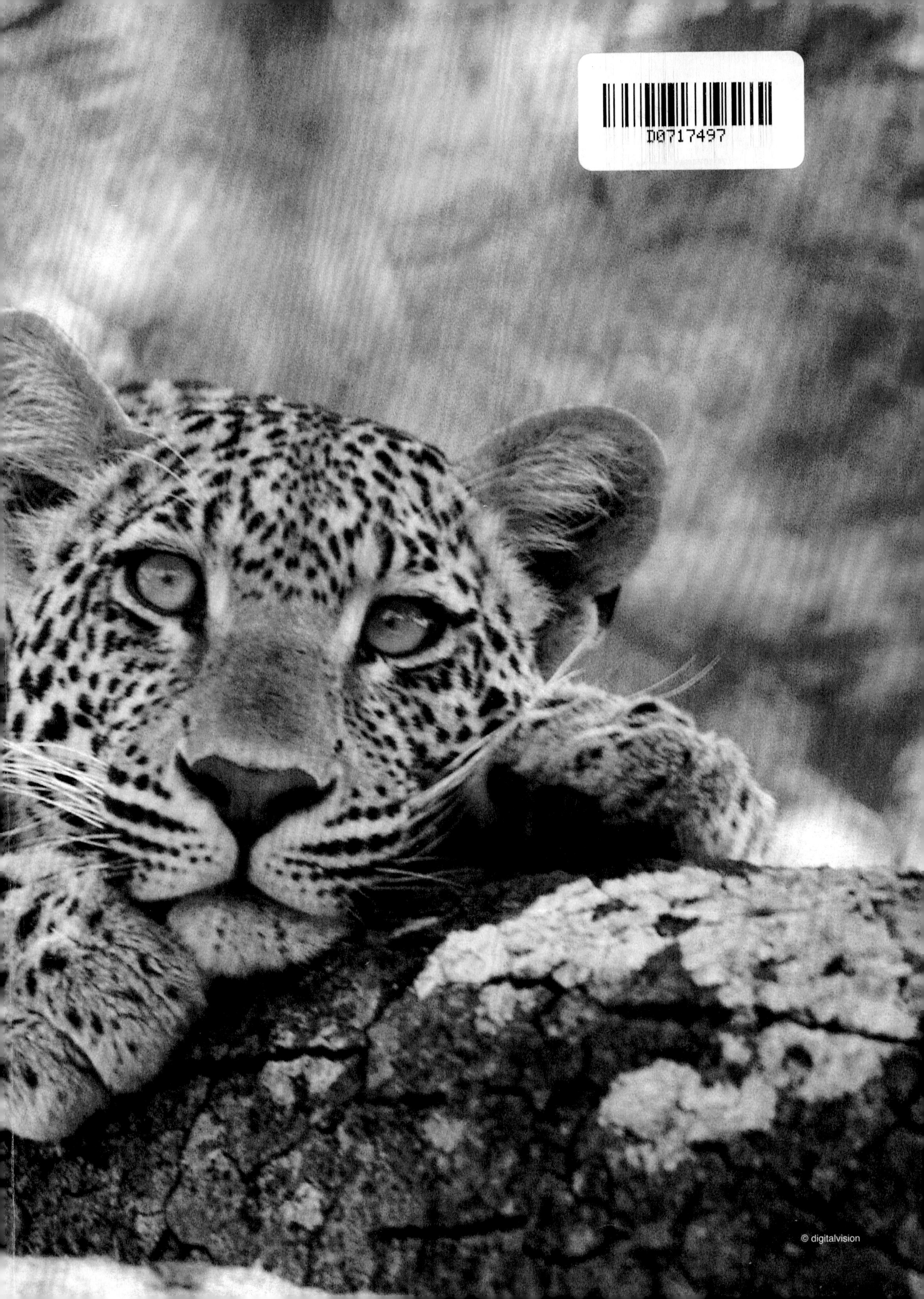

Look What's Inside!

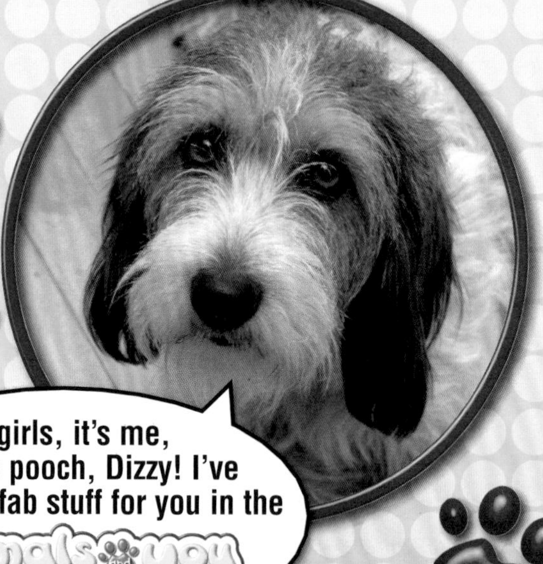

Hi, girls, it's me, your fave pooch, Dizzy! I've got loads of fab stuff for you in the Animals and you Annual!

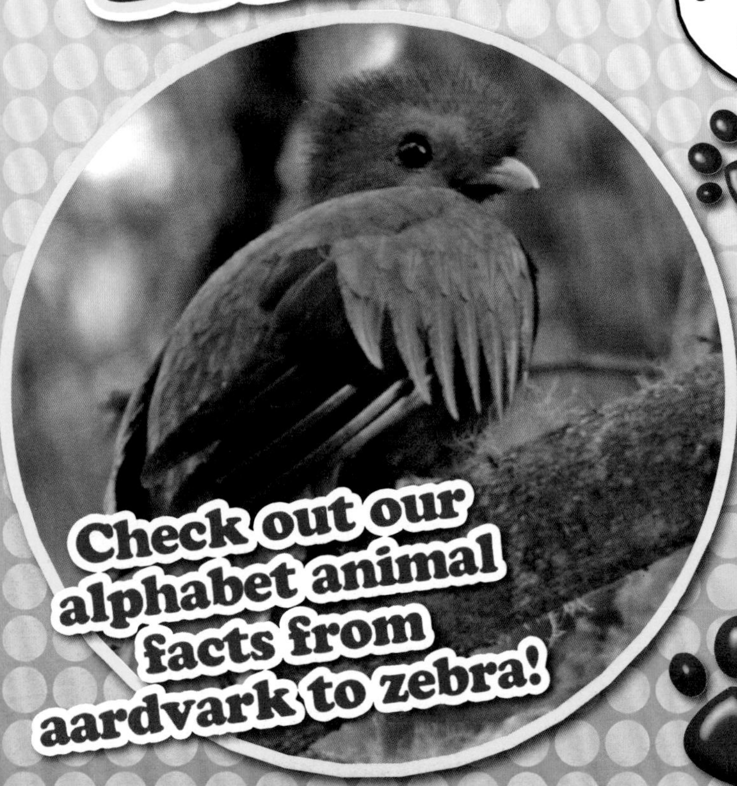

Check out our alphabet animal facts from aardvark to zebra!

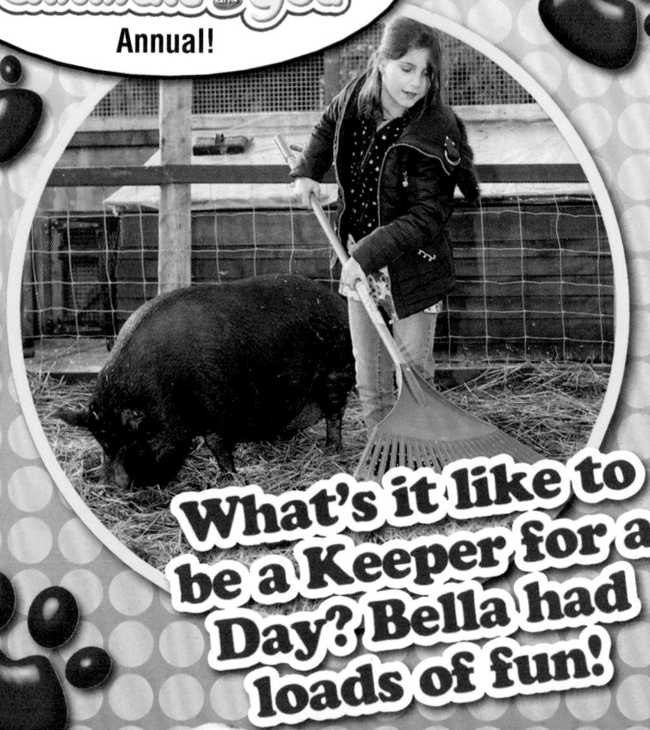

What's it like to be a Keeper for a Day? Bella had loads of fun!

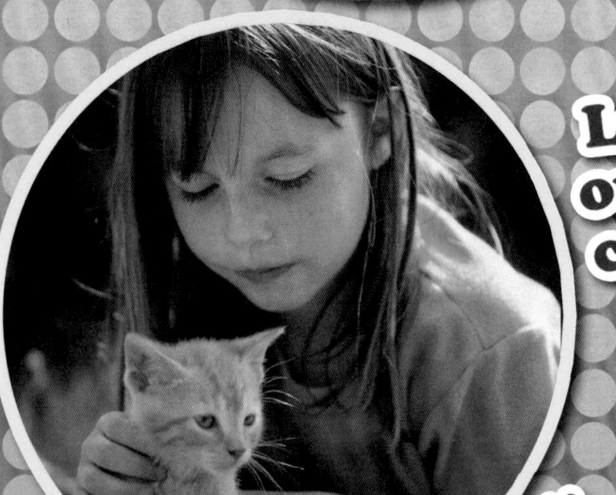

Choosing a pet!

Laugh at our crazy captions!

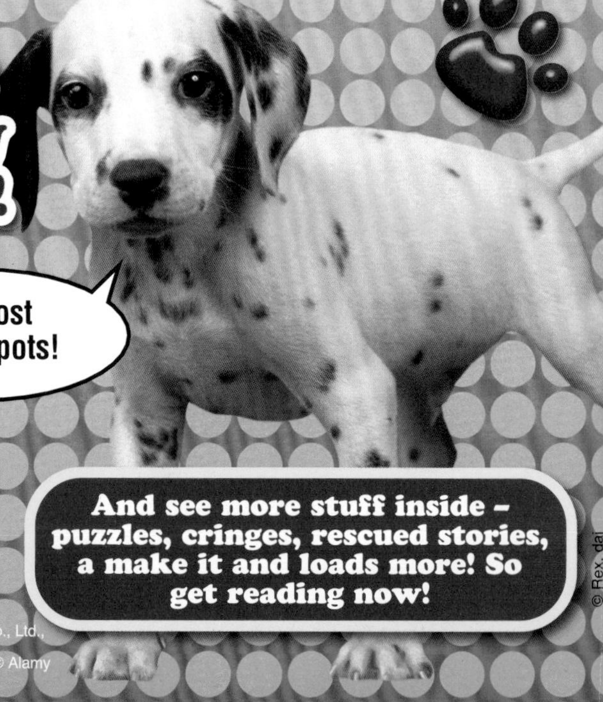

I've lost some spots!

And see more stuff inside – puzzles, cringes, rescued stories, a make it and loads more! So get reading now!

Printed and Published in Great Britain by D. C. Thomson & Co., Ltd.,185 Fleet Street, London, EC4A 2HS.

ABC animals

We've given you a cool creature for every letter of the alphabet! How many more can you come up with? (You might want to Google some of the weirder ones we've listed!!).

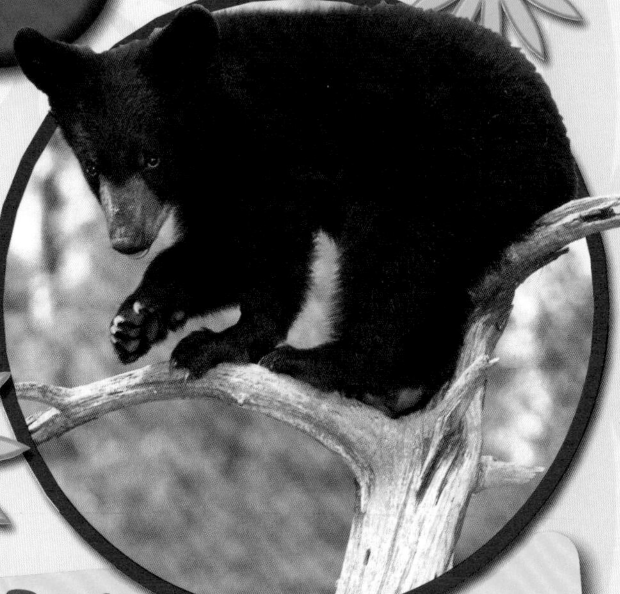

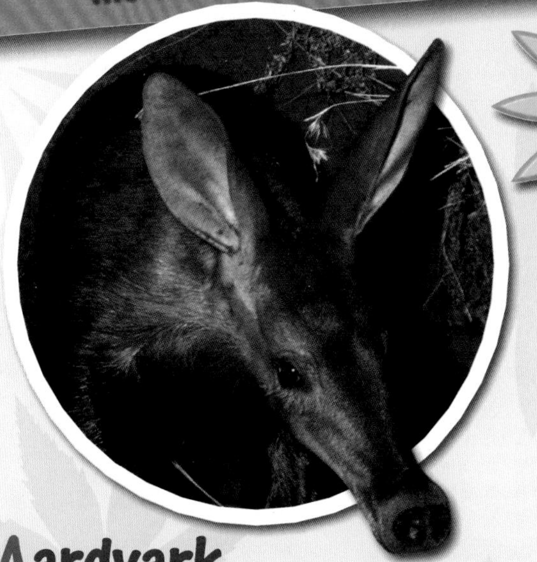

Brown Bear

You'll mainly find these in North America. They can go six months without eating, drinking or going to the loo(!), but love to use their big paws to catch salmon for tea!

Beaver, Bush Baby, Blue-footed booby

Aardvark

This crazy-looking creature's name means 'earth pig'. It lives in Africa and munches termites, using its long snout to suck them out of their mounds.

Armadillo, Antelope, Aye-aye

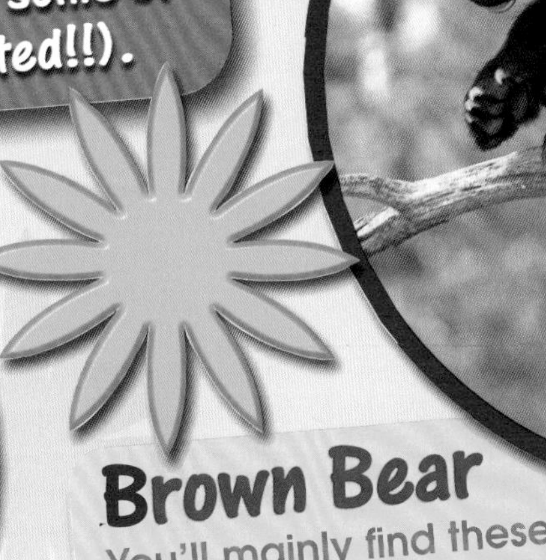

Chimpanzee

These cheeky *apes* (not monkeys!) are mainly veggie and are great at DIY! Chimps use twigs as tools to build cosy nests to sleep in at night!

Capybara, Crocodile, Coyote

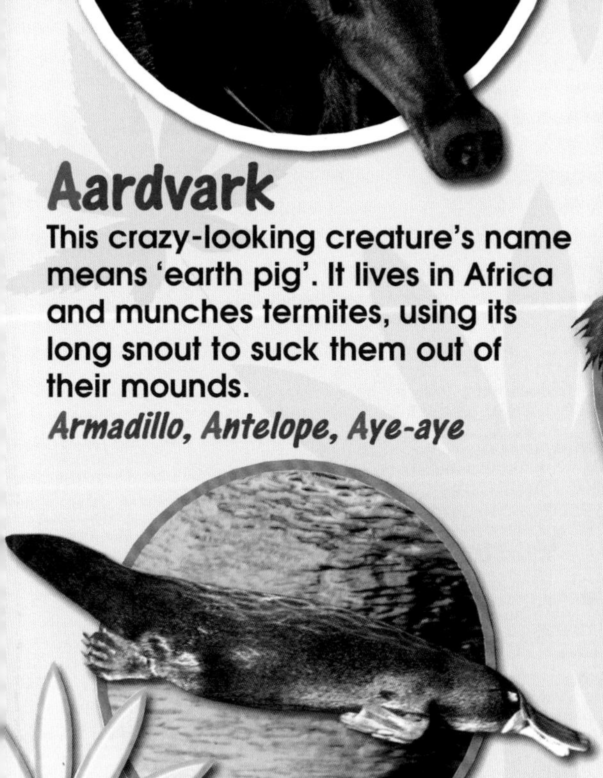

Duck-billed Platypus

Platypus is Greek for 'flat feet' and their flat webbed feet make them brilliant swimmers! Males have a poisonous claw on their ankle for fighting — ouch!

Dolphin, Dormouse, Dik-dik

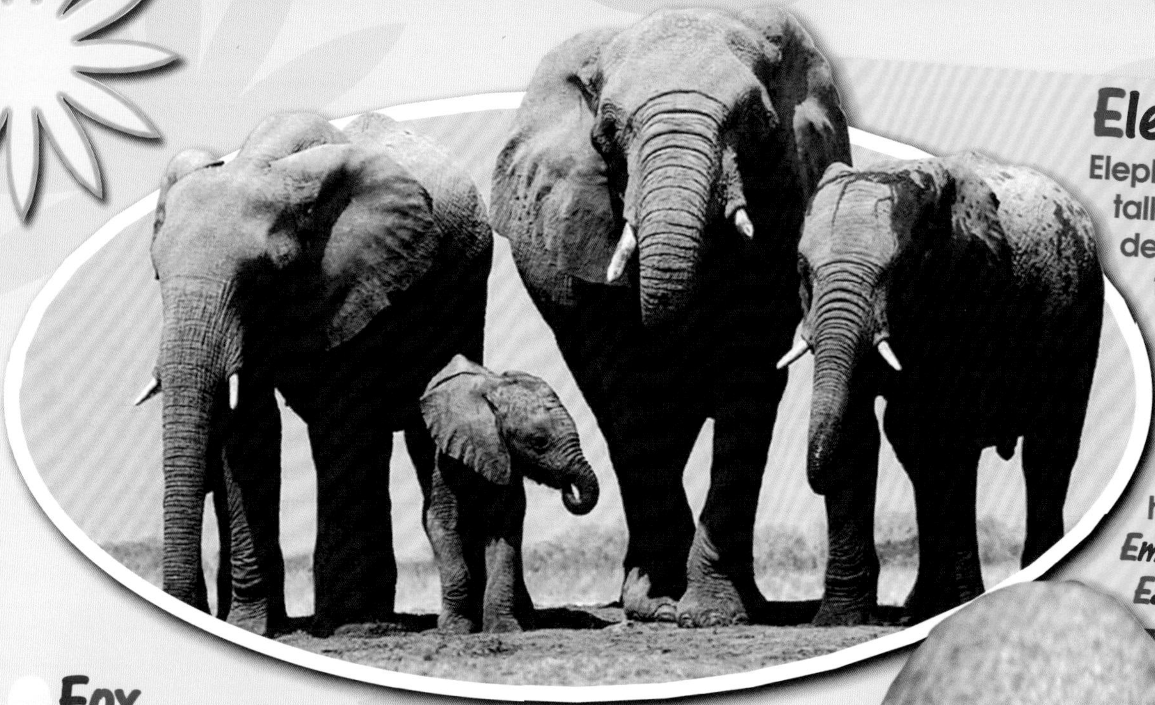

Elephant

Elephants can be as tall as a double-decker bus — now that's *tall*! They chat to each other by making low growling noises which humans can't hear!

Emperor Penguin, Eagle, Electric Eel

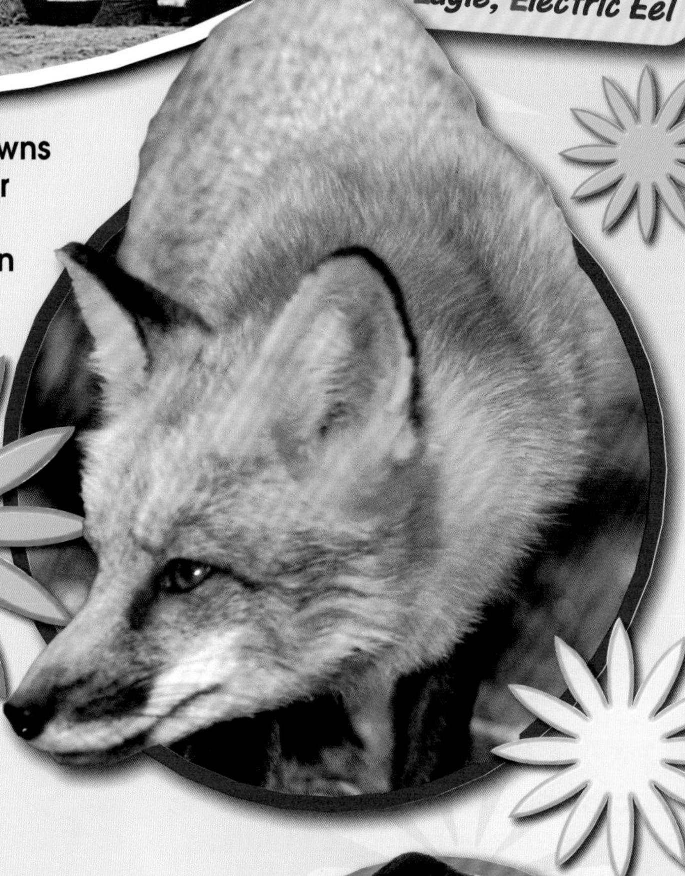

Fox

Foxes can live almost anywhere and love towns and cities where they munch on our left-over food! Fox cubs are born with blue eyes and chocolate-coloured fur which changes when they're about a month old.

Flamingo, Frog, Flying Lemur

Gorilla

These gentle giants live in groups and spend ages grooming each other. You'll know if a gorilla's mad at you cos it'll stand upright and roar while beating its chest. Yikes!

Giraffe, Gecko, Great White Shark

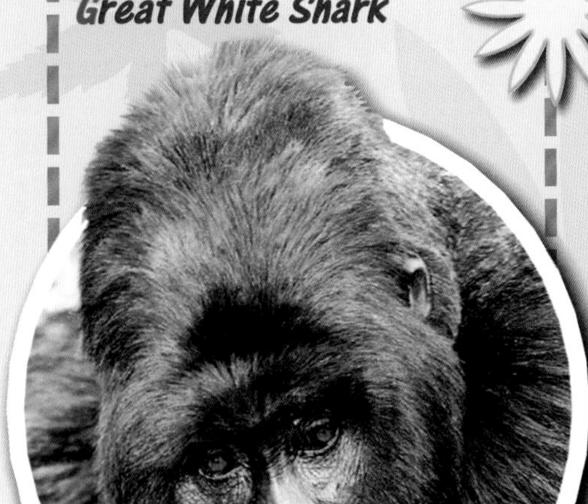

Hyena

These cackling creatures are clever hunters and scavengers (which means they feed on animals killed by other predators). As well as a distinctive giggle, they have powerful jaws and teeth.

Hedgehog, Hippo, Hammerhead Shark

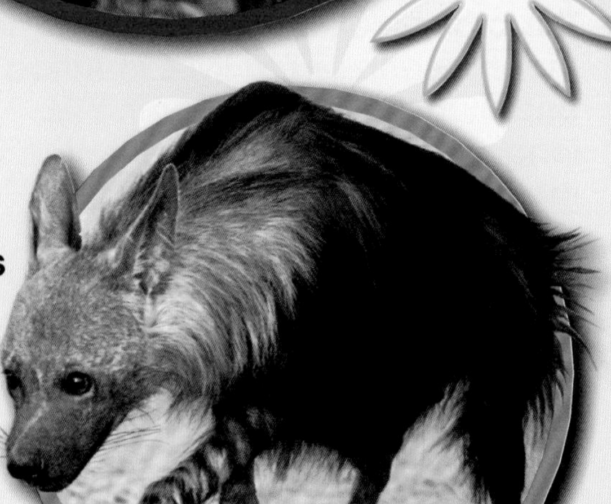

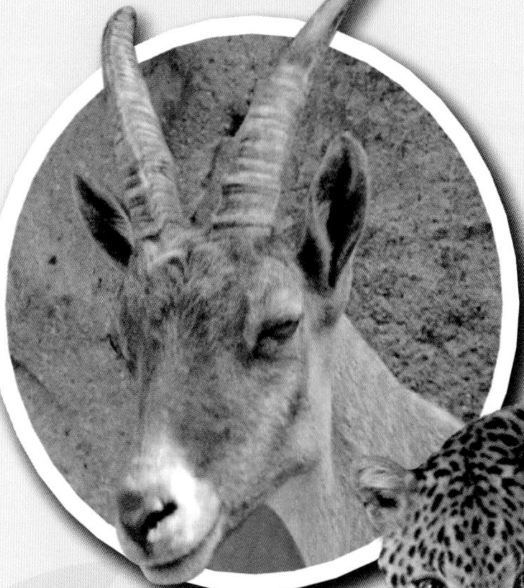

Ibex

Ibexes are wild mountain goats. They can climb higher than any other mammal! Males use their huge horns to fight each other to become leader.

Impala, Indian Elephant

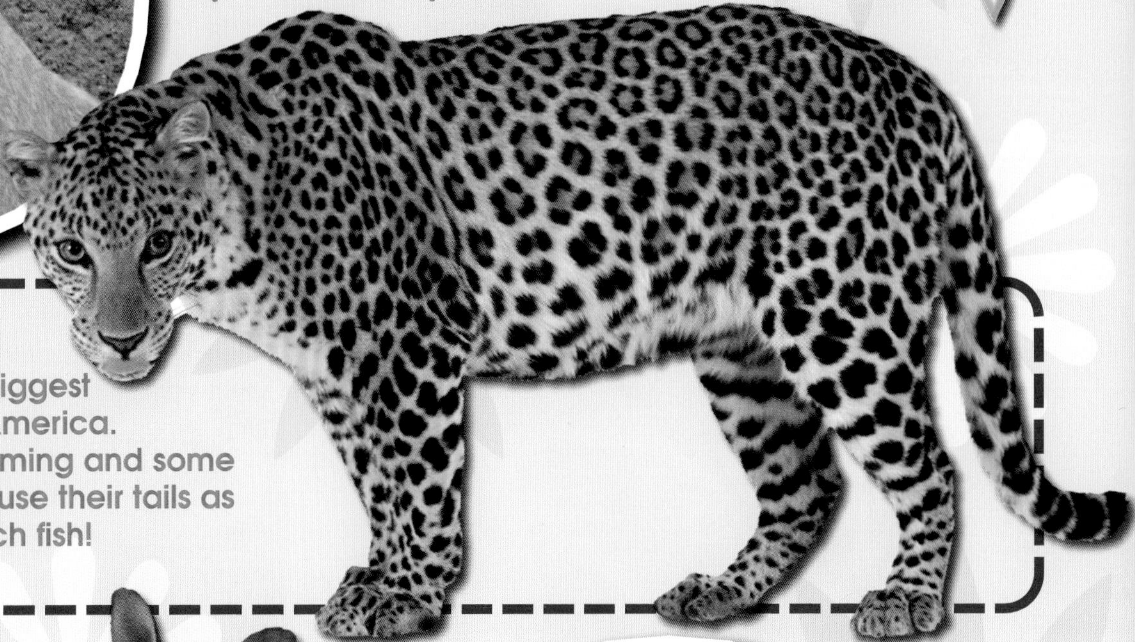

Jaguar

The jaguar is the biggest wild cat in South America. Jaguars love swimming and some people think they use their tails as fishing rods to catch fish!

Jackal, Jellyfish

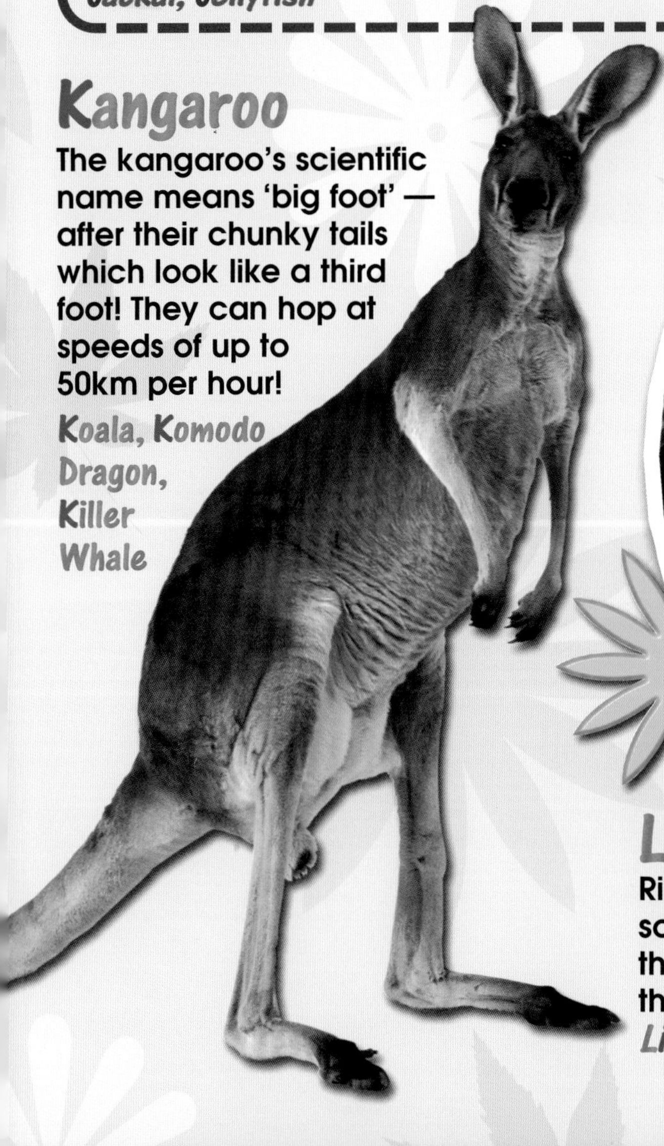

Kangaroo

The kangaroo's scientific name means 'big foot' — after their chunky tails which look like a third foot! They can hop at speeds of up to 50km per hour!

Koala, Komodo Dragon, Killer Whale

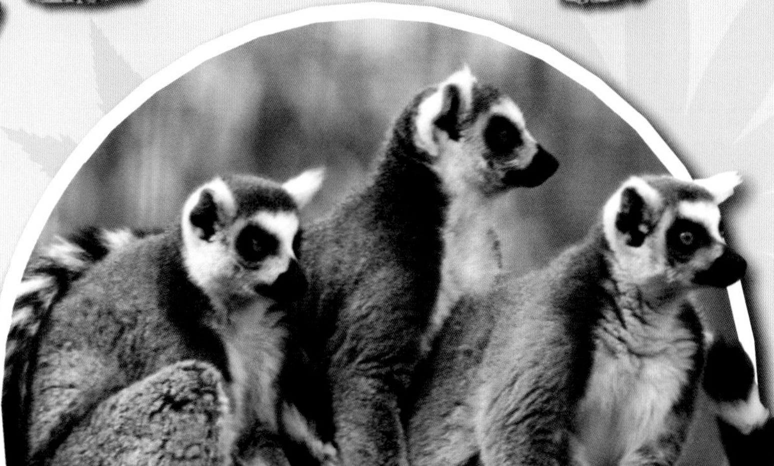

Lemur

Ring-tailed lemurs live in groups called troops. They sometimes hold stink fights over territory by rubbing the scent glands on their tails then waving them at their enemies — pheew!

Lion, Leopard, Lynx

Continued on page 66

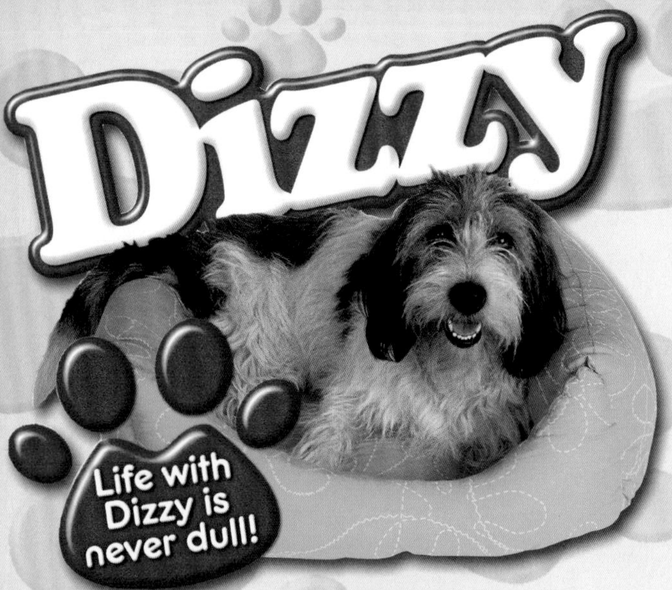
Dizzy
Life with Dizzy is never dull!

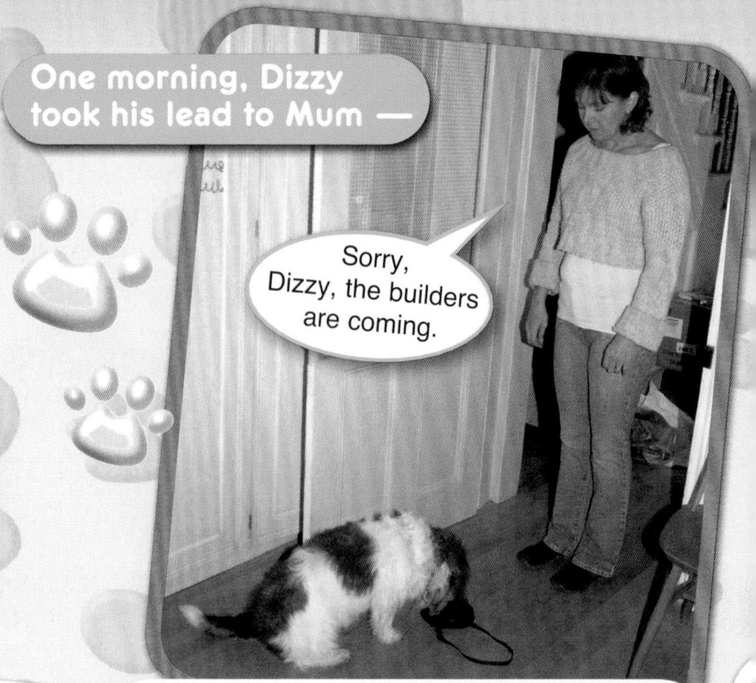
One morning, Dizzy took his lead to Mum —
Sorry, Dizzy, the builders are coming.

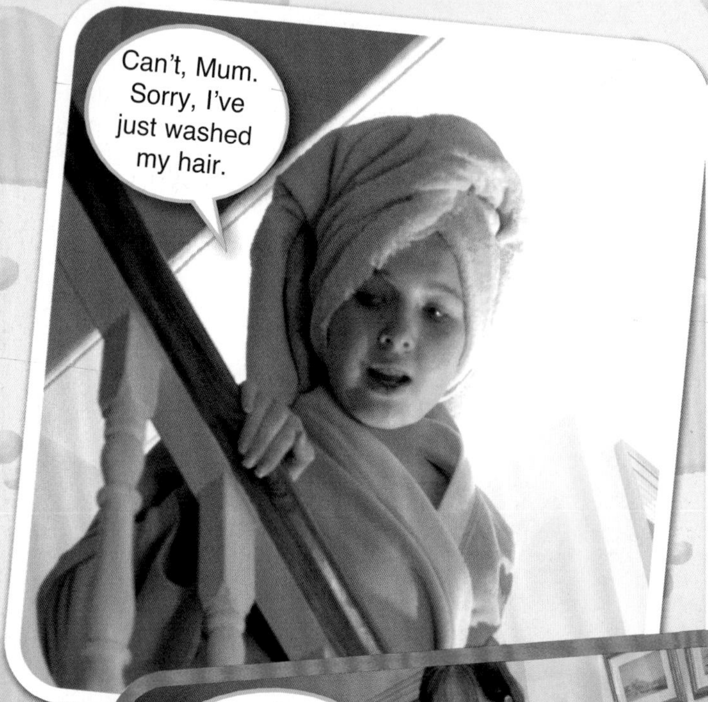
Can't, Mum. Sorry, I've just washed my hair.

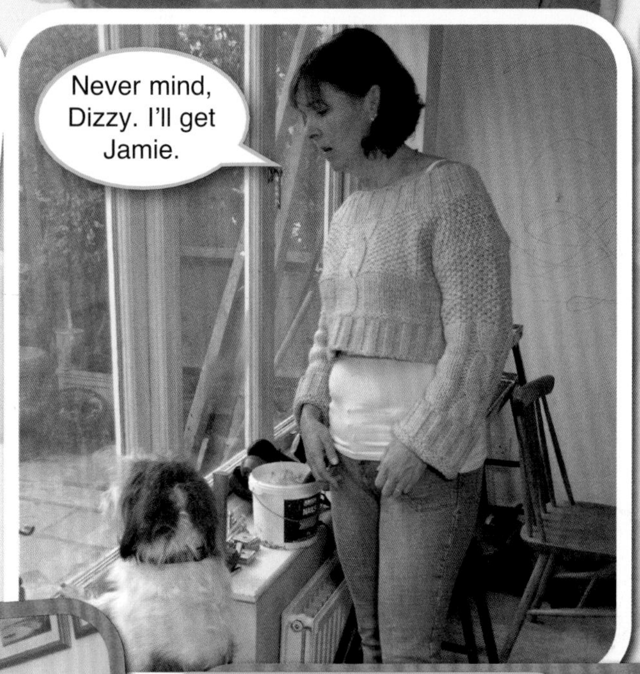
Never mind, Dizzy. I'll get Jamie.

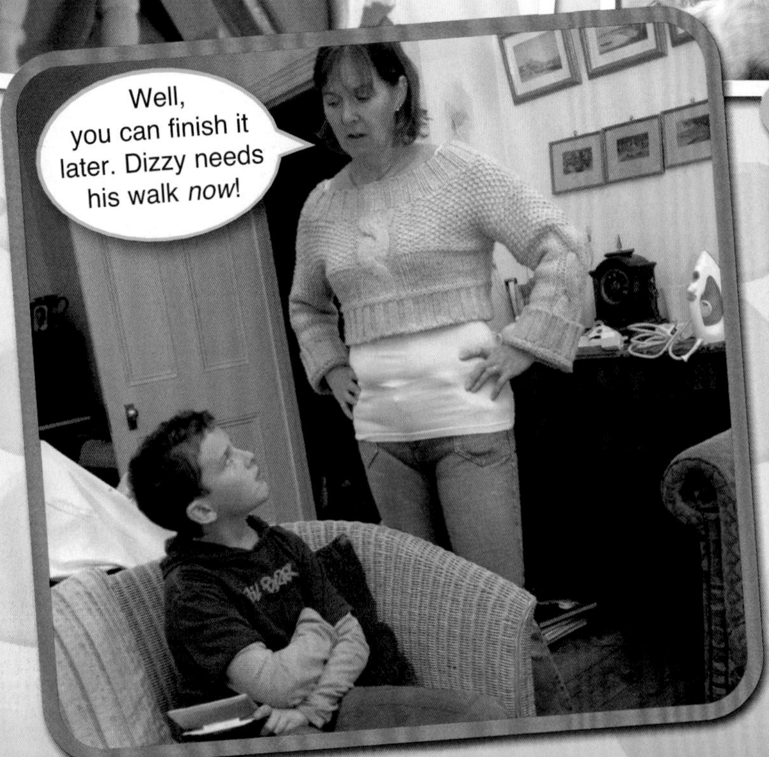
Well, you can finish it later. Dizzy needs his walk *now*!

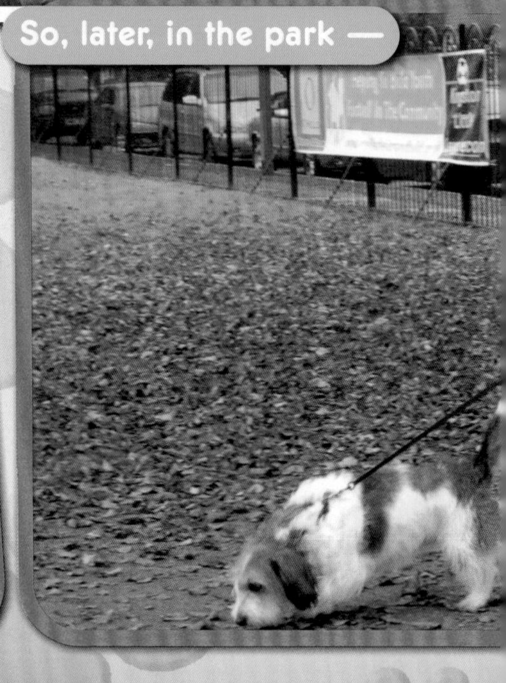
So, later, in the park —

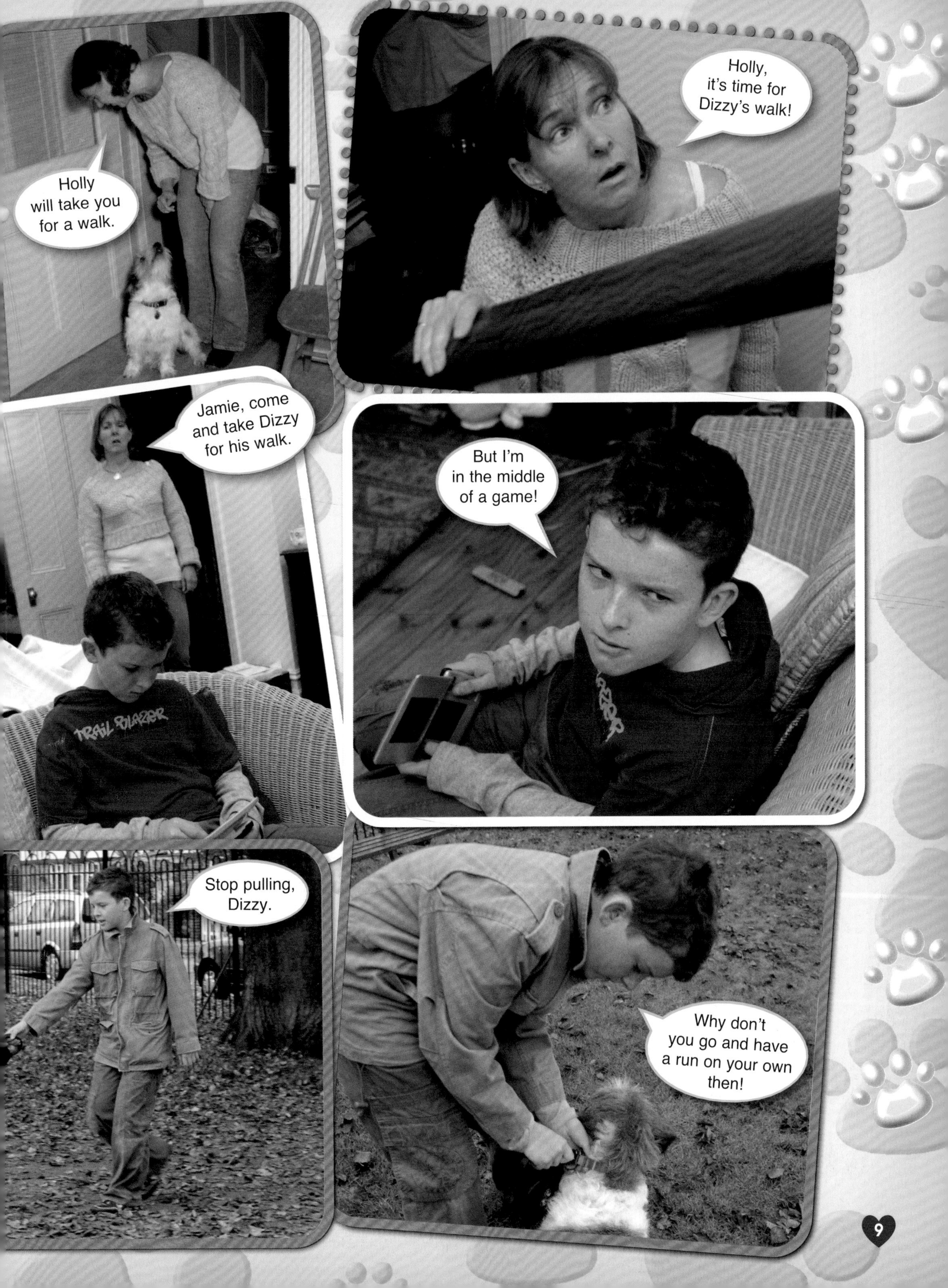
Holly will take you for a walk.
Holly, it's time for Dizzy's walk!
Jamie, come and take Dizzy for his walk.
But I'm in the middle of a game!
Stop pulling, Dizzy.
Why don't you go and have a run on your own then!

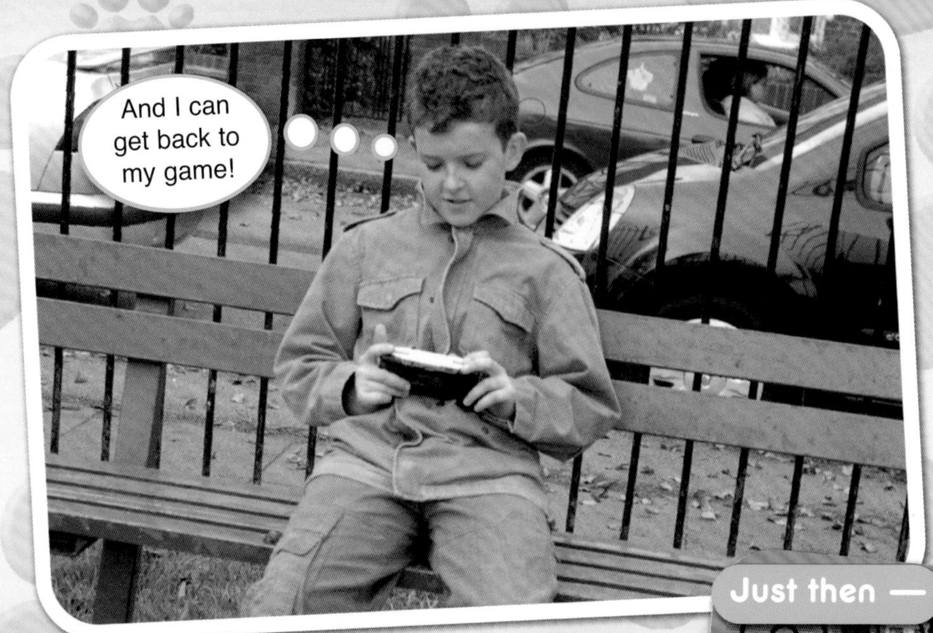
And I can get back to my game!

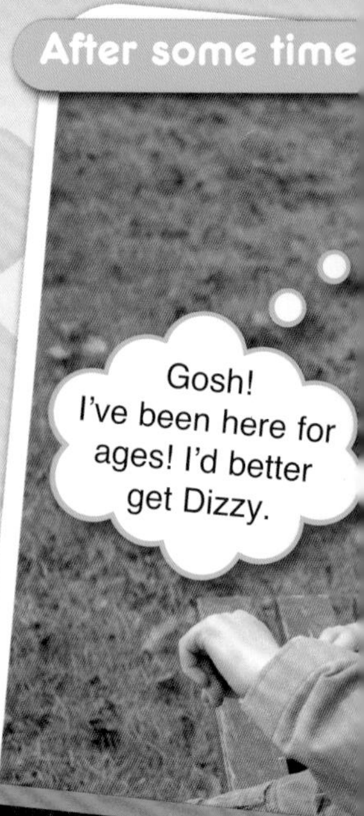
After some time
Gosh! I've been here for ages! I'd better get Dizzy.

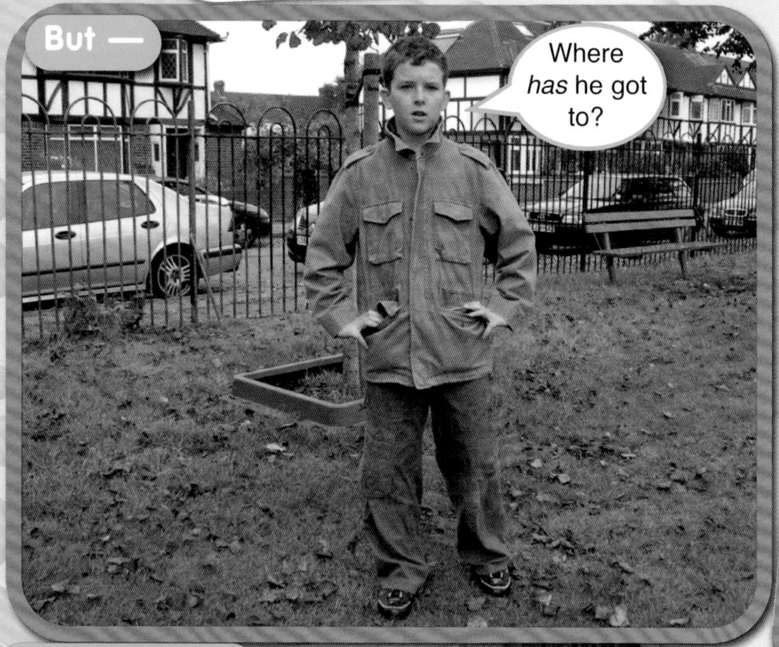
But —
Where *has* he got to?

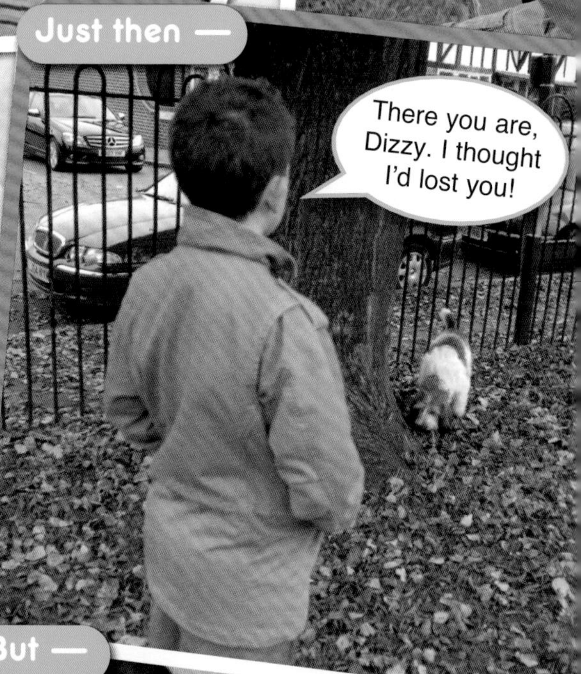
Just then —
There you are, Dizzy. I thought I'd lost you!

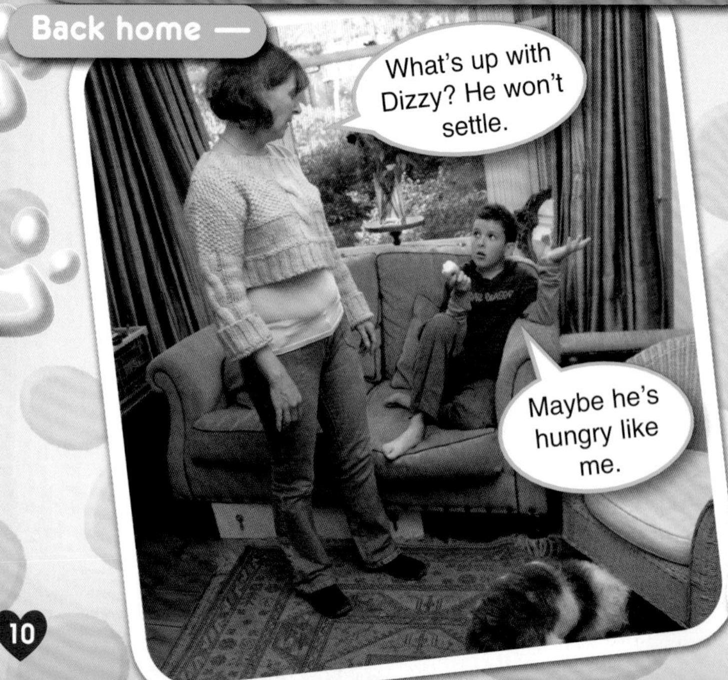
Back home —
What's up with Dizzy? He won't settle.
Maybe he's hungry like me.

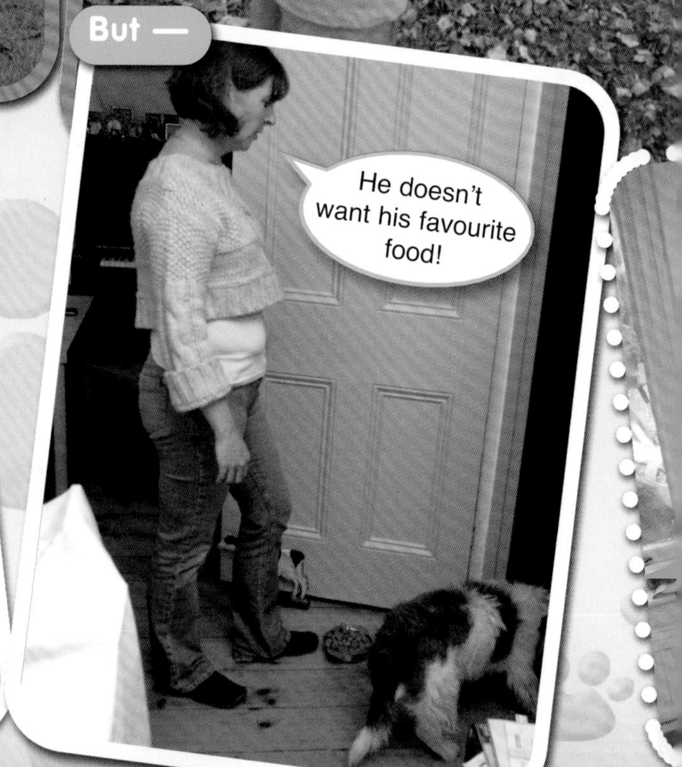
But —
He doesn't want his favourite food!

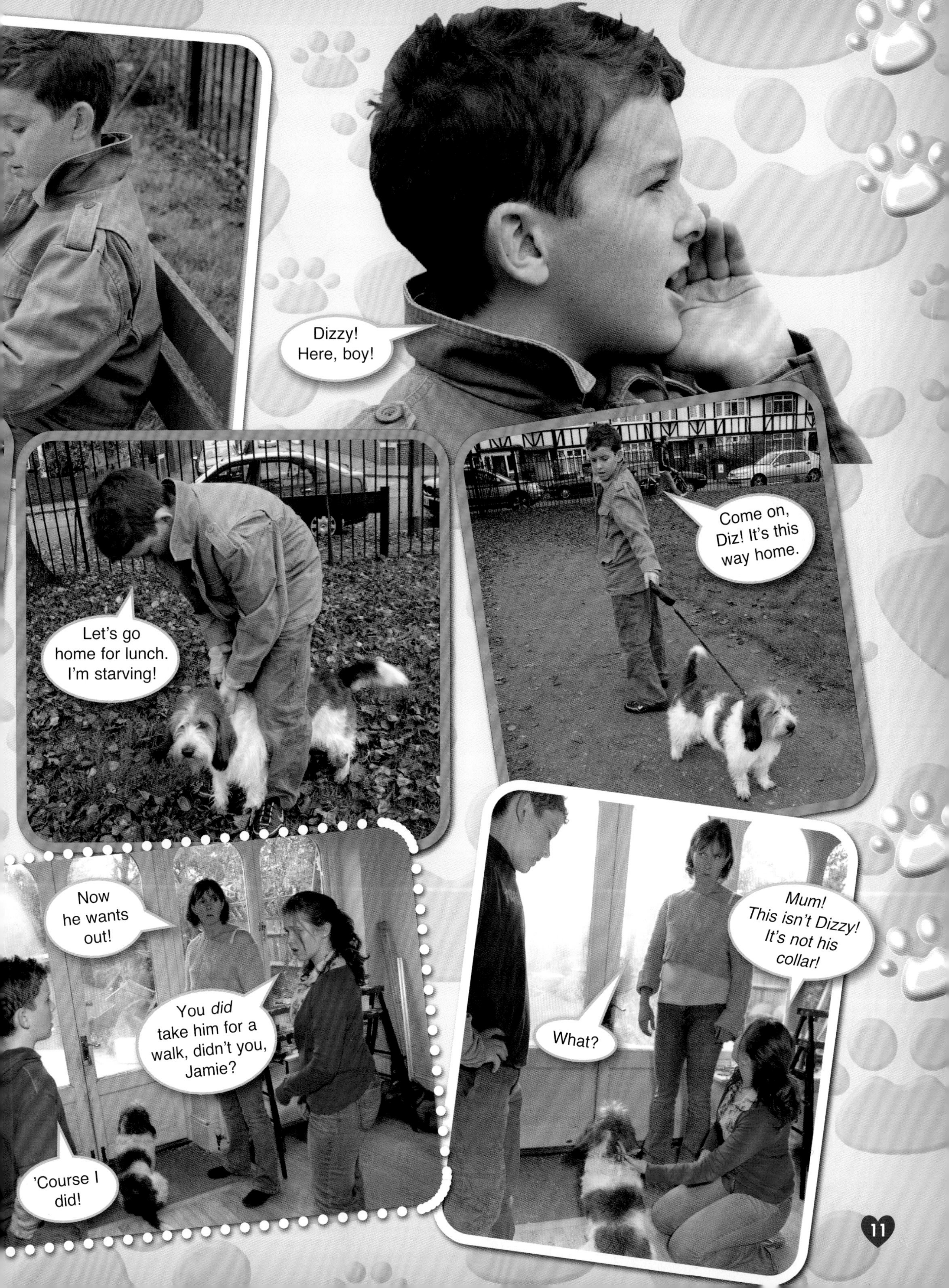
Dizzy! Here, boy!
Let's go home for lunch. I'm starving!
Come on, Diz! It's this way home.
Now he wants out!
You *did* take him for a walk, didn't you, Jamie?
'Course I did!
Mum! This isn't Dizzy! It's not his collar!
What?

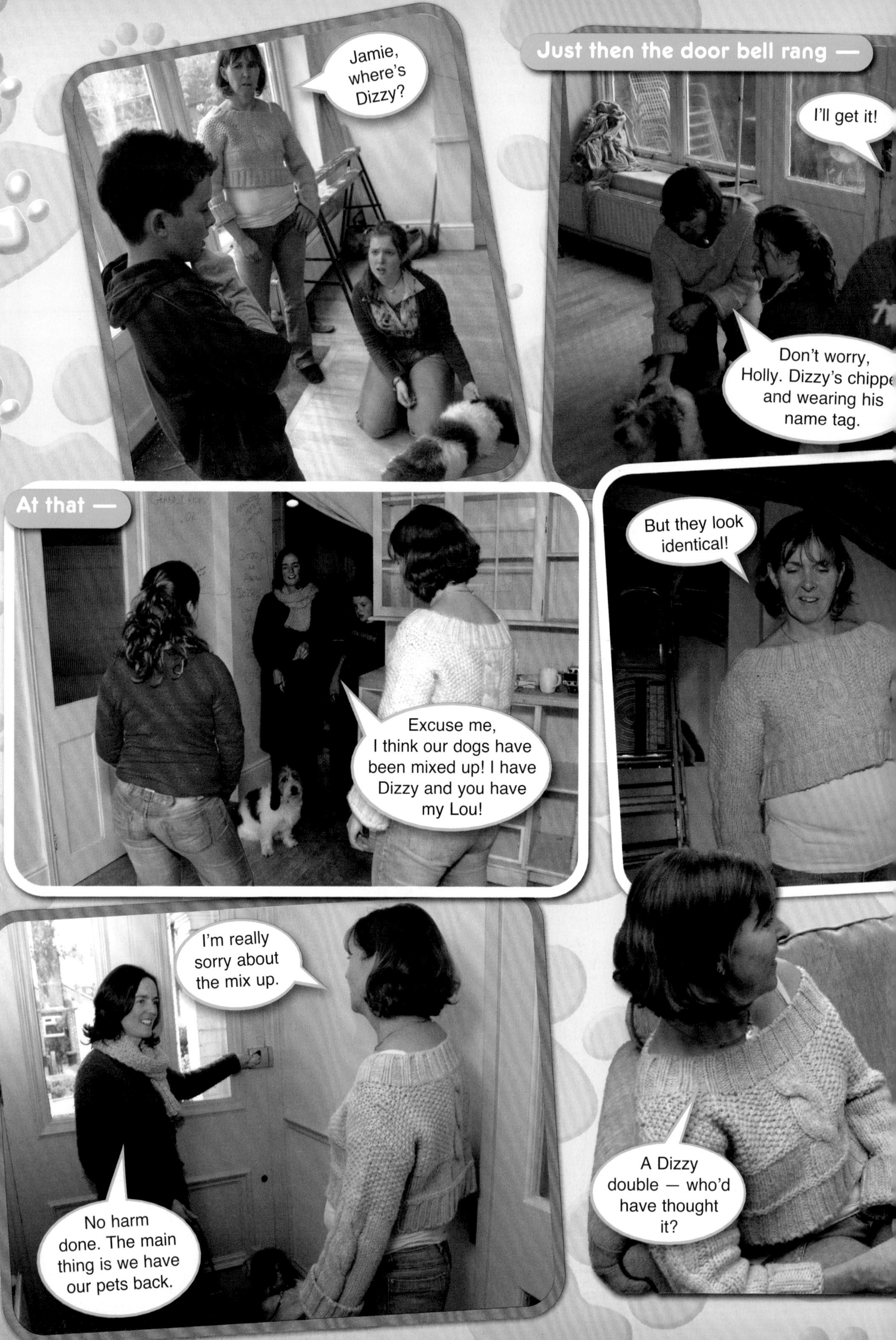

Jamie, where's Dizzy?
Just then the door bell rang —
I'll get it!
Don't worry, Holly. Dizzy's chippe and wearing his name tag.
At that —
Excuse me, I think our dogs have been mixed up! I have Dizzy and you have my Lou!
But they look identical!
I'm really sorry about the mix up.
No harm done. The main thing is we have our pets back.
A Dizzy double — who'd have thought it?

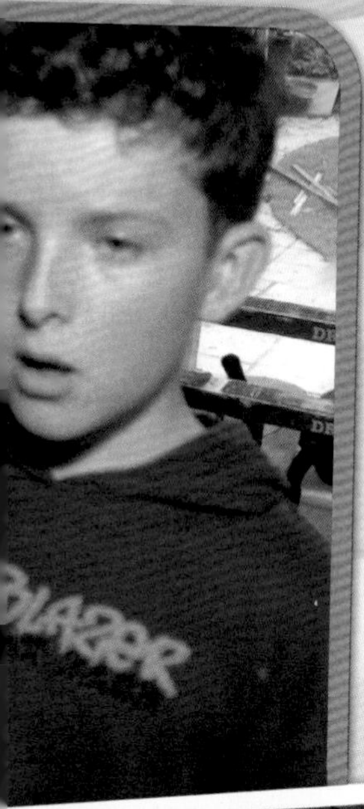

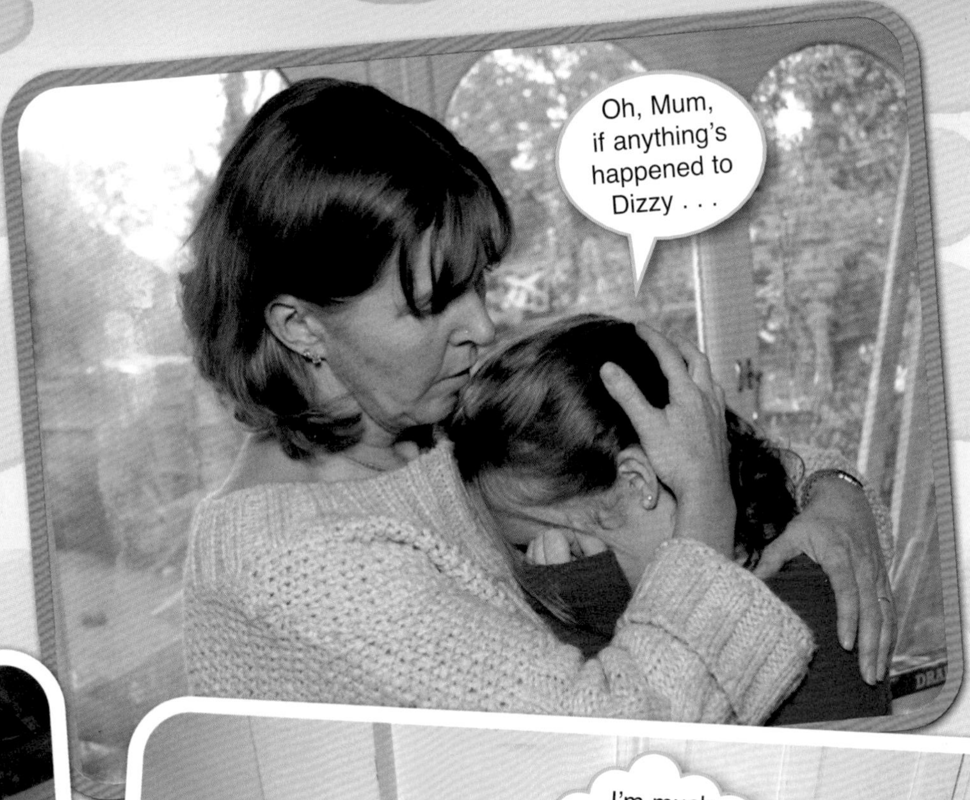
Oh, Mum, if anything's happened to Dizzy . . .

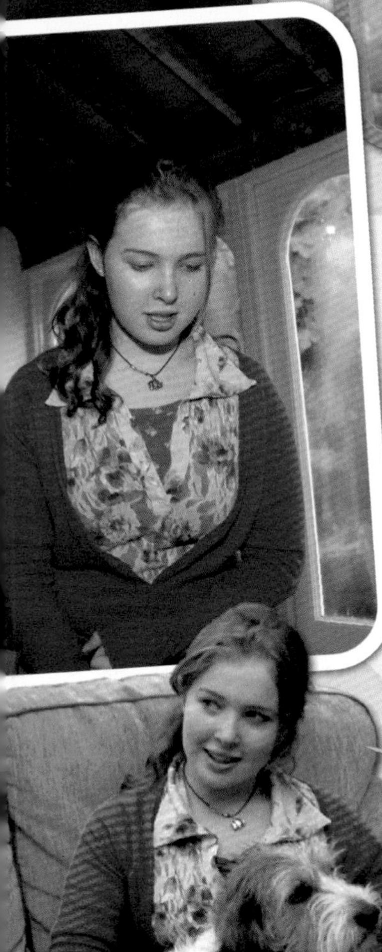

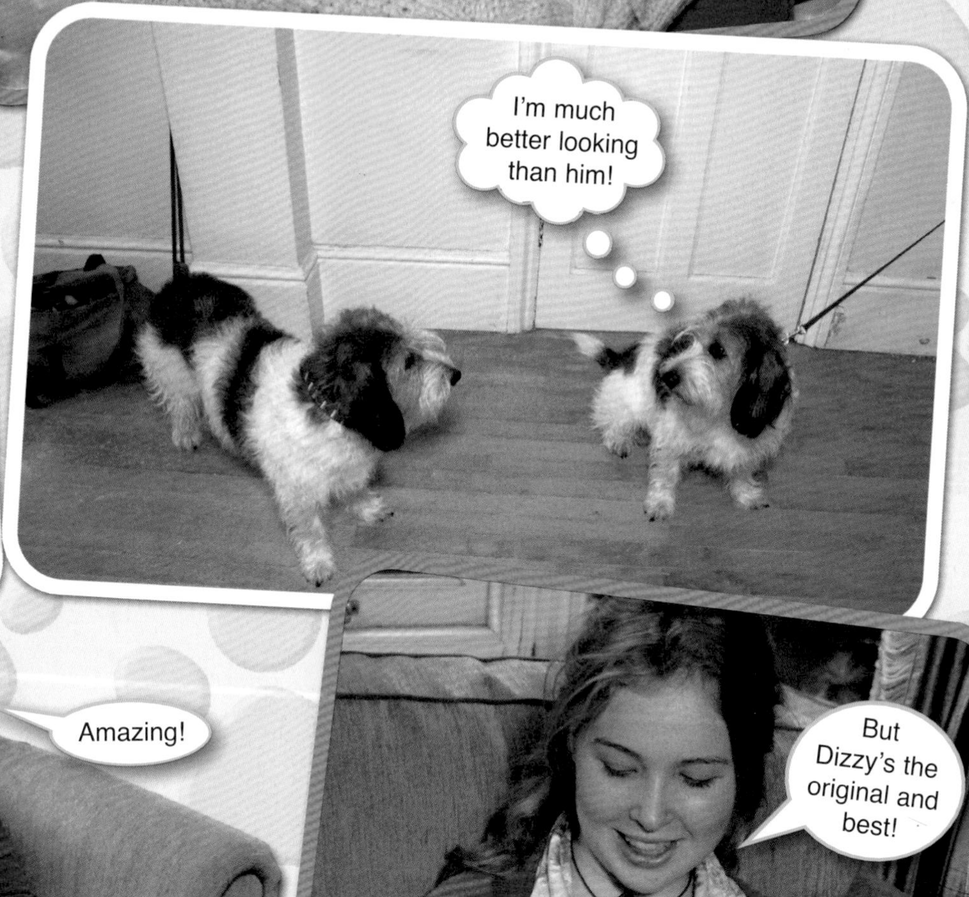
I'm much better looking than him!

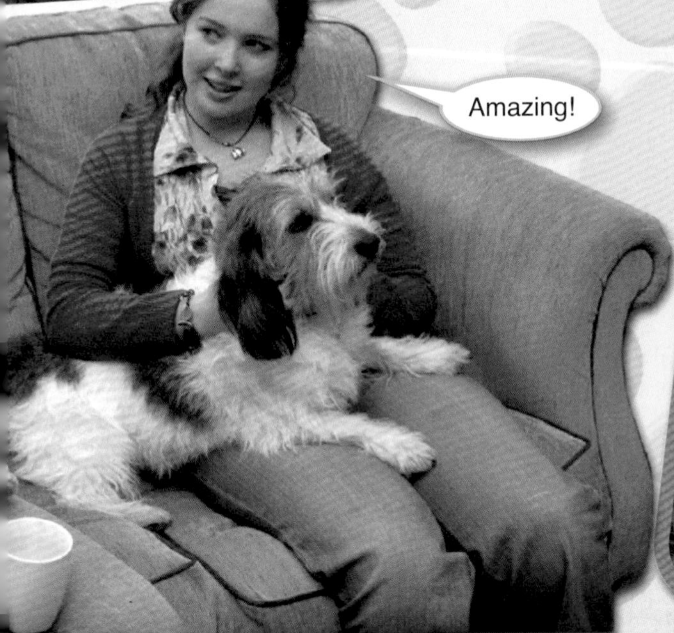
Amazing!

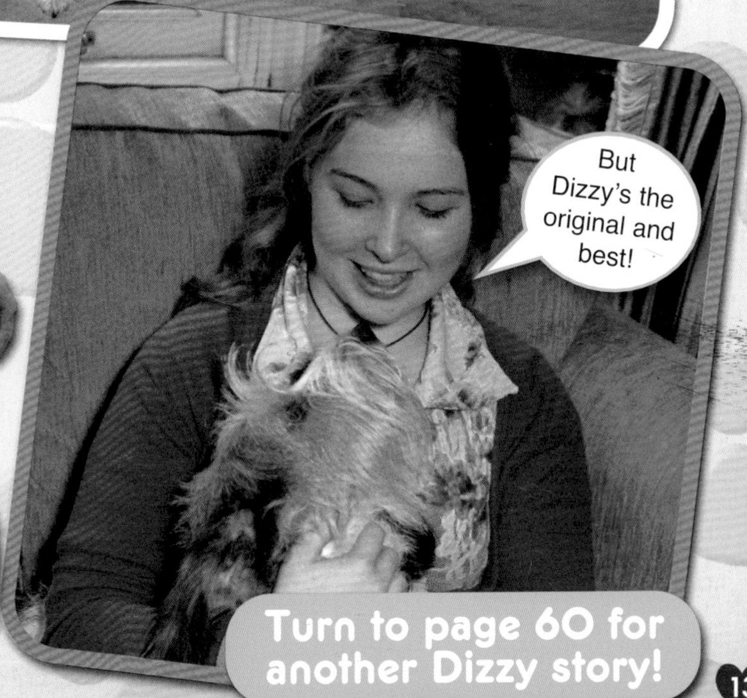
But Dizzy's the original and best!

Turn to page 60 for another Dizzy story!

Rescued!

Meet Dumpling, Suet and Muffin, three sweet donkeys rescued by The Donkey Sanctuary!

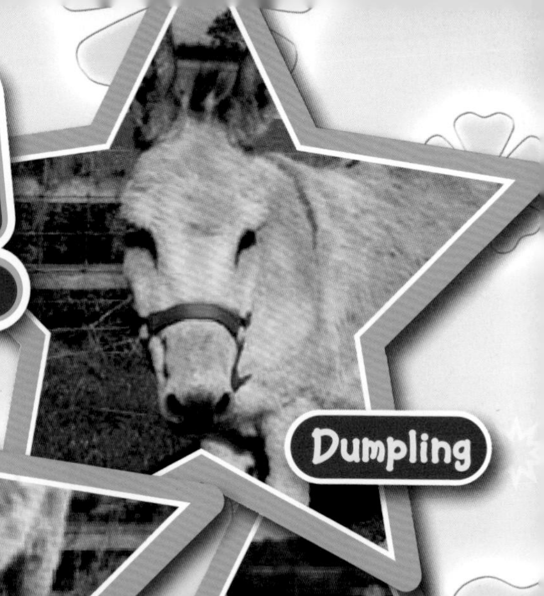
Dumpling

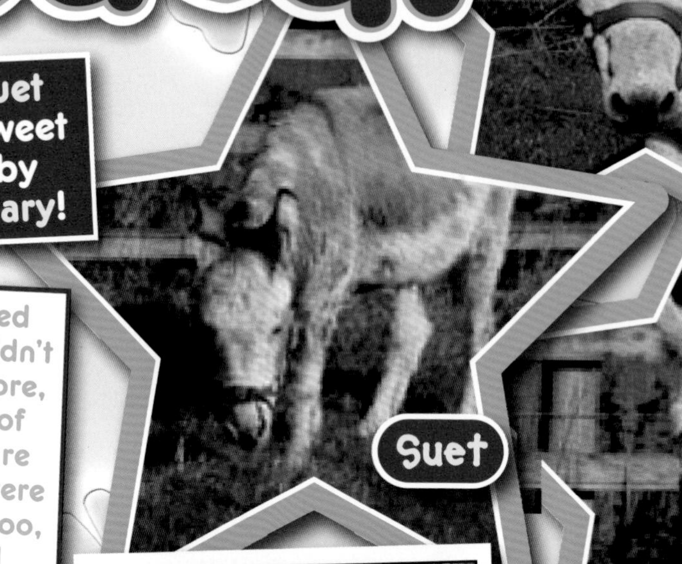
Suet

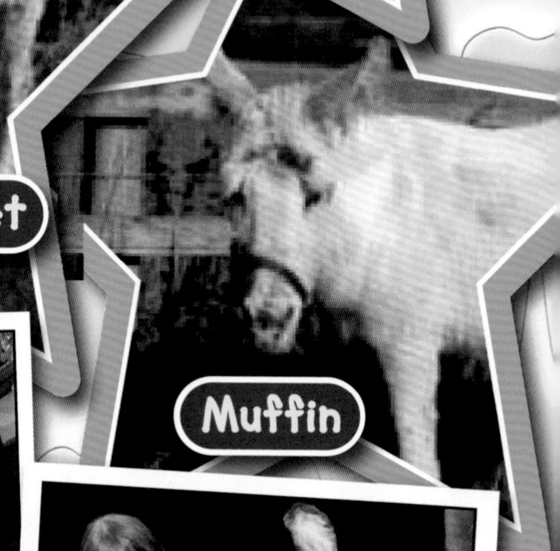
Muffin

1 When they were rescued from an owner who couldn't take care of them anymore, **Dumpling** was in a lot of pain and needed vet care straight away. Her feet were in very poor condition, too, but the farrier worked wonders reshaping them. **Suet** had to have a tooth removed as it was growing into the side of her cheek. **Muffin** was treated for lice and minor injuries.

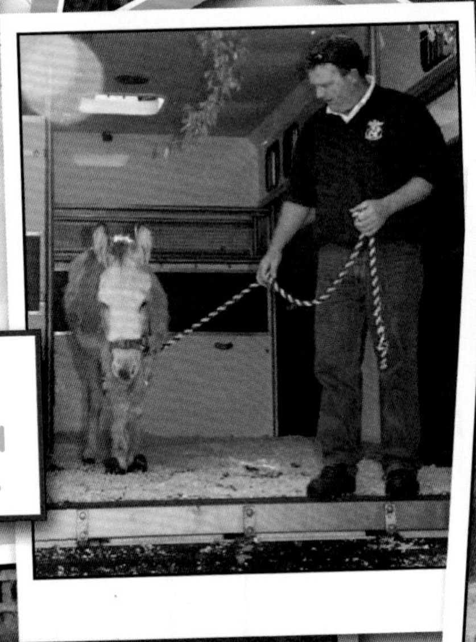

2 After a few weeks of vet treatment, the donkeys were moved to the home of **Sue** and **Ron Sharples** who live nearby.

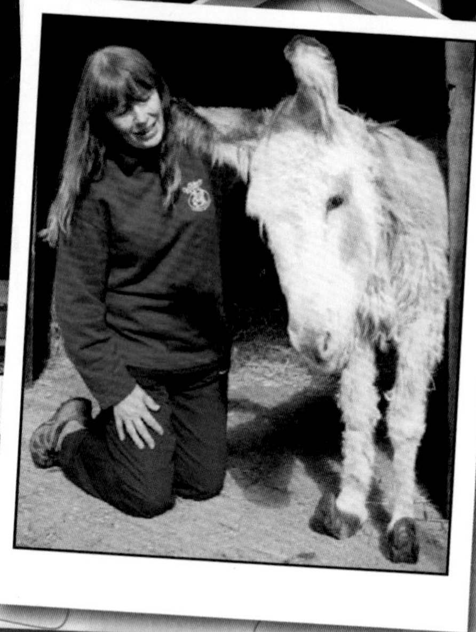

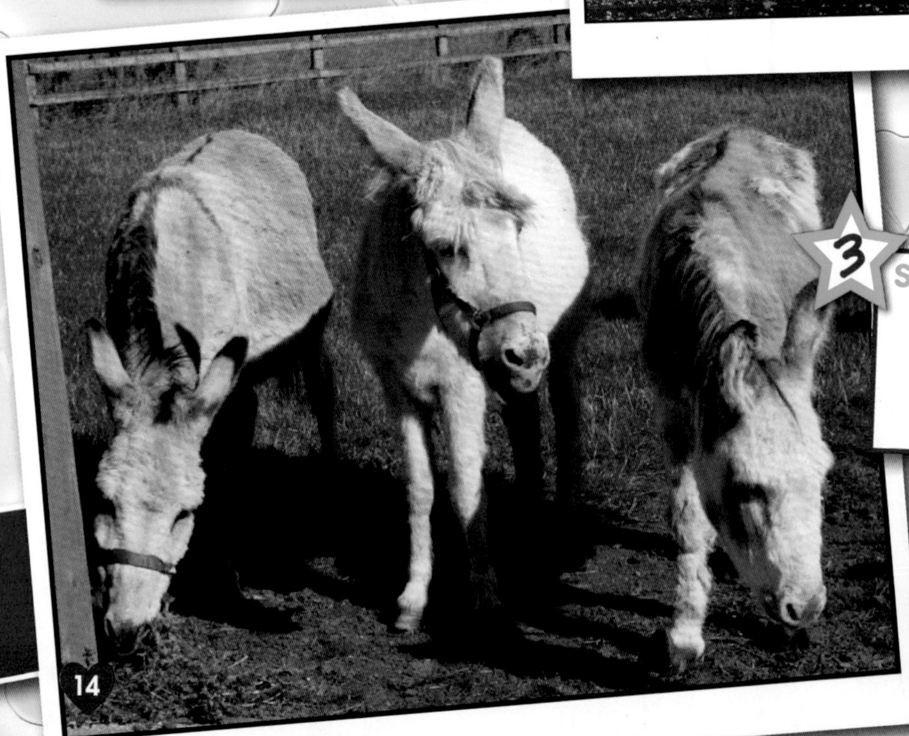

3 Sue and Ron looked after the donkeys until they were well enough to be moved to the **Sidmouth Sanctuary** where they'll receive all the **TLC** (**T**ender **L**oving **C**are) they'll need!

Visit www.thedonkeysanctuary.org.uk for more info.

Dizzy's Challenge – Spots V Stripes

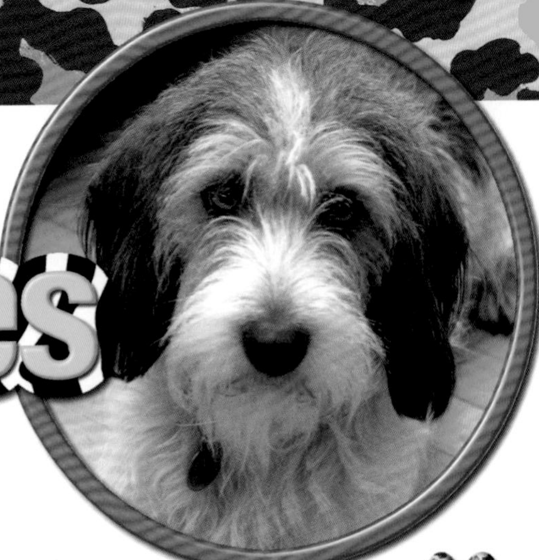

Do you know which cool creatures have SPOTS and which have STRIPES? Check out the clues below and tick the correct boxes.

1. You might find me when crossing a road! _ _ _ _ _

2. There are 101 of these in a film! _ _ _ _ _ _ _ _ _ _

3. These are on my tail only. See me on page 24. _ _ _ _ _ _ _ _ _ _ _ _ _ _ _ _ _

4. I'm pretty purrr-fect! _ _ _ _ _ _ _

5. I'm a bit smelly! _ _ _ _ _

6. I'm a bird you'll see in your garden. _ _ _ _ _ _

7. Unscramble the letters to find my name. COOLET

8. I'm sometimes known as sabre-toothed! _ _ _ _ _

Answers: 1. Zebra/stripes, 2. Dalmatians/spots, 3. Ring tailed lemur/stripes, 4. Leopard/spots, 5. Skunk/stripes, 6. Thrush/spots, 7. Ocelot/spots, 8. Tiger/stripes.

Otterly Cute!

Find out the facts on otters!

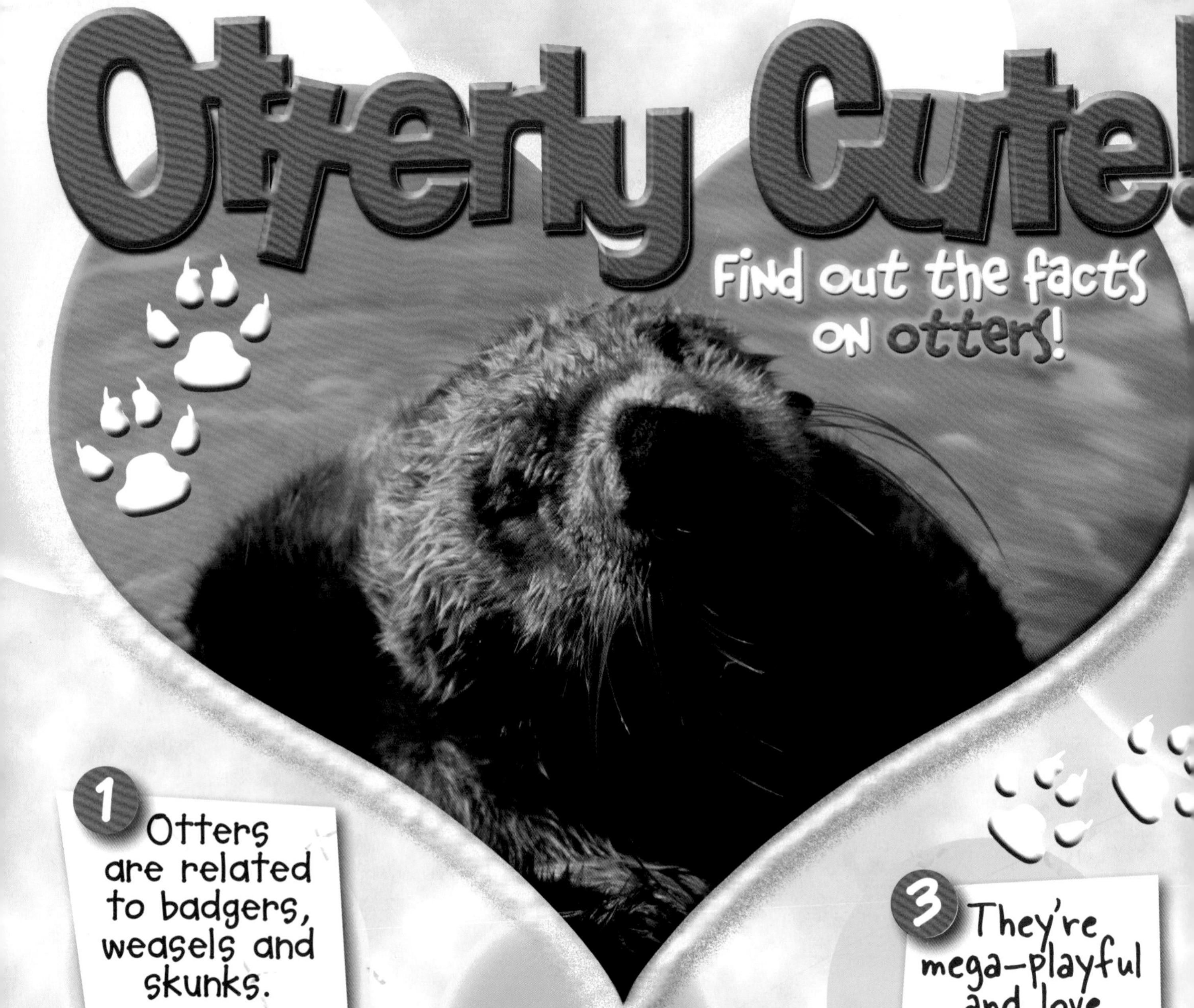

1 Otters are related to badgers, weasels and skunks.

2 They can live for up to 10 years.

3 They're mega-playful and love sliding down muddy river banks!

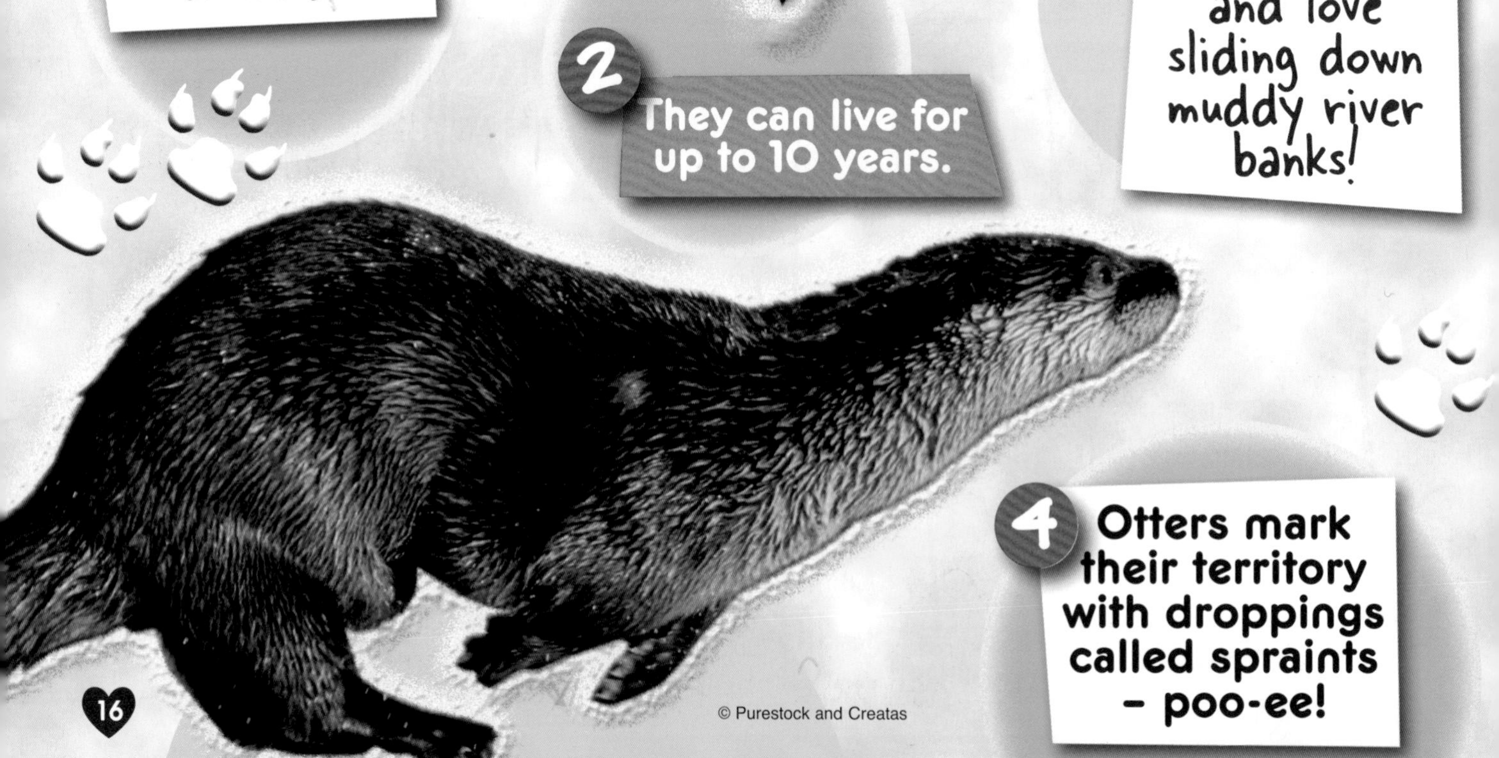

4 Otters mark their territory with droppings called spraints – poo-ee!

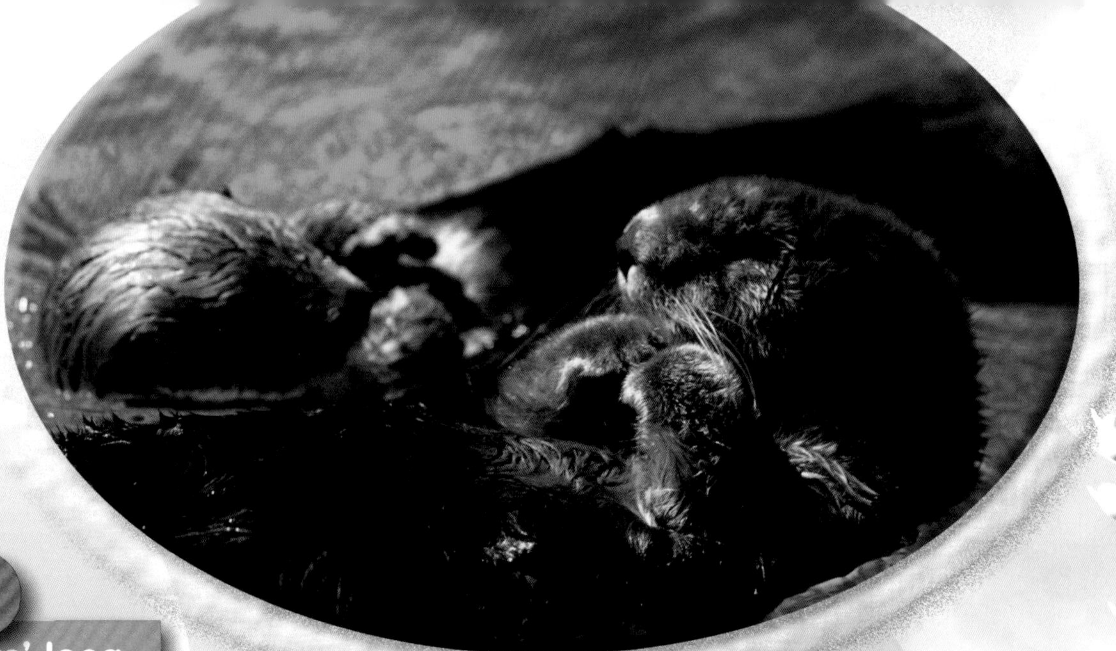

5
Otters' long whiskers help them catch their food by sensing the movements of frogs and fish underwater.

6
They're super-speedy swimmers cos of their strong tails and webbed feet.

7
Otters mainly come out at night. In daytime they usually stay in their cosy dens which are called holts.

8
They have 2–3 babies, called cubs, at a time. Cubs are born blind and stay in the holt with their mum for the first few weeks.

9
They can close their ears and noses under water!

10
Otters have become extinct in some areas and numbers of these cute creatures are still falling. They're strictly protected by the Wildlife And Countryside Act.

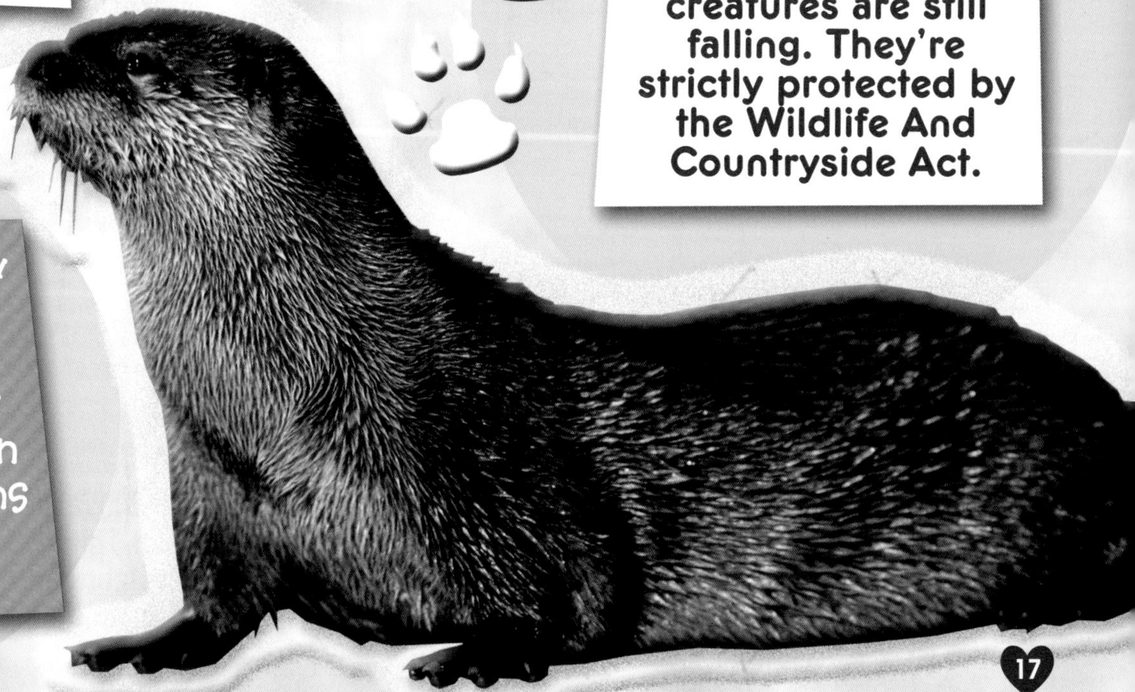

Wanna Help Endangered Animals?

Adopting an animal can be your way of helping animals that are in danger of becoming extinct. Here are a few to choose from –

Elephant

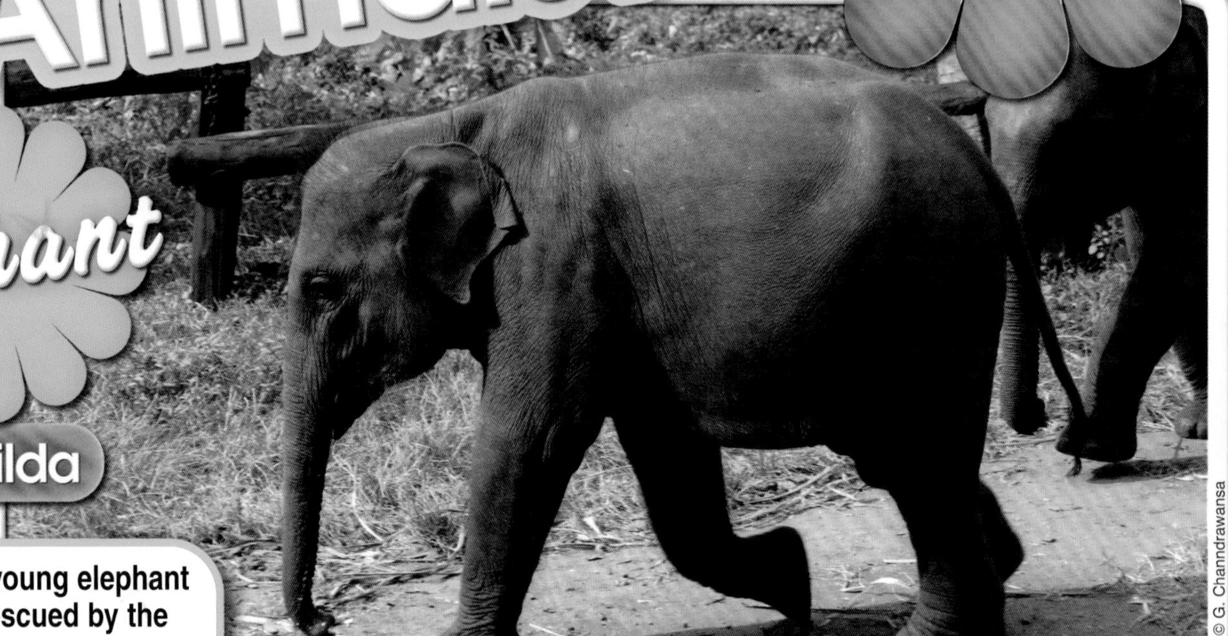

© G. Channdrawansa

Matilda

Matilda is a young elephant who was rescued by the Born Free Foundation. She was found exhausted and hungry, roaming with a herd of water buffalo after she lost her mother.

Adopt an animal with Born Free and you'll help give the care and protection each animal needs. Adopters receive a great gift pack including a framed photo of your animal, adoption papers with your animal's story plus regular news updates. For more info go to

www.bornfree.org.uk/give/adopt-an-animal/

Dolphin

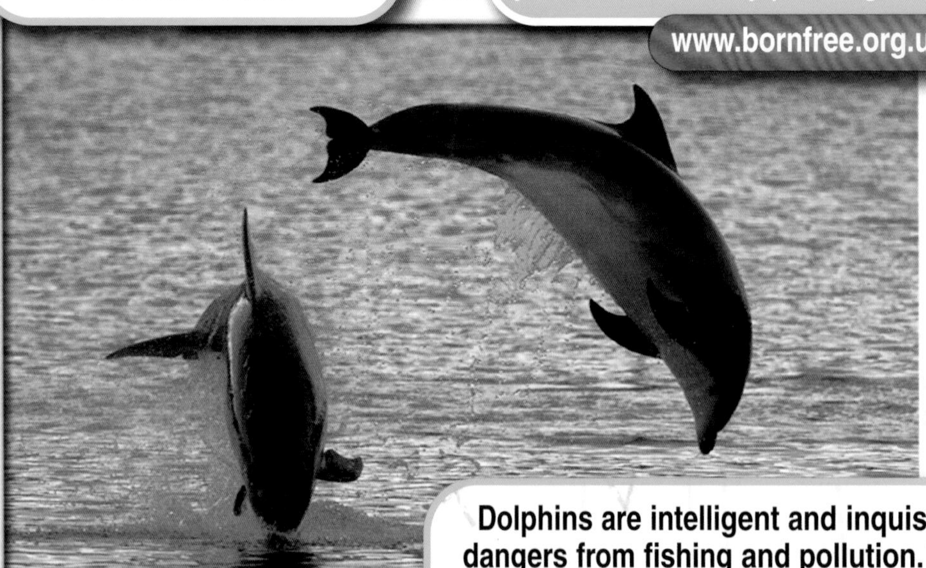

© P. Flackett

Dolphins are intelligent and inquisitive creatures. They face many dangers from fishing and pollution. This pod of bottlenose dolphins live in the waters around the Inner Hebrides, off the coast of Scotland. Adopting them through WWF helps to protect them where they live.

Leopard

Sami, Alam and Namira

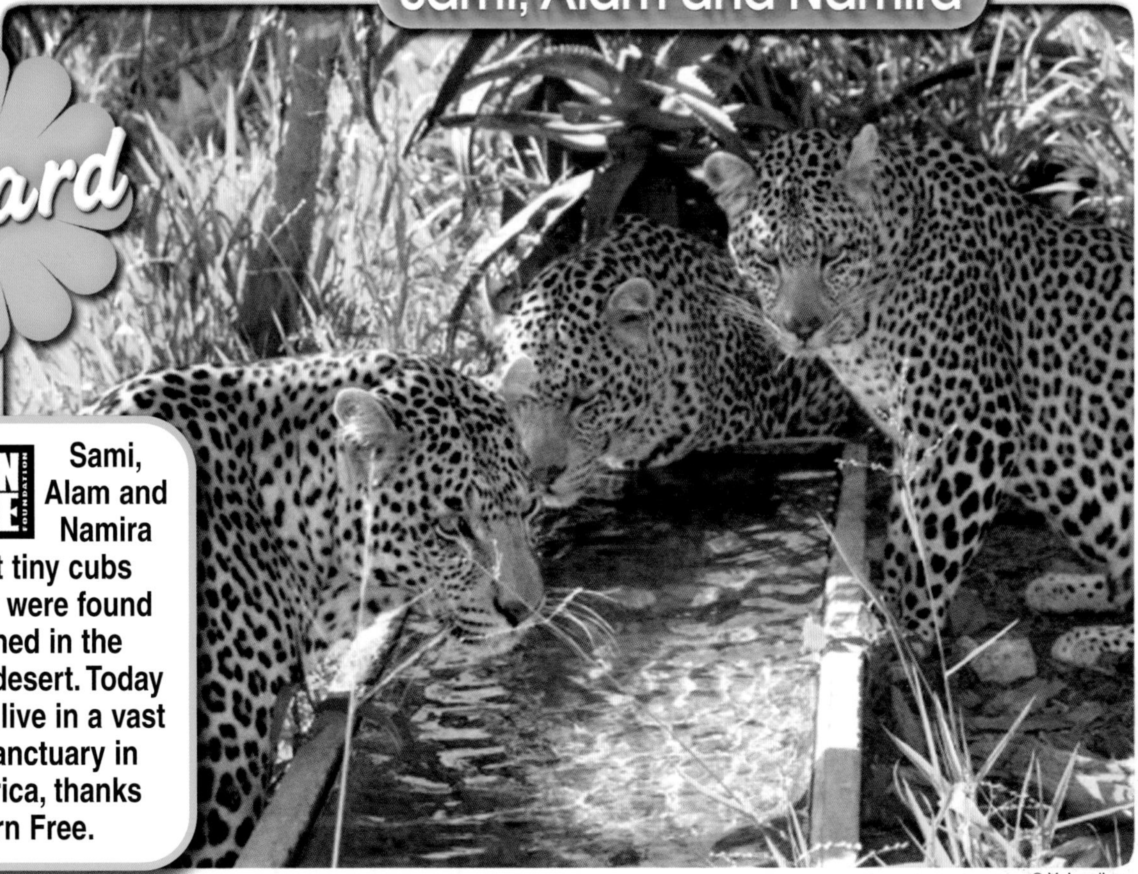

© V. Lundian

Sami, Alam and Namira were just tiny cubs when they were found abandoned in the Sudanese desert. Today the triplets live in a vast big cat sanctuary in South Africa, thanks to Born Free.

Polar Bear

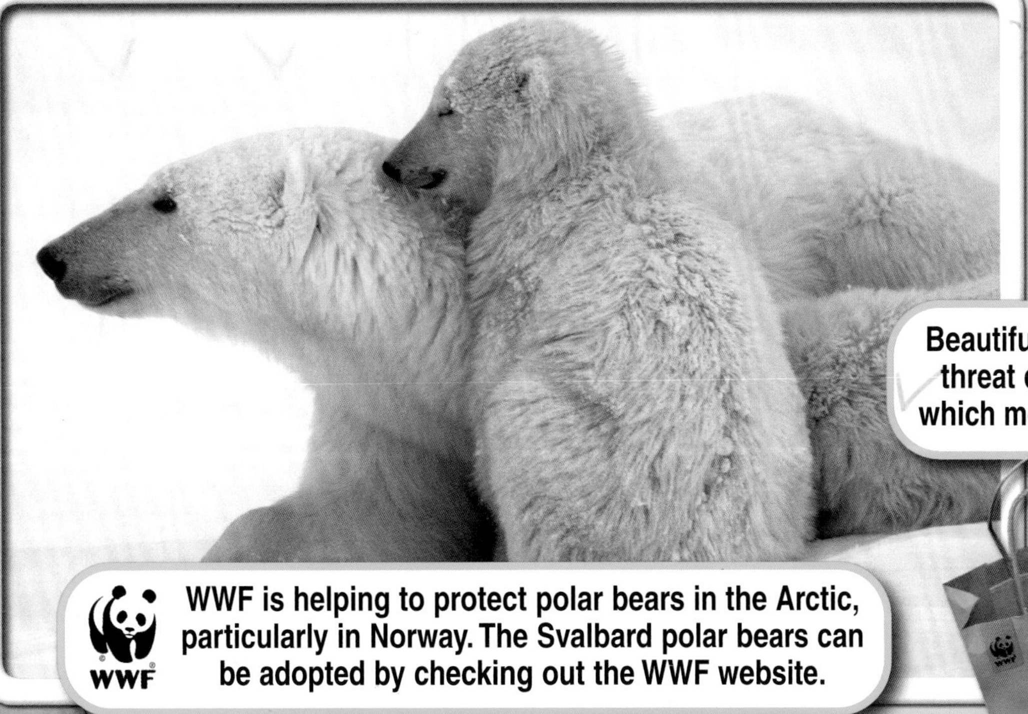

Beautiful polar bears are under threat due to global warming which melts the ice they live on.

WWF is helping to protect polar bears in the Arctic, particularly in Norway. The Svalbard polar bears can be adopted by checking out the WWF website.

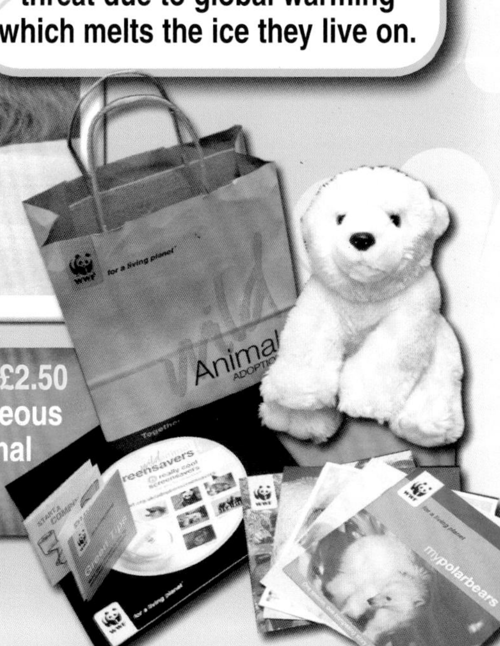

Help safeguard the future of these animals and others for as little as £2.50 a month. Adoption packs make a lovely gift, too. They include a gorgeous soft toy of your animal, a fact booklet, a print of your adopted animal and you'll receive a regular newsletter. Details can be found at

www.wwf.org.uk/adoption

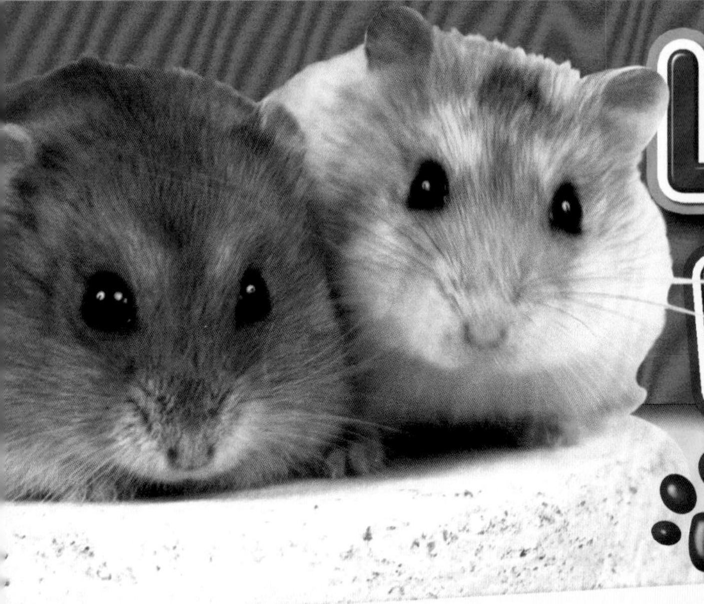

Little Pet Puzzles

Try these cute pet puzzles for loadsa fun!

Wordsearch!

G	S	H	E	L	L	T	R	M	R
I	I	C	L	L	L	W	A	A	E
P	E	U	T	S	I	H	G	R	T
A	L	O	V	E	B	I	R	D	S
E	C	P	T	A	R	S	P	W	M
N	T	A	T	E	E	K	H	T	A
I	A	A	G	F	G	E	A	R	H
U	R	D	I	E	E	R	A	T	A
G	U	S	Y	L	E	S	U	O	M
B	H	S	R	E	H	T	A	E	F

Score out the words listed in the wordsearch as you find them. Rat appears seven times. Got them all? If you're right, the remaining letters will spell out a budgie's fave treat!

- BUDGERIGAR
- CAGE
- MOUSE
- FEATHERS
- LOVEBIRDS
- HAMSTER
- SHELL
- WHISKERS
- WHEEL
- POUCH
- GUINEA PIG
- GERBIL
- FISH

Spot the Differences!

There are six differences between these pictures of this cute hamster. Can you spot them?

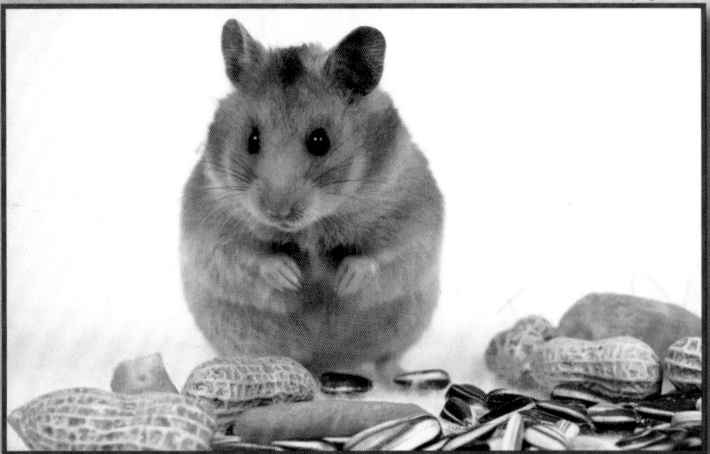

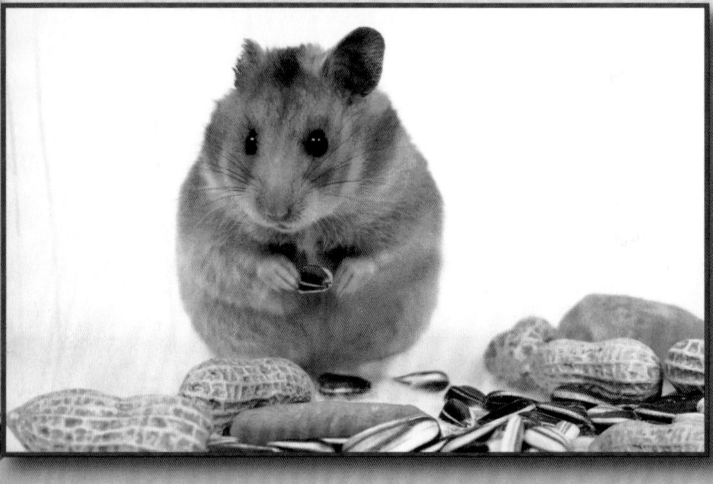

Cute!

Score out the letters in each grid that appear three or more times to find cute pets' features.

A

M	N	O	P
Q	U	M	S
P	E	Q	U
U	Q	P	M

B

N	E	C	D
C	L	N	A
D	R	L	C
S	N	D	L

C

B	R	O	T
O	R	A	O
R	B	O	I
O	B	L	B

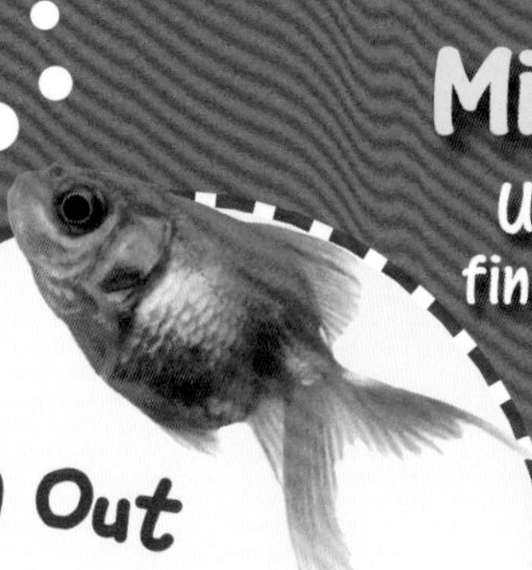

Fish Out Of water!

There are ten fish out of water on these pages, can you see them?

Mixed up Toys!

Unscramble the letters to find Billy Budgie's fave toys.

WINGS

LEBL

ROMIRR

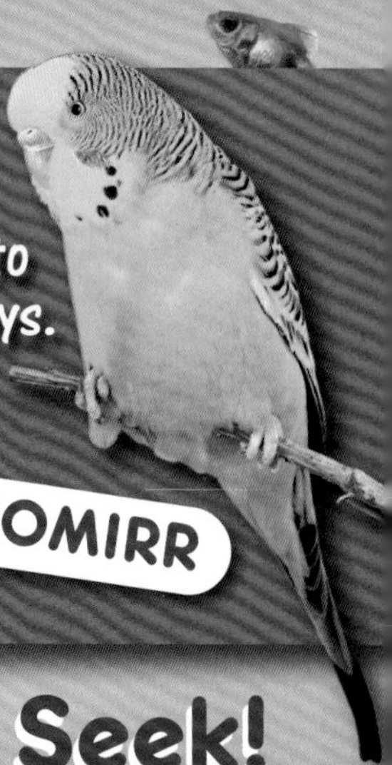

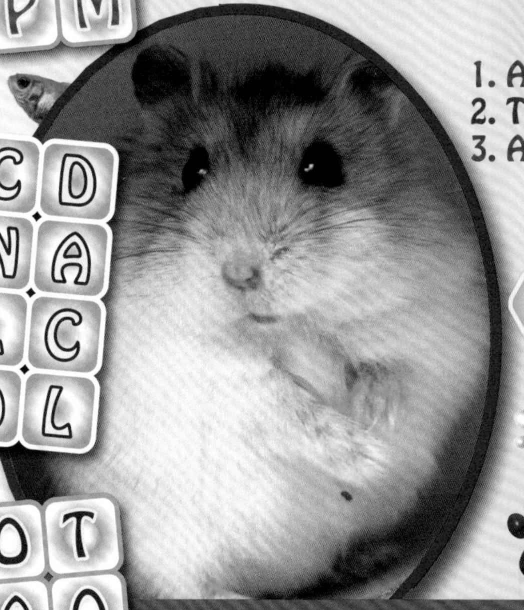

Hide and Seek!

Fill in the answers to the pet clues reading across to find a little pet hidden in the pink panel reading down.

1. A small budgerigar?
2. This pig doesn't say oink!
3. A chatty bird.
4. Thumper's one.
5. They swim a lot.
6. Bird's toes?

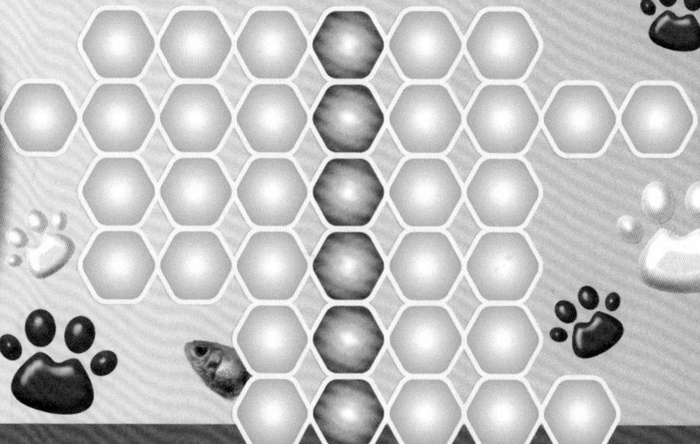

Which Two?

These five parrots all look alike but only two are identical. Which two?

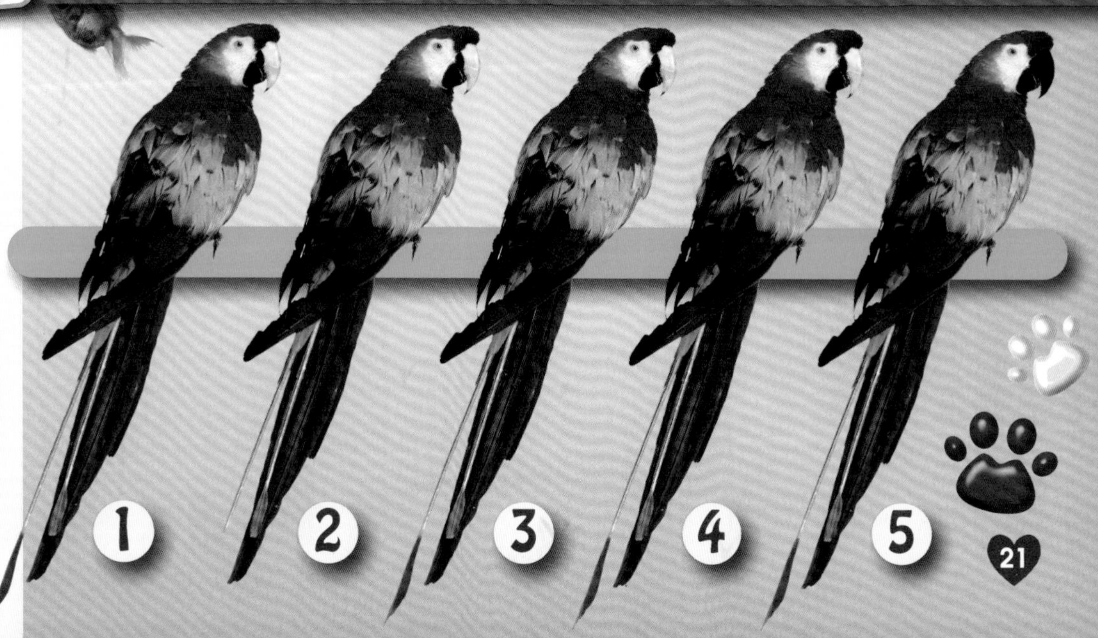

1
2
3
4
5

Answers:

Wordsearch - Fave treat is millet spray

Spot the Differences - 1. Left ear missing 2. Extra stripe on right side of body. 3. Seed between paws. 4. Extra peanut in bottom right corner 5. Piece of veg missing to left of hamster 6. Foot missing.

Cute! a) Nose, b) Ears, c) Tail.

Mixed up toys - Swing, bell, mirror.

Hide and Seek - Across: 1. Budgie, 2. Guinea pig, 3. Parrot, 4. Rabbit, 5. Fish, 6. Claws. Down - Gerbil.

Which two? 1&4.

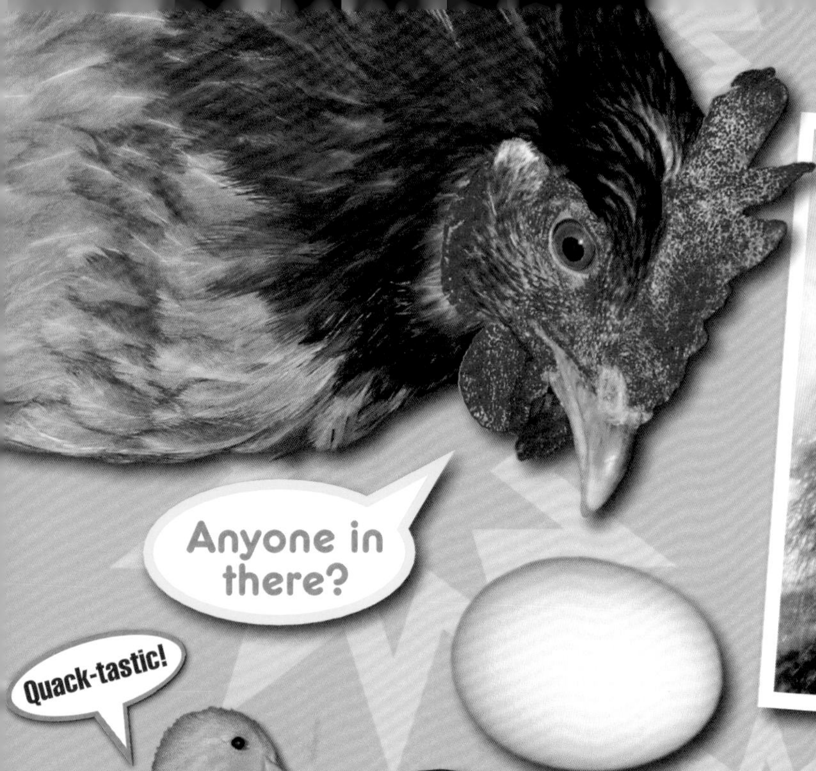
Anyone in there?

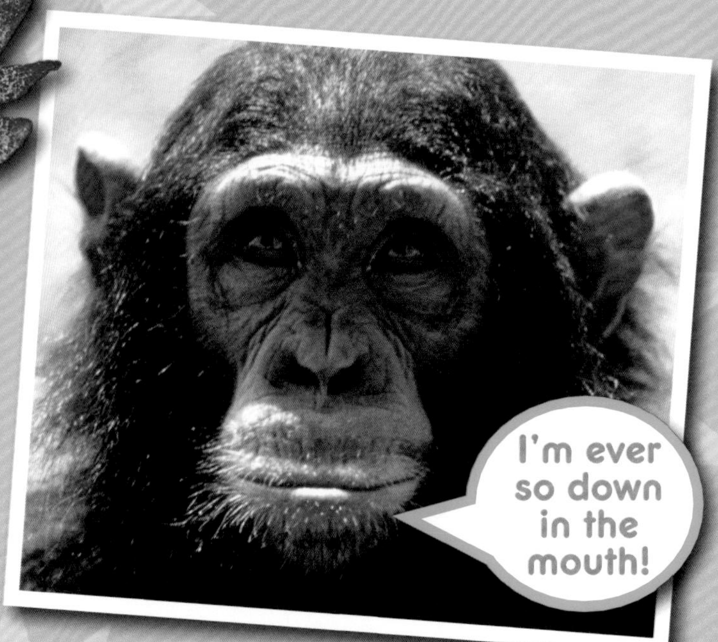
I'm ever so down in the mouth!

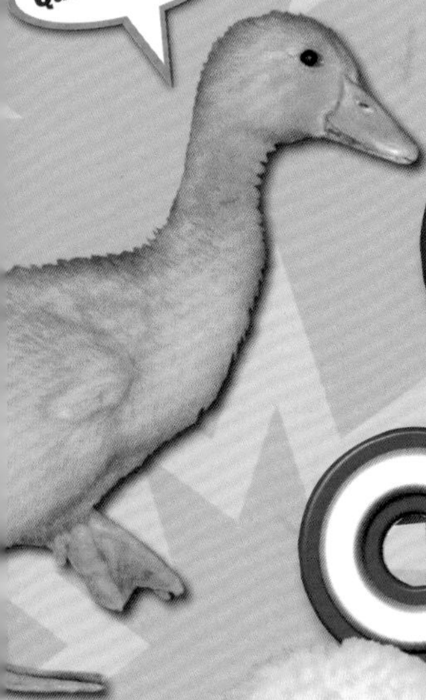
Quack-tastic!

Crazy Captions!

What animals would say if only they could talk!

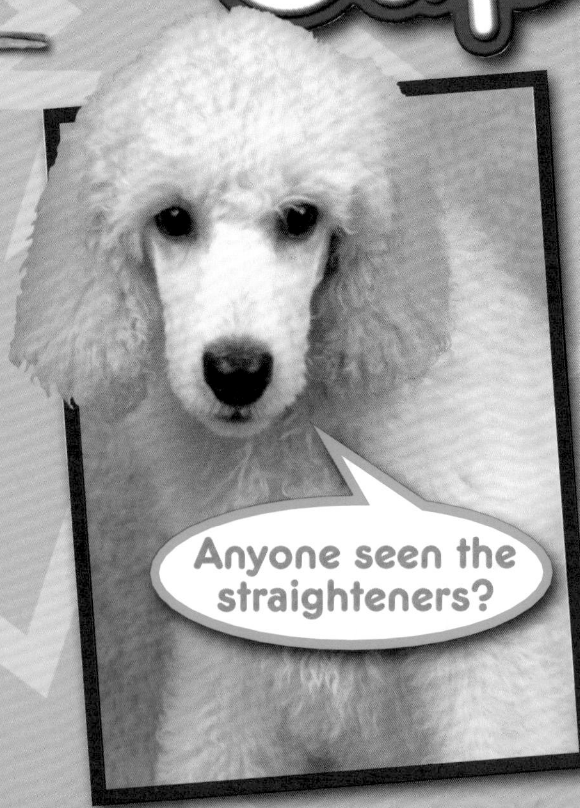
Anyone seen the straighteners?

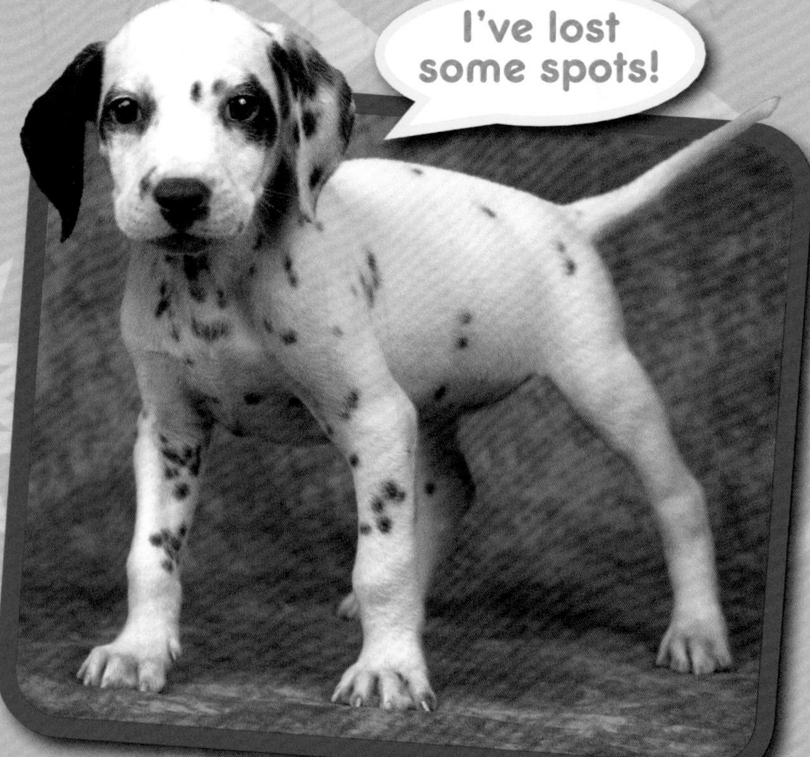
I've lost some spots!

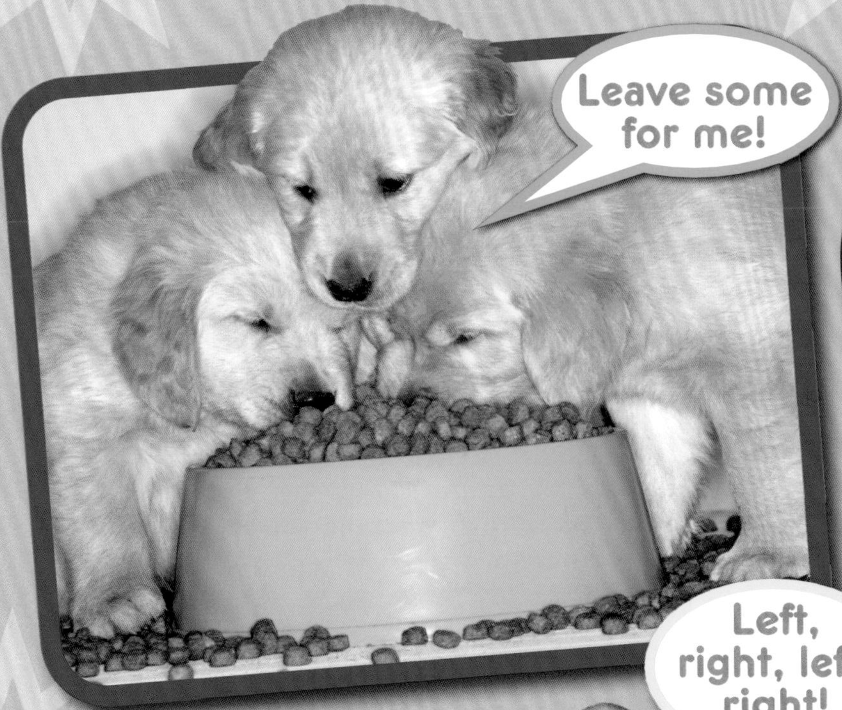
Leave some for me!

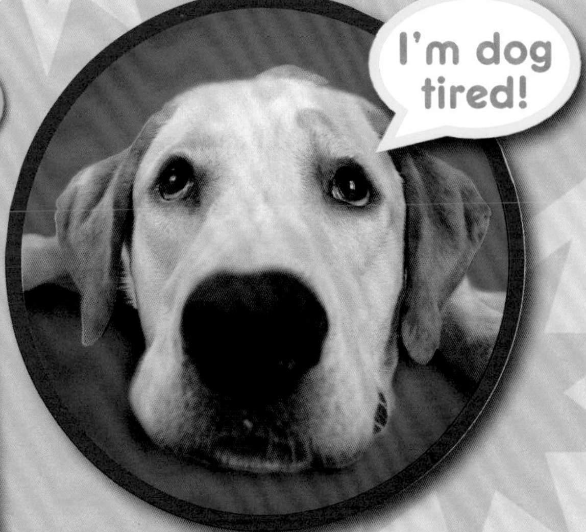
I'm dog tired!

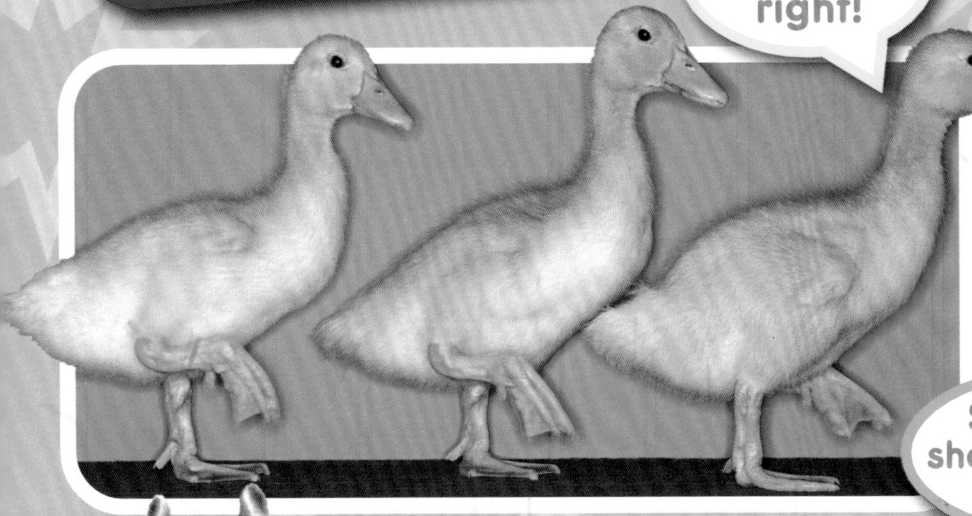
Left, right, left, right!

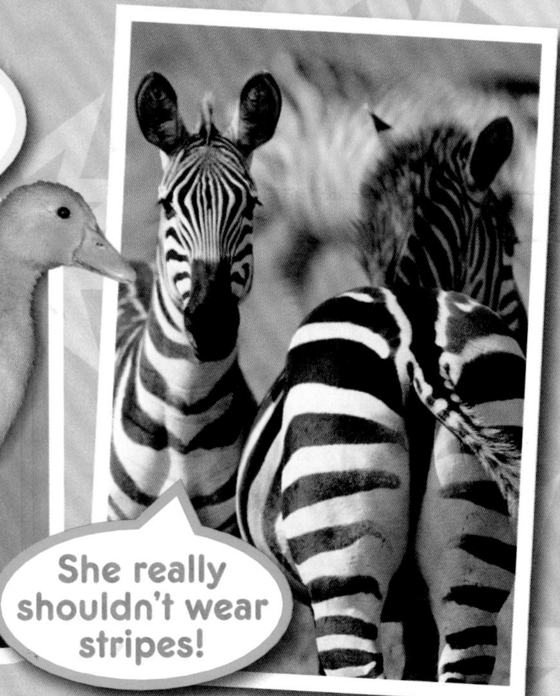
She really shouldn't wear stripes!

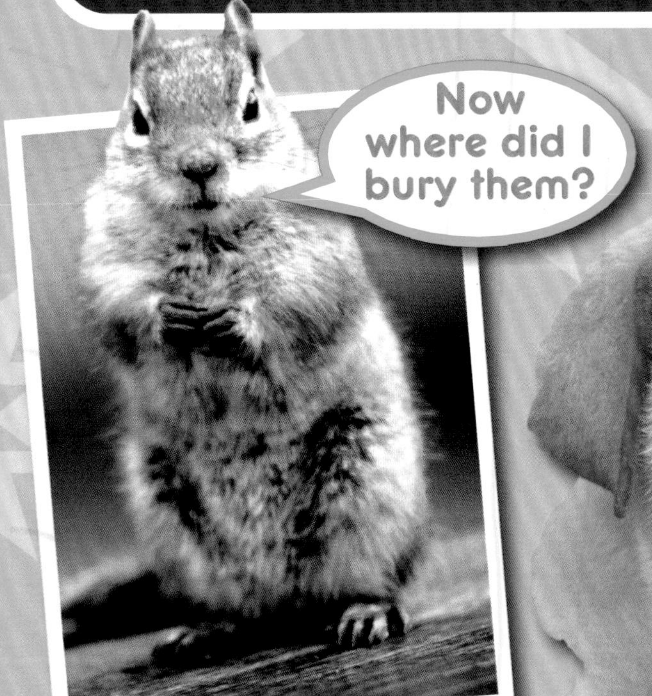
Now where did I bury them?

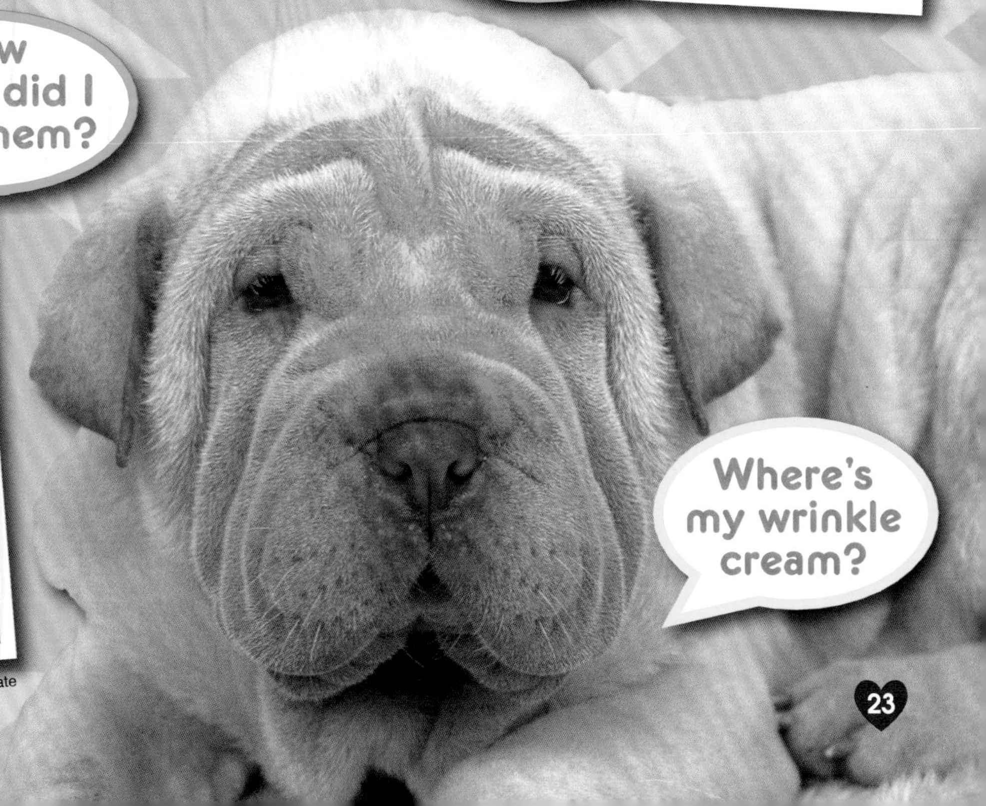
Where's my wrinkle cream?

On Safari

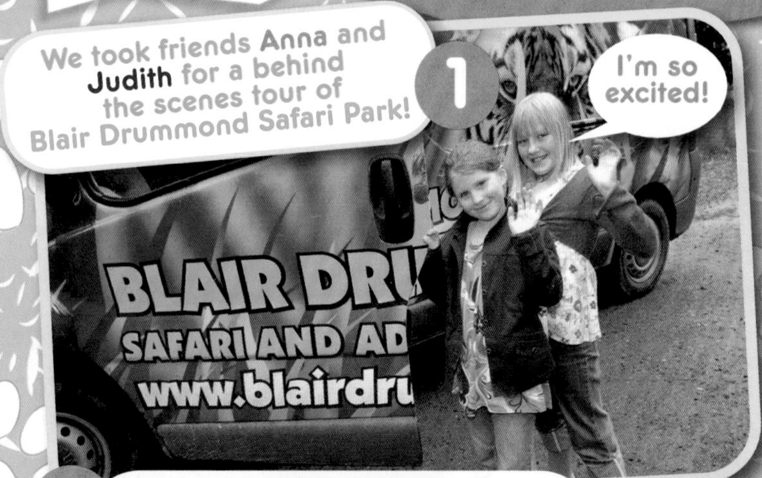
1
We took friends Anna and Judith for a behind the scenes tour of Blair Drummond Safari Park!
I'm so excited!
BLAIR DRU
SAFARI AND AD
www.blairdru

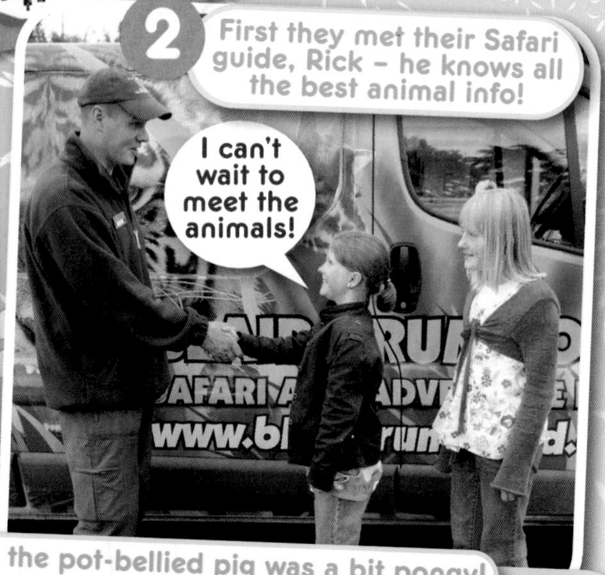
2
First they met their Safari guide, Rick – he knows all the best animal info!
I can't wait to meet the animals!

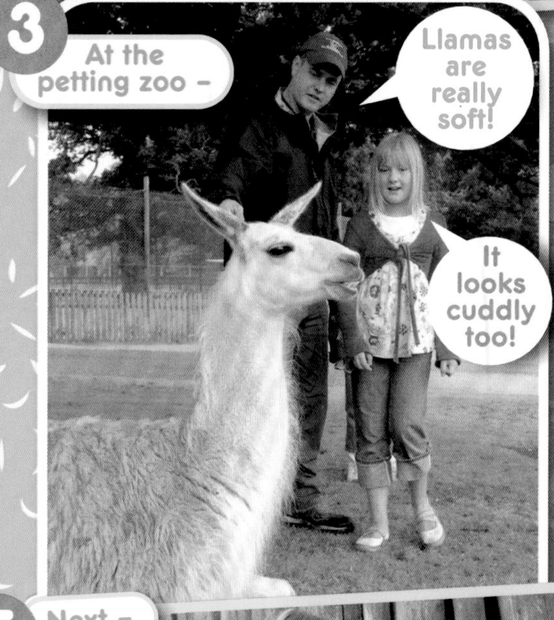
3
At the petting zoo –
Llamas are really soft!
It looks cuddly too!

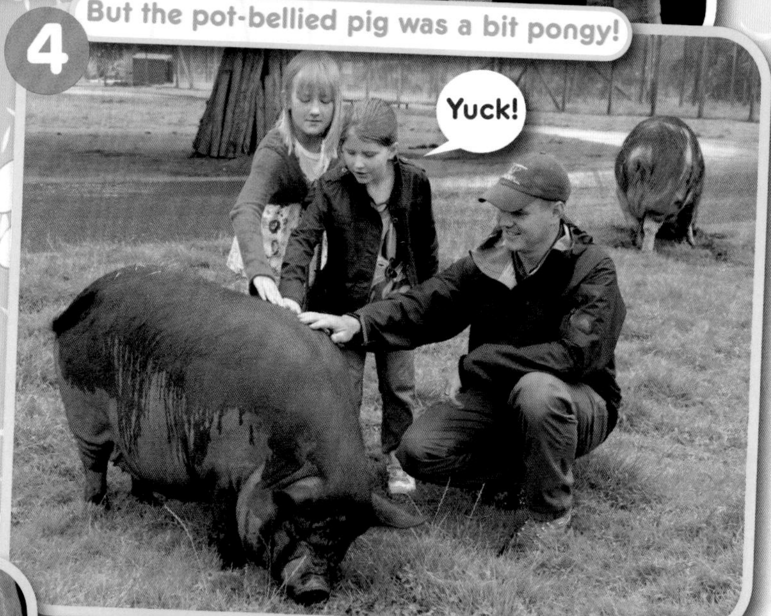
4
But the pot-bellied pig was a bit pongy!
Yuck!

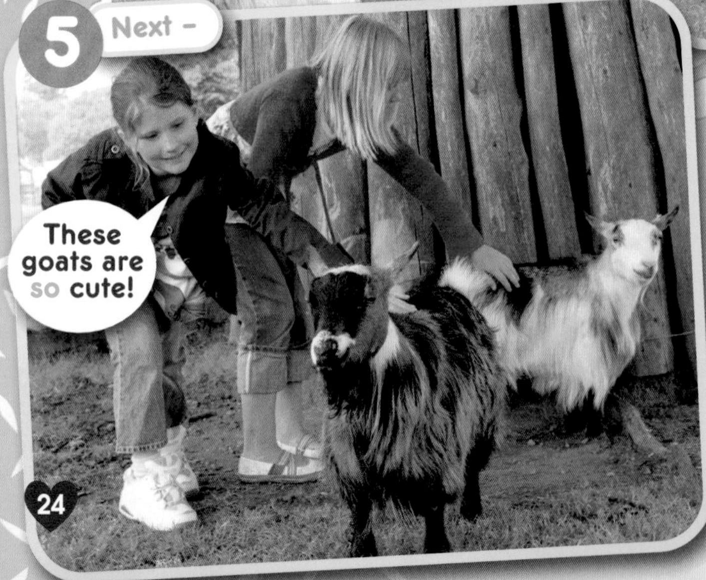
5
Next –
These goats are so cute!

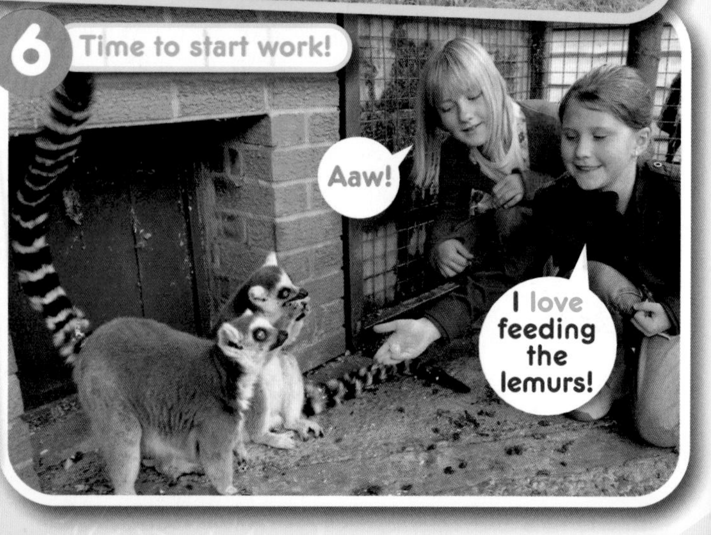
6
Time to start work!
Aaw!
I love feeding the lemurs!

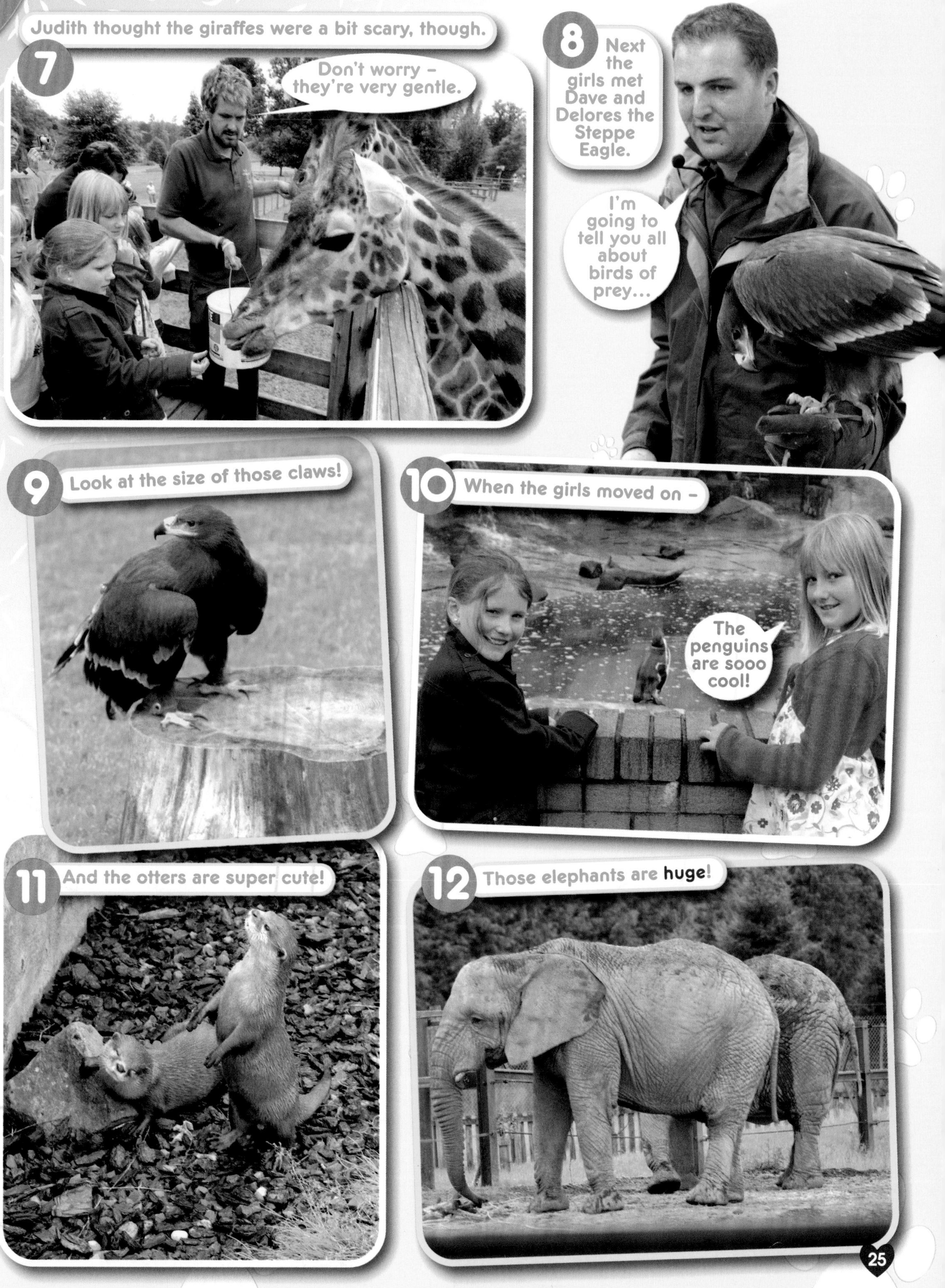
Judith thought the giraffes were a bit scary, though.
7
Don't worry – they're very gentle.
8
Next the girls met Dave and Delores the Steppe Eagle.
I'm going to tell you all about birds of prey...
9
Look at the size of those claws!
10
When the girls moved on –
The penguins are sooo cool!
11
And the otters are super cute!
12
Those elephants are **huge**!

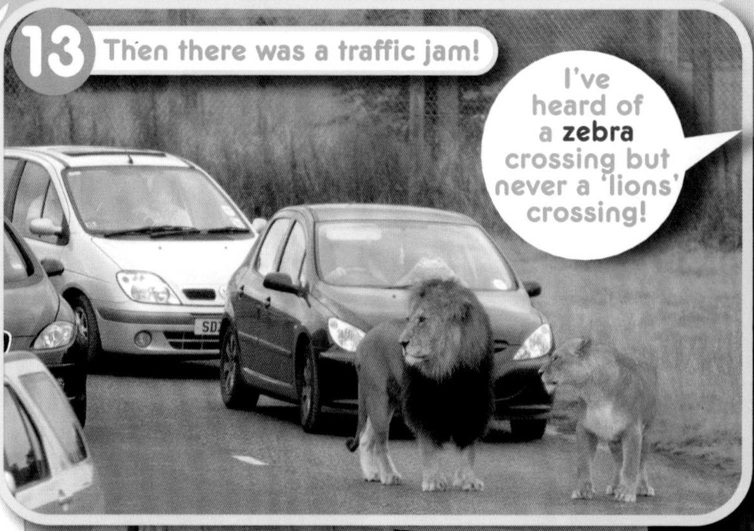
13
Then there was a traffic jam!
I've heard of a **zebra** crossing but never a 'lions' crossing!

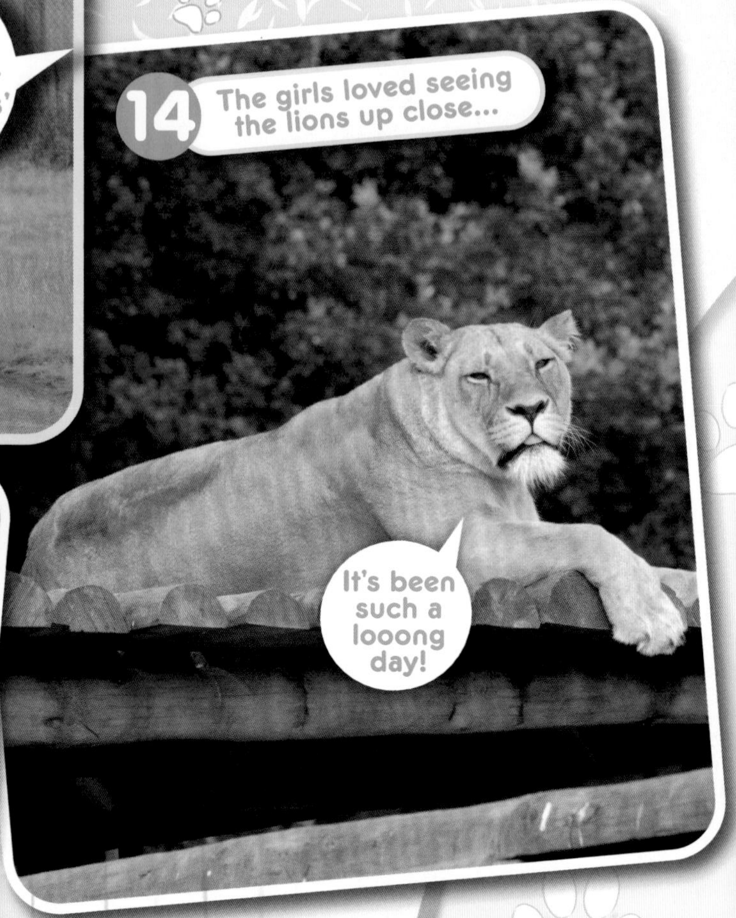
14
The girls loved seeing the lions up close...
It's been such a looong day!

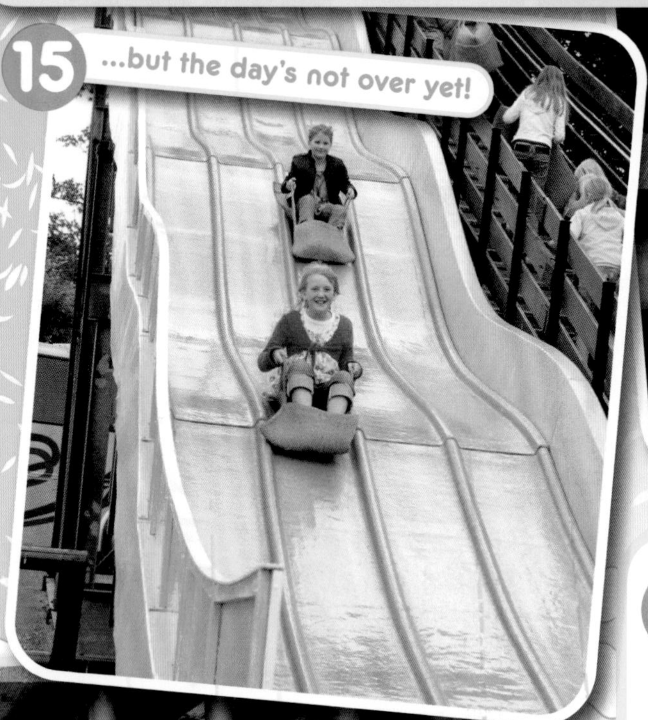
15
...but the day's not over yet!

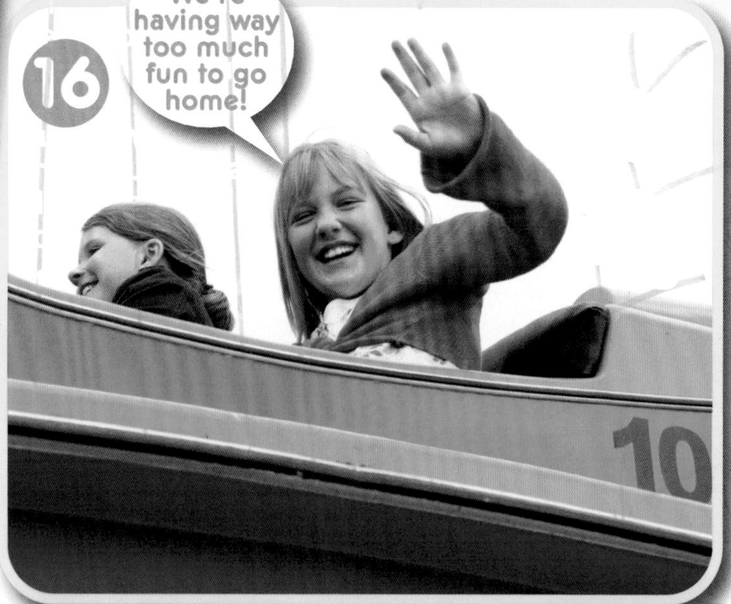
16
We're having way too much fun to go home!
10

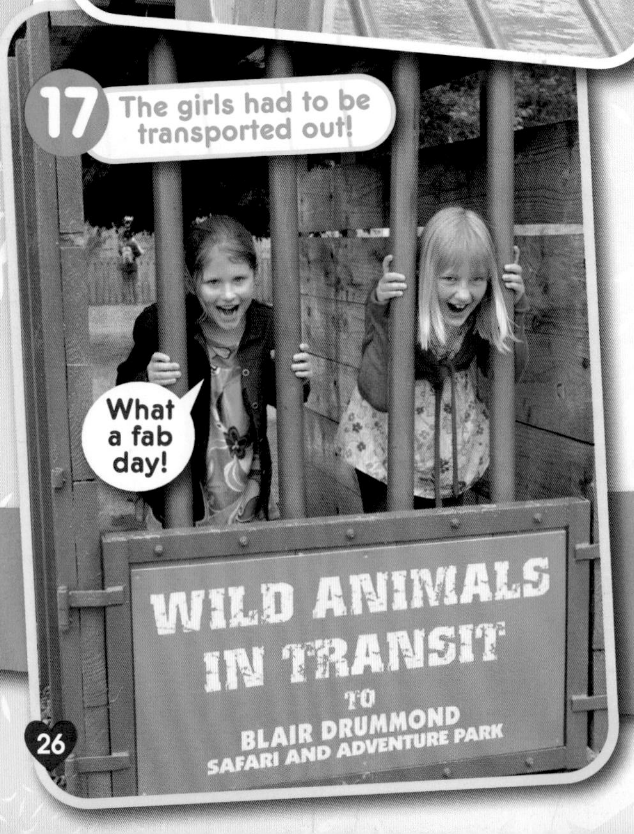
17
The girls had to be transported out!
What a fab day!
WILD ANIMALS
IN TRANSIT
TO
BLAIR DRUMMOND
SAFARI AND ADVENTURE PARK

For a great day out or more info visit
www.blairdrummond.com

BLAIR DRUMMOND SAFARI AND ADVENTURE PARK

cringe!

Had an embarrassing moment? These Animals and You readers have!

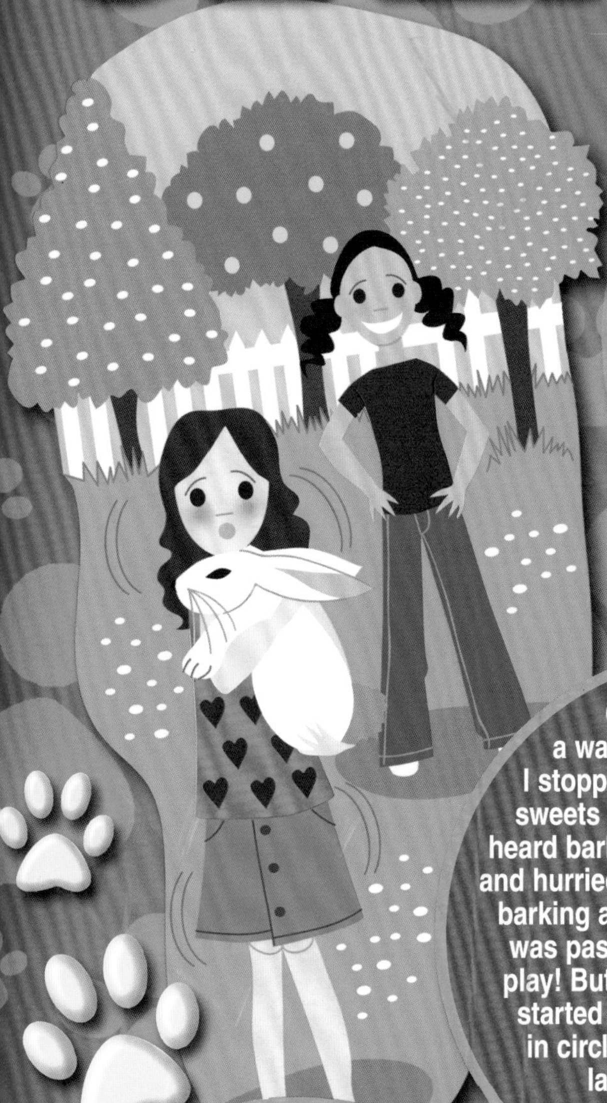

I've got a white rabbit called Muffin and one day, he managed to escape. I looked over the fence and saw him hopping around in my neighbour's garden so I ran round and picked him up. Just as I was going back through the gate, my neighbour called out, "Where are you going with Snowball?" My face was so red when I realised I'd picked up their rabbit by mistake! A few minutes later, Muffin turned up safe and sound.

Laura Porter, Durham

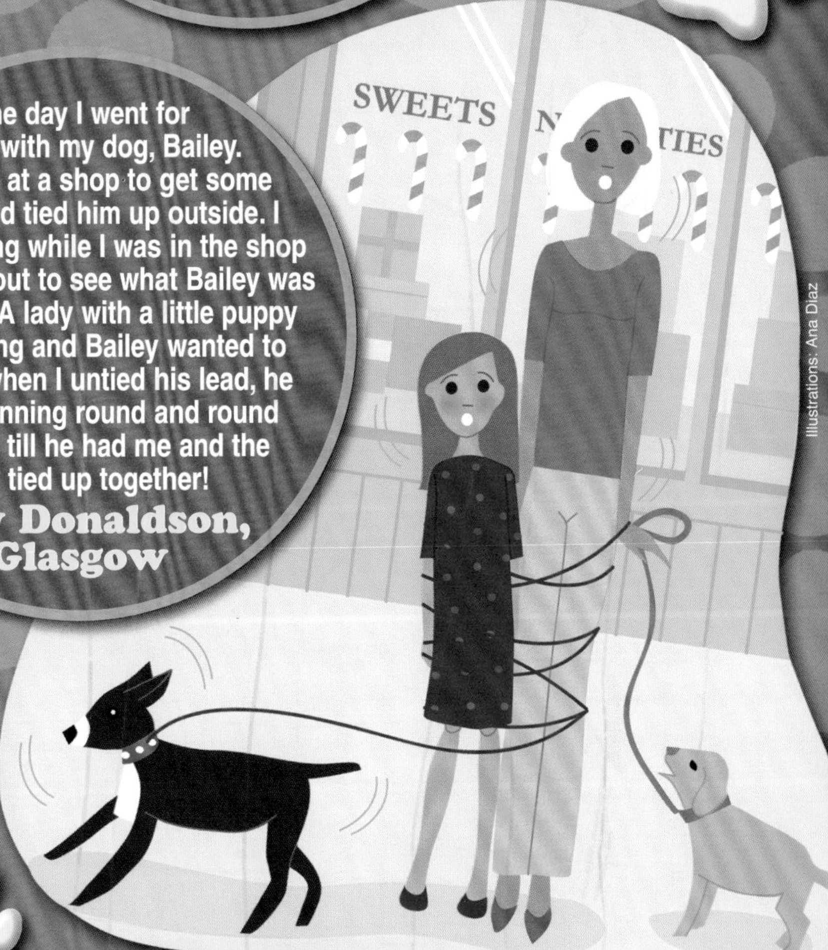

SWEETS

One day I went for a walk with my dog, Bailey. I stopped at a shop to get some sweets and tied him up outside. I heard barking while I was in the shop and hurried out to see what Bailey was barking at. A lady with a little puppy was passing and Bailey wanted to play! But when I untied his lead, he started running round and round in circles till he had me and the lady tied up together!

Amy Donaldson, Glasgow

My friend Lauren's mum and dad took me and Lauren to a safari park for the day. It was great. But just as we were driving through the area where the baboons were, one of them climbed on the car and stuck its bottom out at us in front of the windscreen! I didn't know where to look and neither did Lauren!

Georgia Thomas, Bromley

Illustrations: Ana Diaz

WIN £10! If you've had an embarrassing moment with an animal, why not tell us? If your cringe is printed in the mag, you'll win £10! Send your stories to **Cringe! Animals and You, PO Box 305, London NW1 1TX**

Sea Search

Can you *see* all these creatures that can be found swimming in the *sea*? They can be read up, down, forwards, backwards or diagonallly.

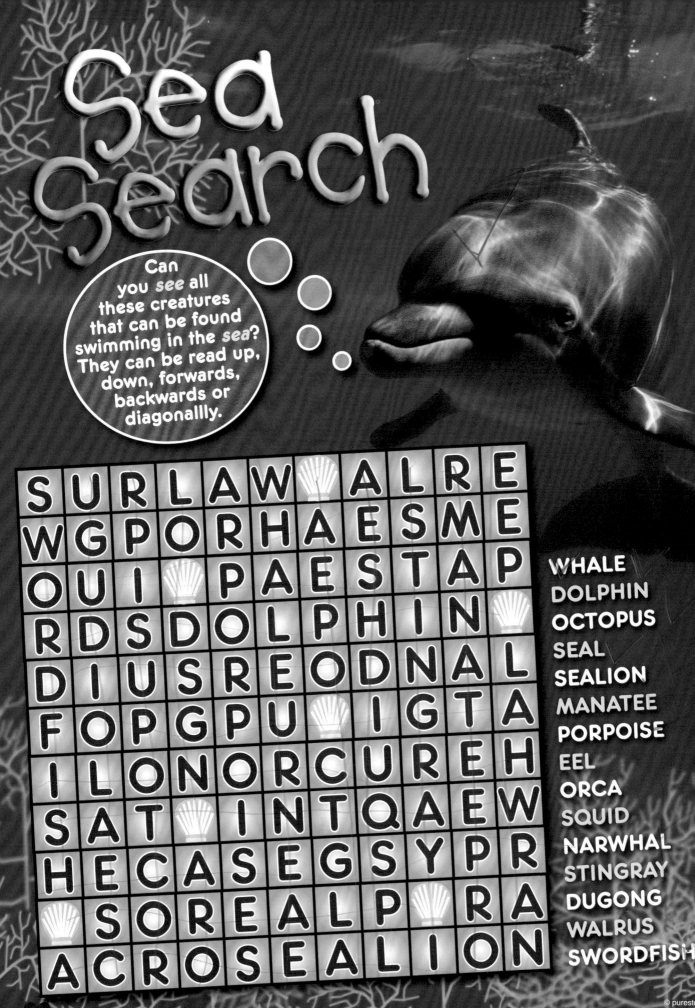

S	U	R	L	A	W		A	L	R	E
W	G	P	O	R	H	A	E	S	M	E
O	U	I		P	A	E	S	T	A	P
R	D	S	D	O	L	P	H	I	N	
D	I	U	S	R	E	O	D	N	A	L
F	O	P	G	P	U		I	G	T	A
I	L	O	N	O	R	C	U	R	E	H
S	A	T		I	N	T	Q	A	E	W
H	E	C	A	S	E	G	S	Y	P	R
	S	O	R	E	A	L	P		R	A
A	C	R	O	S	E	A	L	I	O	N

WHALE
DOLPHIN
OCTOPUS
SEAL
SEALION
MANATEE
PORPOISE
EEL
ORCA
SQUID
NARWHAL
STINGRAY
DUGONG
WALRUS
SWORDFISH

Pretty in Pink

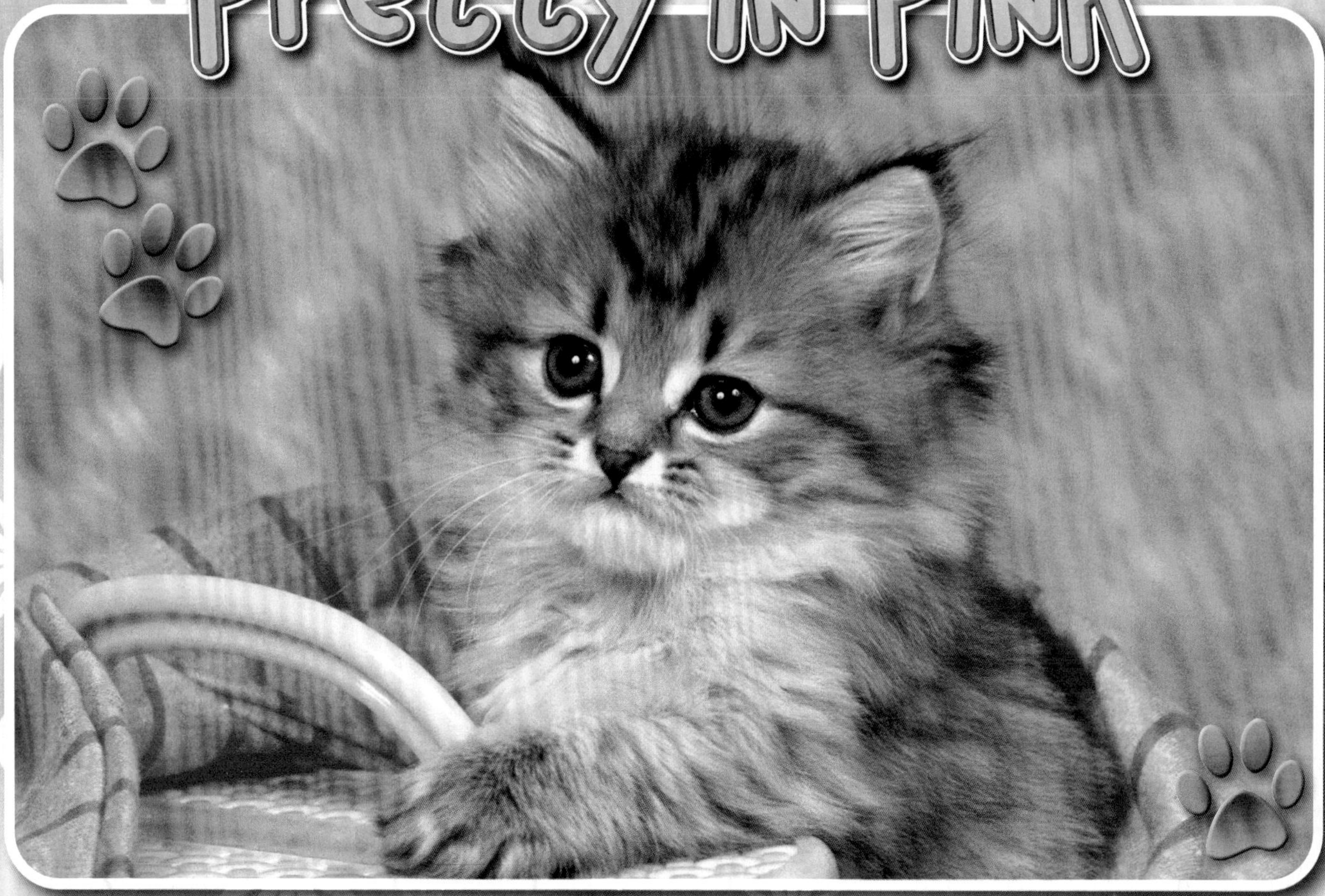

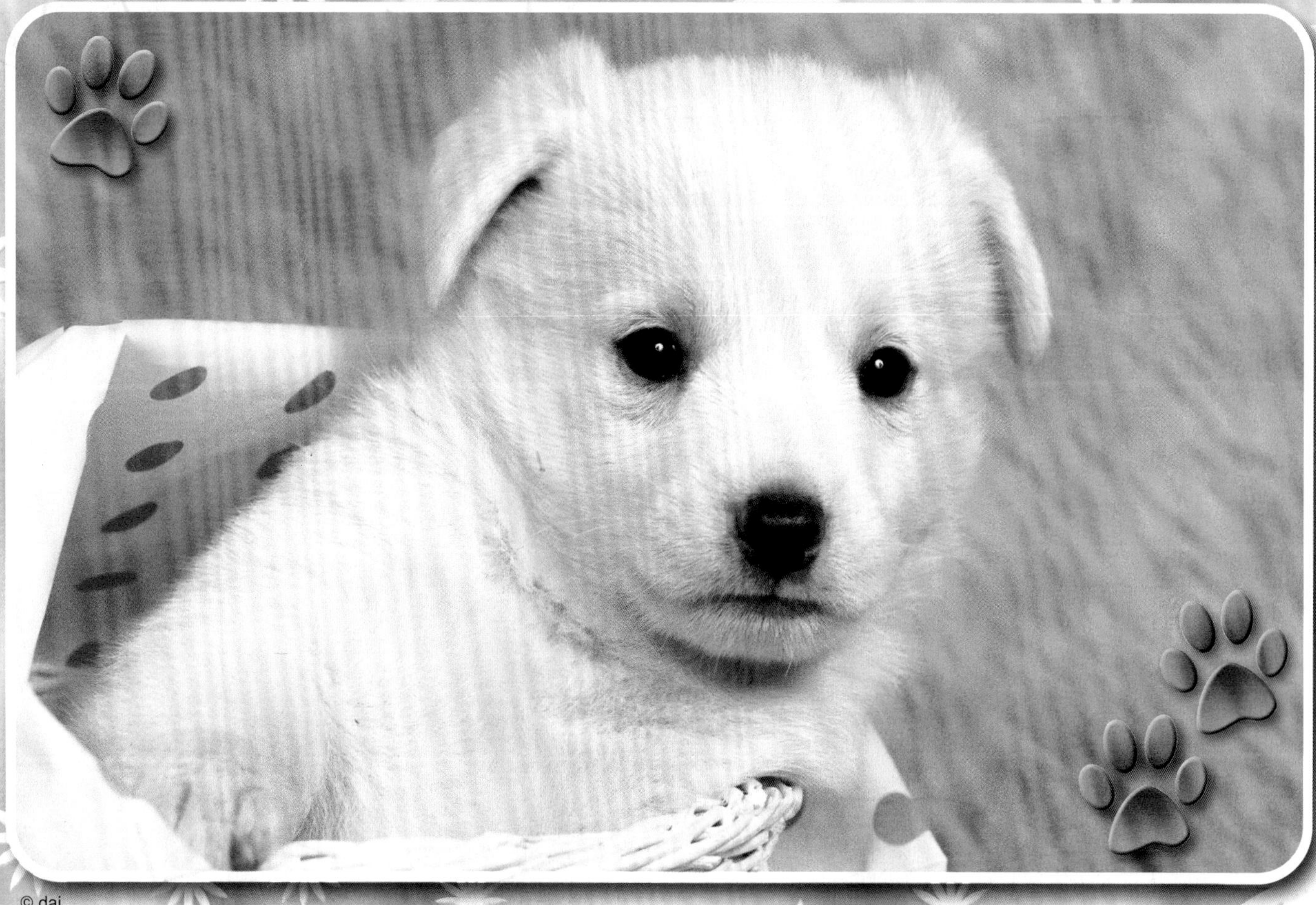

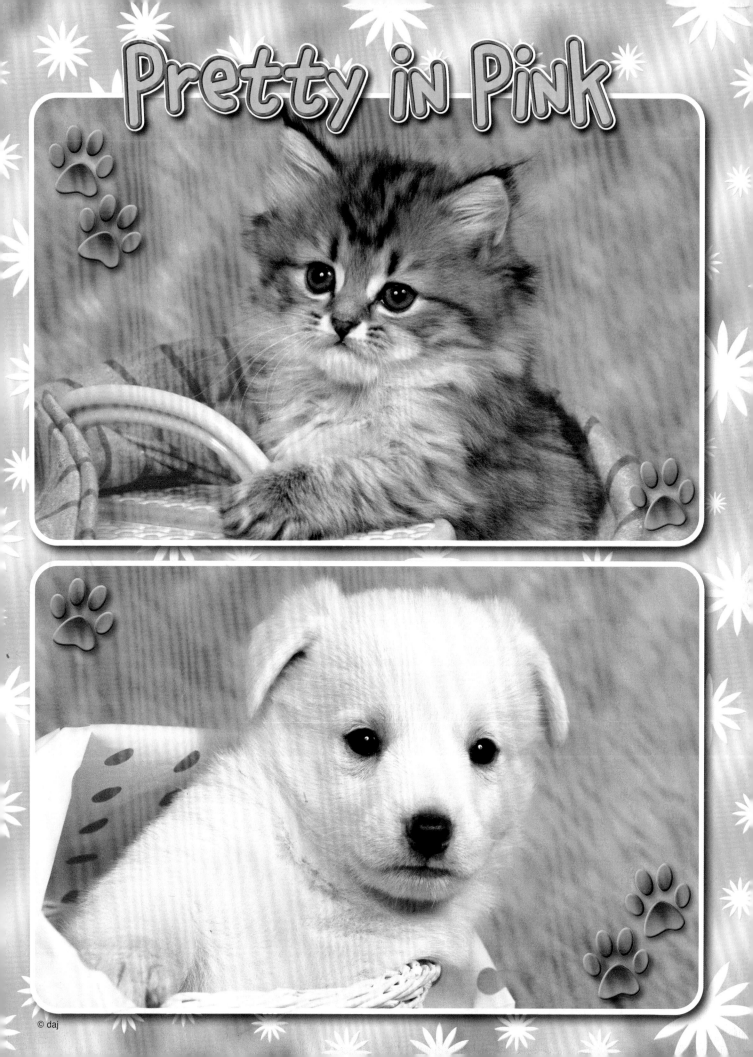

An exciting new pet!

You've always wanted a pet and at last you're allowed to have one. But which pet will you choose? Here are some tips to help you decide.

● If you have room for a dog, look for one that's not too timid.

Dog

You'll need grooming tools to keep your pet's coat and claws in good condition.

● Puppies shouldn't be taken from their mums before they are eight weeks old.

● If you get a puppy from a breeder, they should give you details of the food he needs.

● Puppies will miss their mum at first so it may take them a little while to settle down.

Most pets like to have their own bed but they don't always choose to sleep in it!

● Remember, some puppies grow into very big strong dogs that might take YOU for walks!

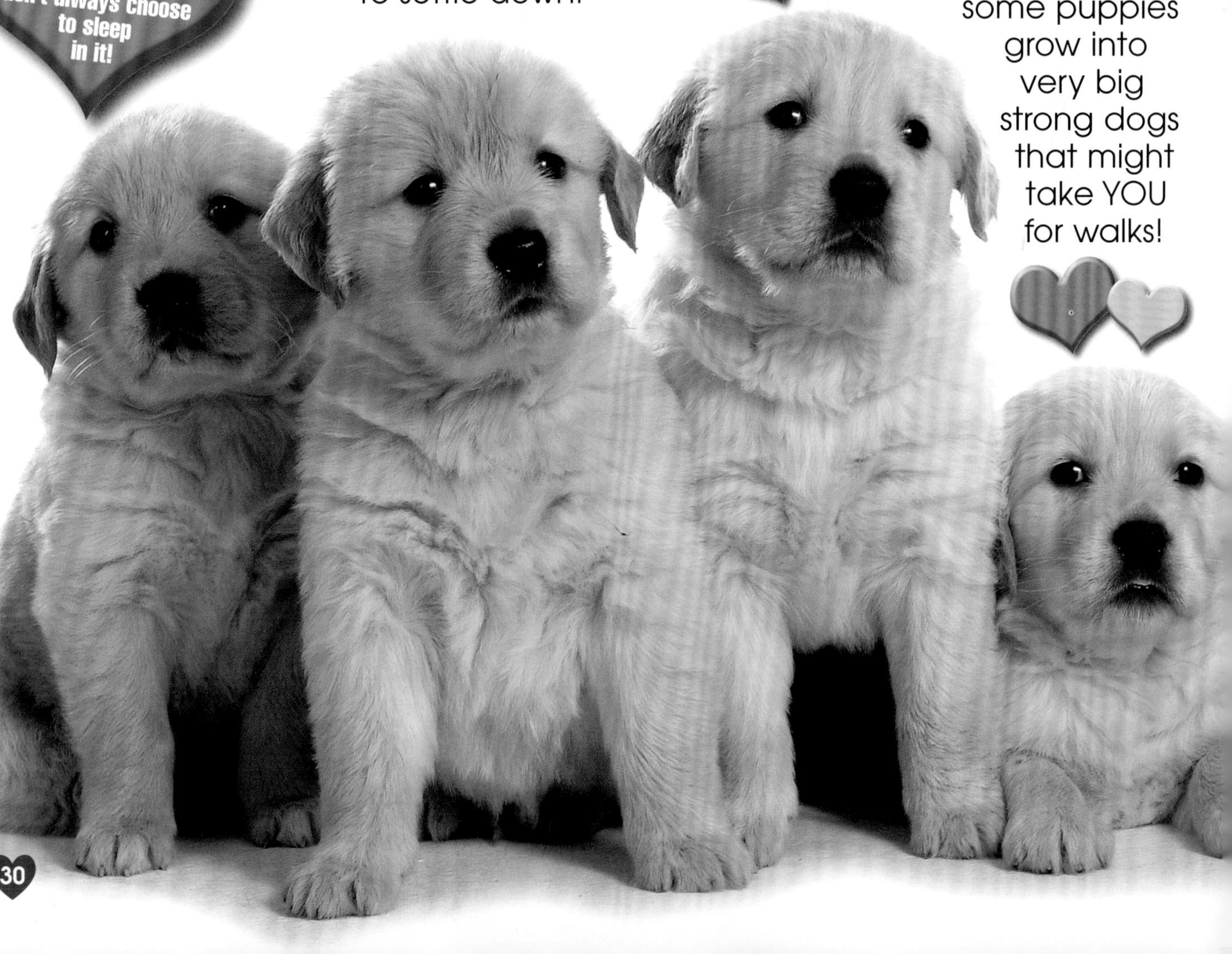

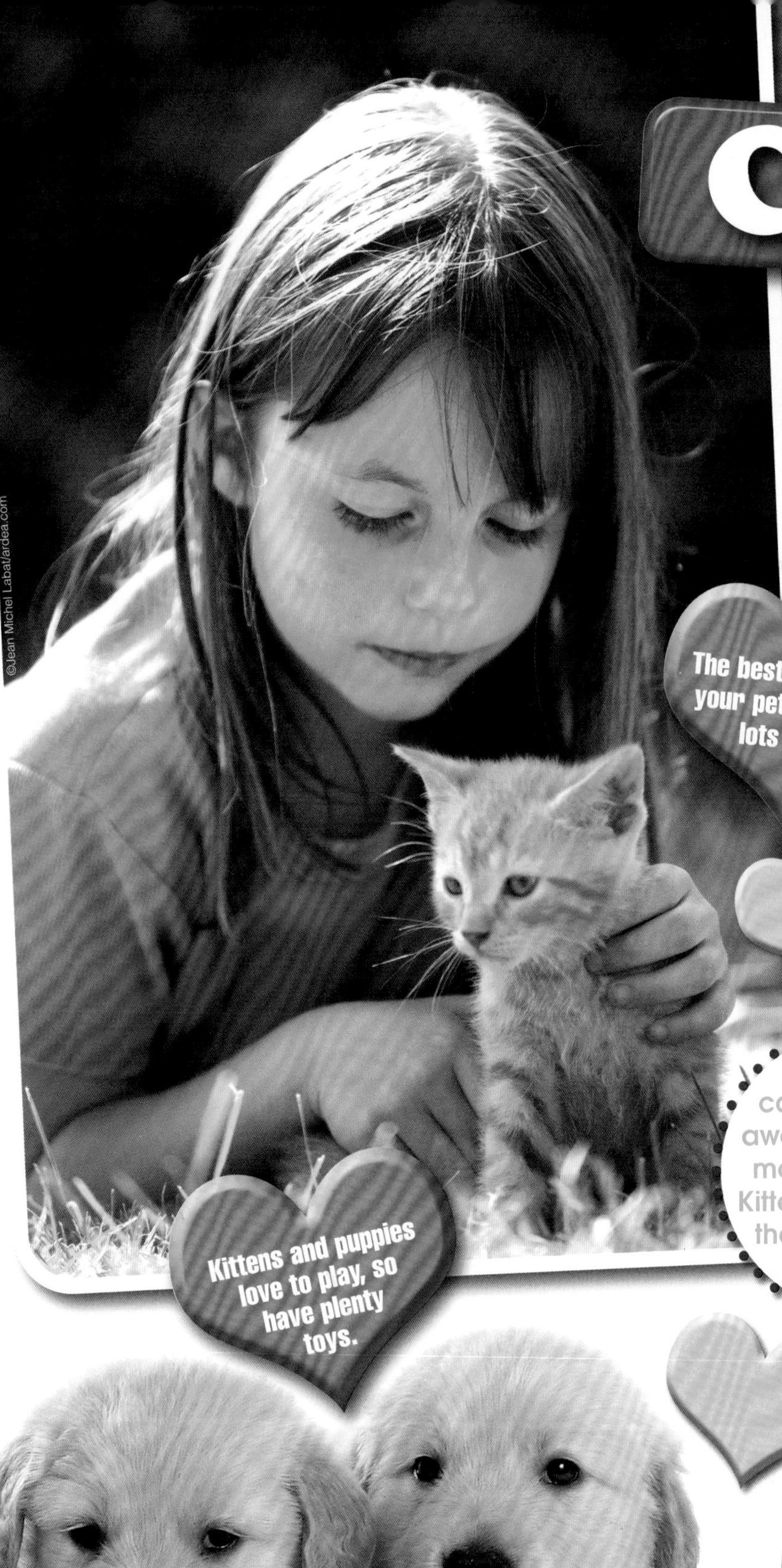

©Jean Michel Labat/ardea.com

Cat

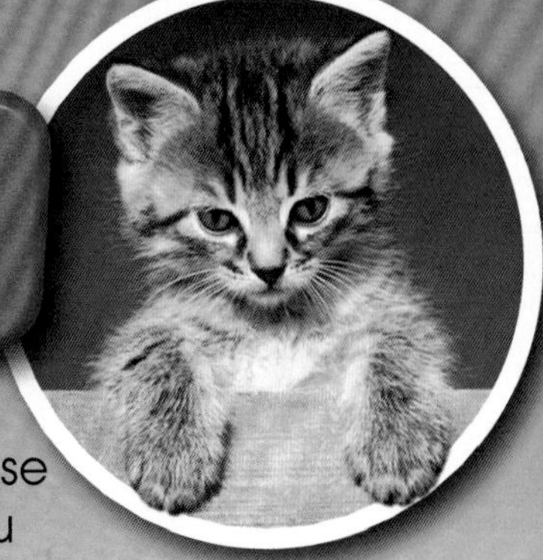

Cats don't need a big house or garden. If you decide to get a kitten or a full-grown cat, look for one that is lively, friendly and gentle. Check that its coat is clean, as well as its eyes, ears and nose.

The best thing to give your pet — lots and lots of love!

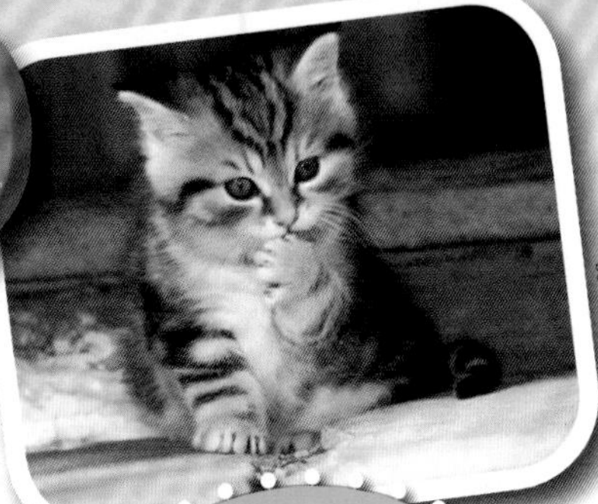

©imagesource

When you take your new pet home, let it get used to its new surroundings and if you have other animals, introduce them carefully.

Grown cats often hide away till they feel more confident. Kittens will inspect their new home slowly.

Make sure you have cat litter and a tray placed nearby to prevent accidents!

Kittens and puppies love to play, so have plenty toys.

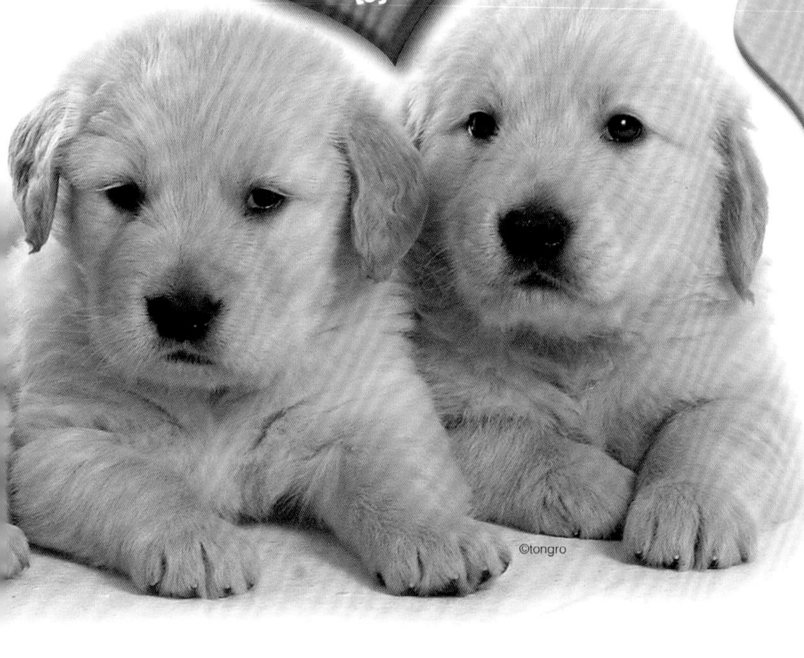

©tongro

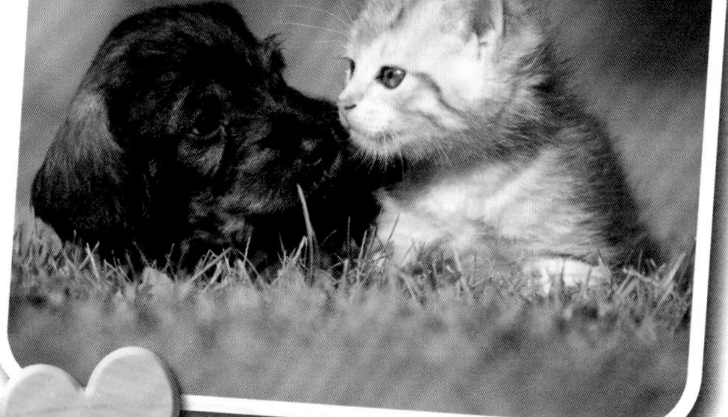

Turn the page for more...

Guinea Pig

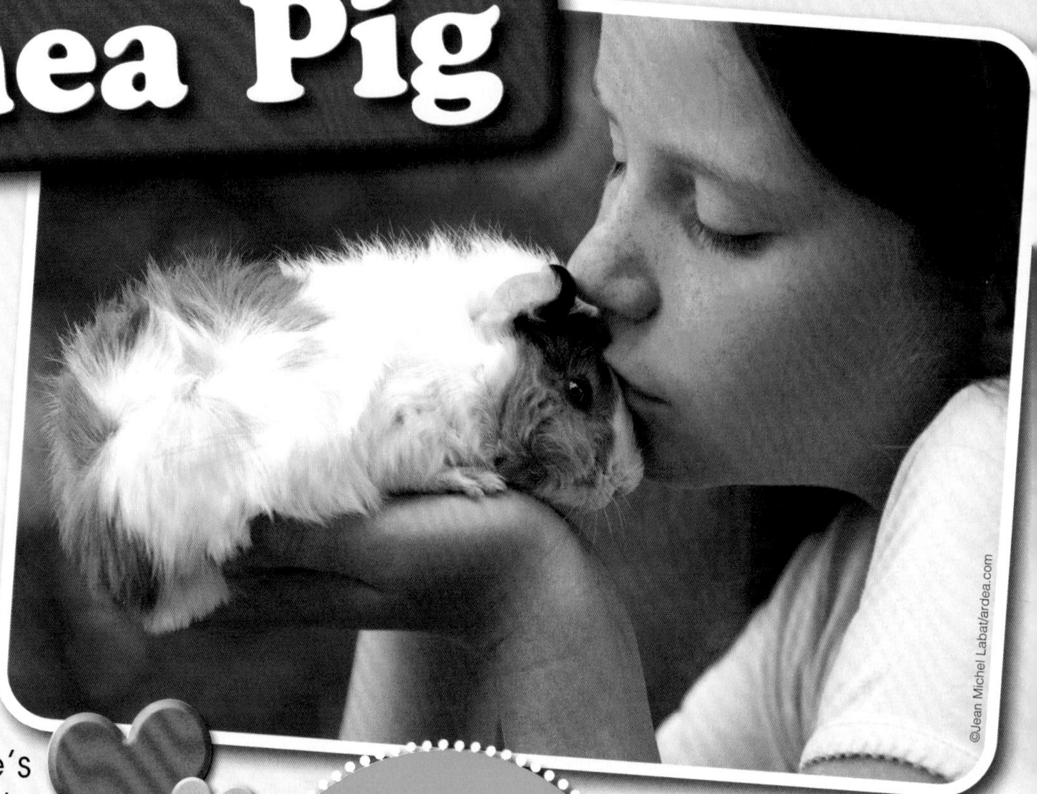

©Jean Michel Labat/ardea.com

- If you'd like a guinea pig, it's best if you have a garden. They should have an outside run where they can eat grass as they LOVE it!

- Make sure the hutch you have is the biggest one possible so that there's lots of room to stretch and move around.

- When you first get your guinea pig home put it into its hutch and leave it alone to get used to its new home. Do not handle it in the first few days as it may be frightened.

- **It's often best to have two guinea pigs to keep each other company.**

- Guinea pigs don't usually play with toys. What they do like are boxes and tunnels to hide and play in!

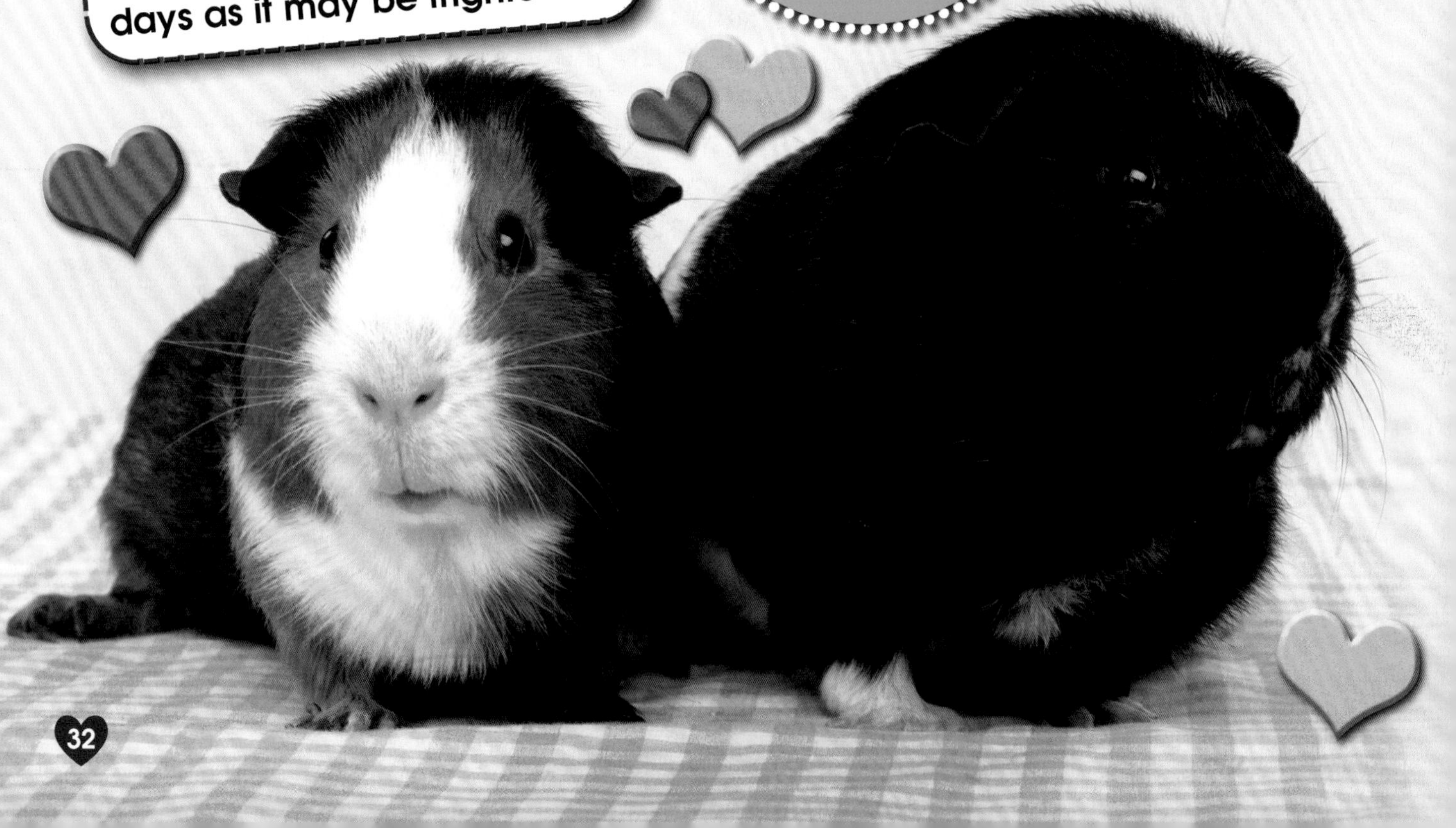

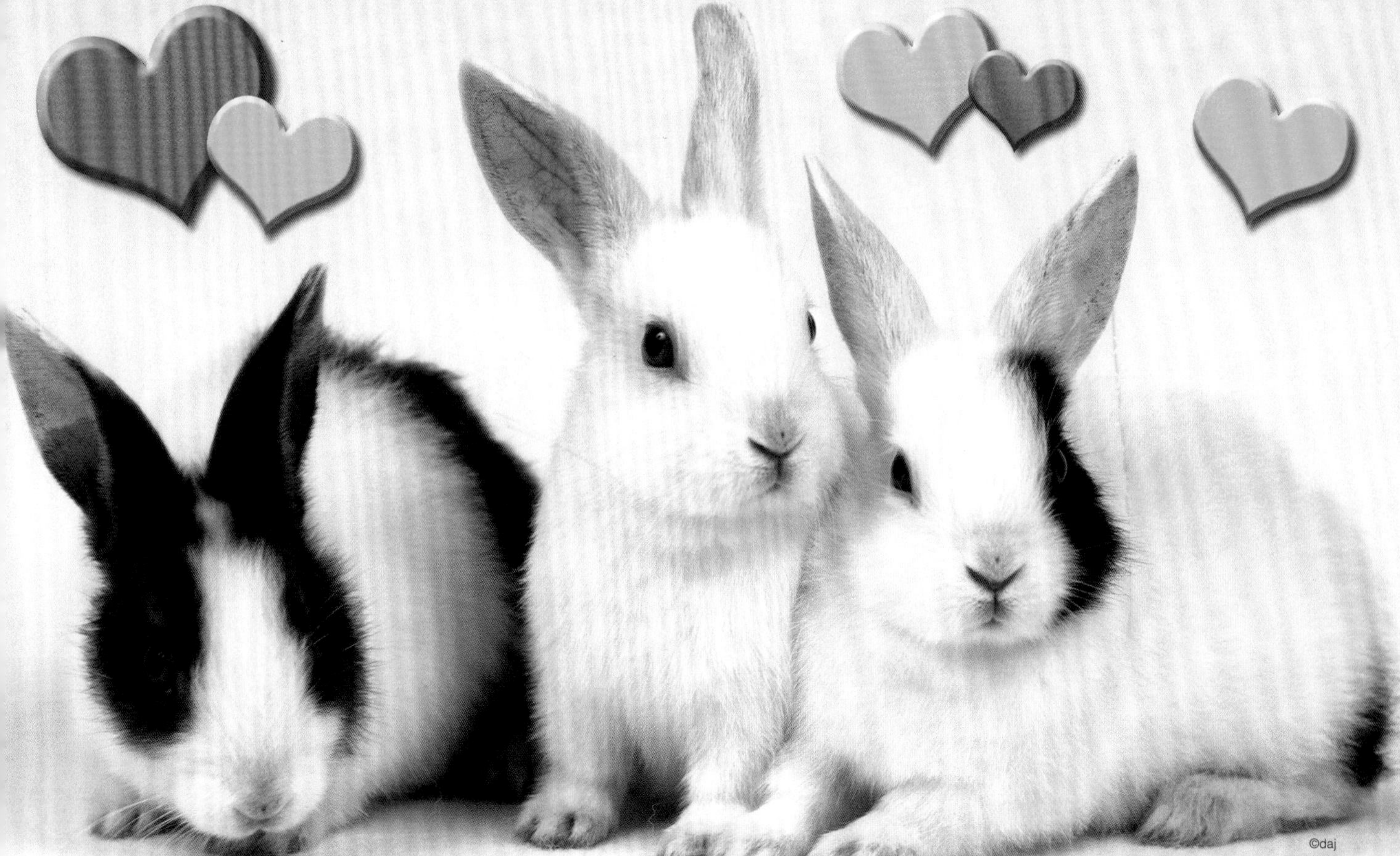

©daj

Rabbit

Rabbits can be house-trained and make great house pets but they do take a lot of looking after.

They love living with other rabbits but don't be tempted to put them with guinea pigs.

Rabbits need as much exercise as a small dog! If you keep them in a hutch, it's best to have a run attached. The hutch should be sheltered from wind, rain and direct sunshine.

A gnawing block will help prevent rabbits' teeth from growing too long.

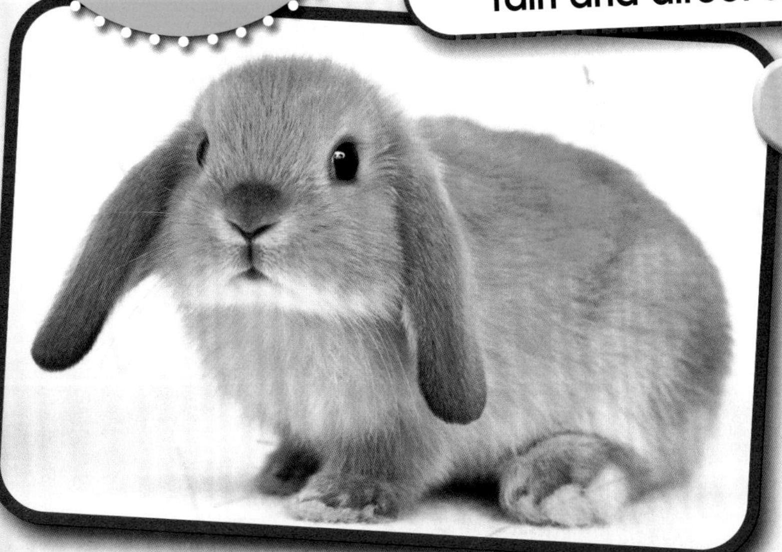

Remember, there are many shelters with animals desperate for a new owner. Perhaps you could offer one a home. Check out your local shelters.

cuddles 'n' snuggles

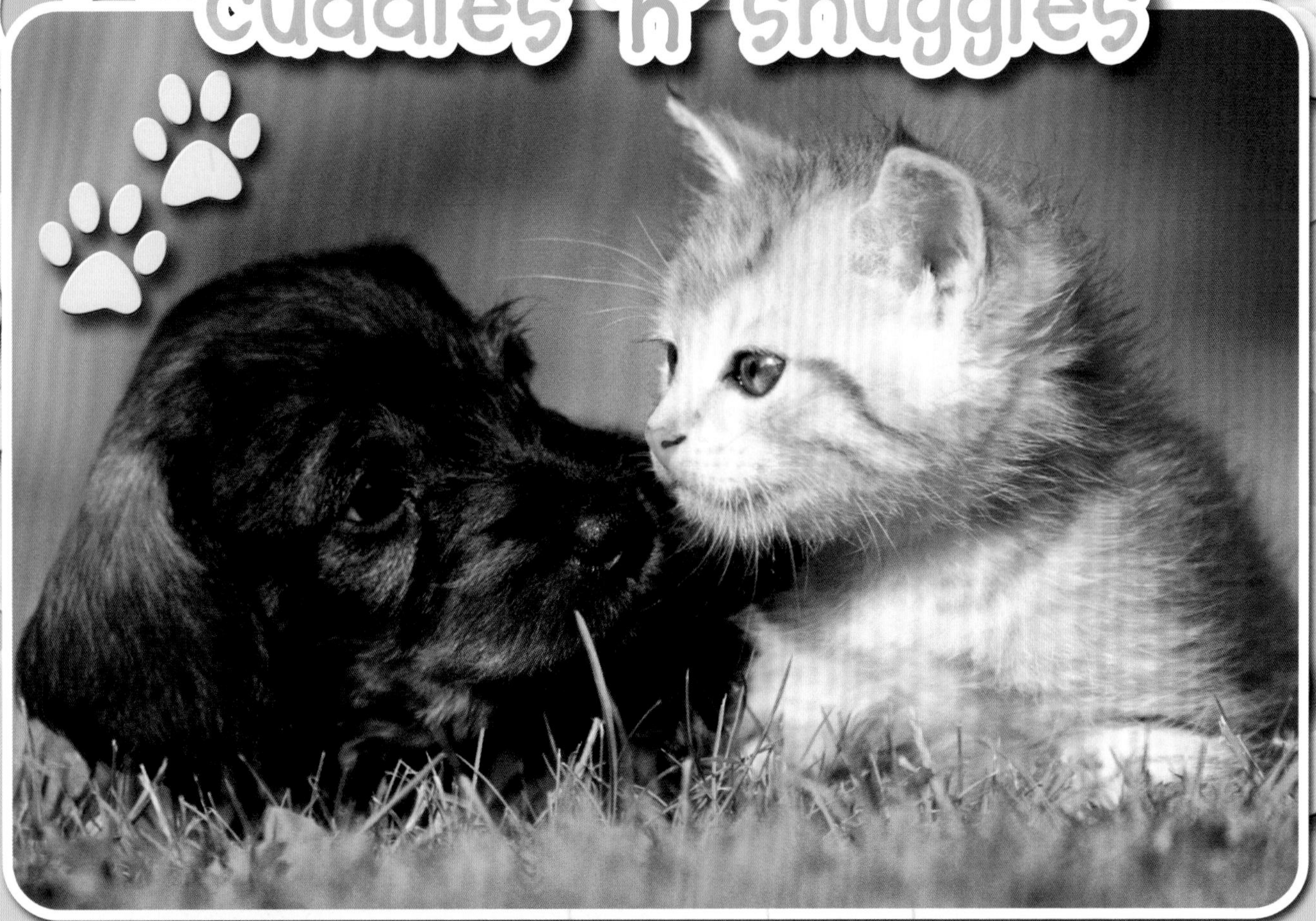

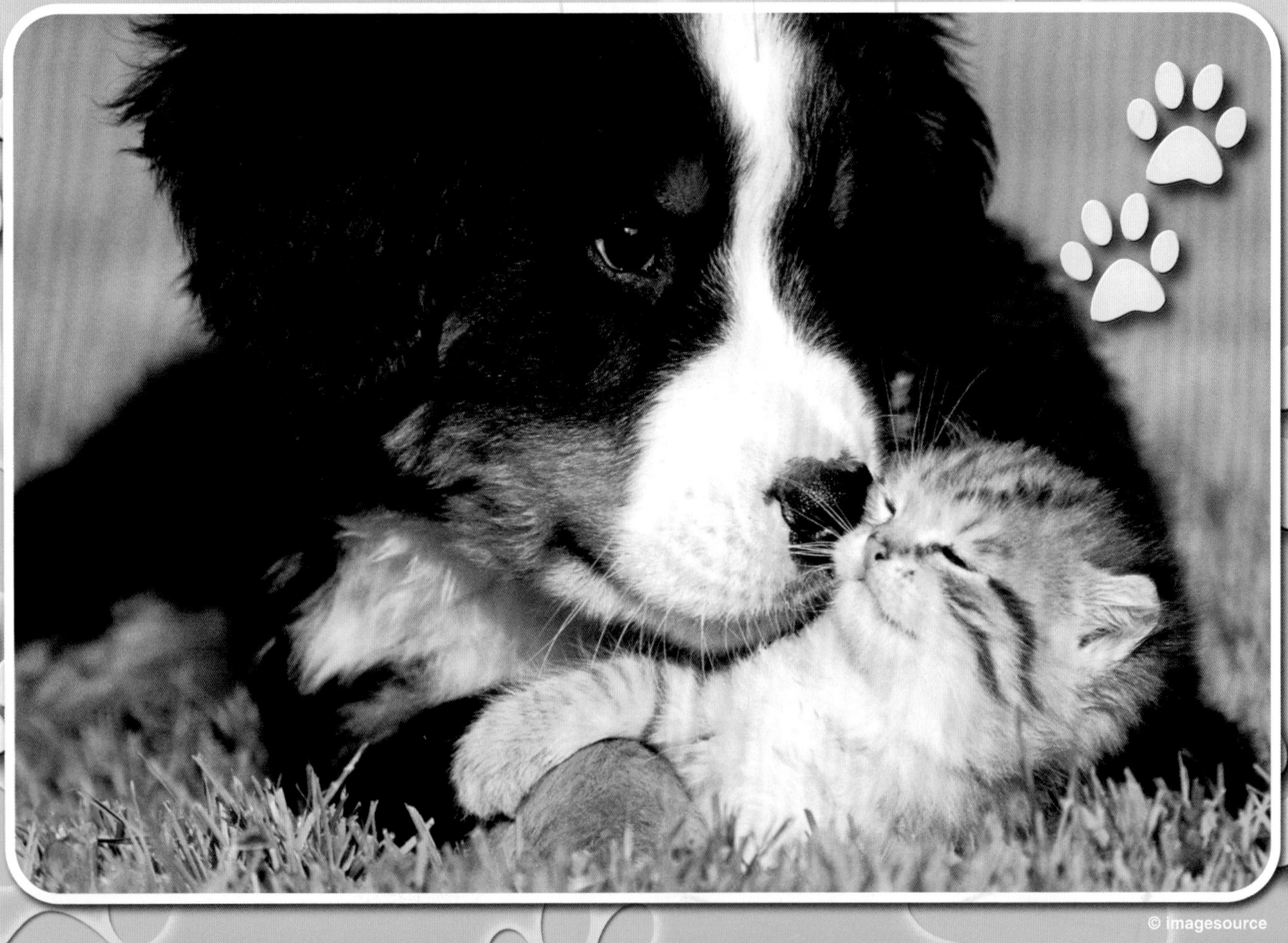

Spot the Differences!

Can you find all 5 differences in these two bunny pics?

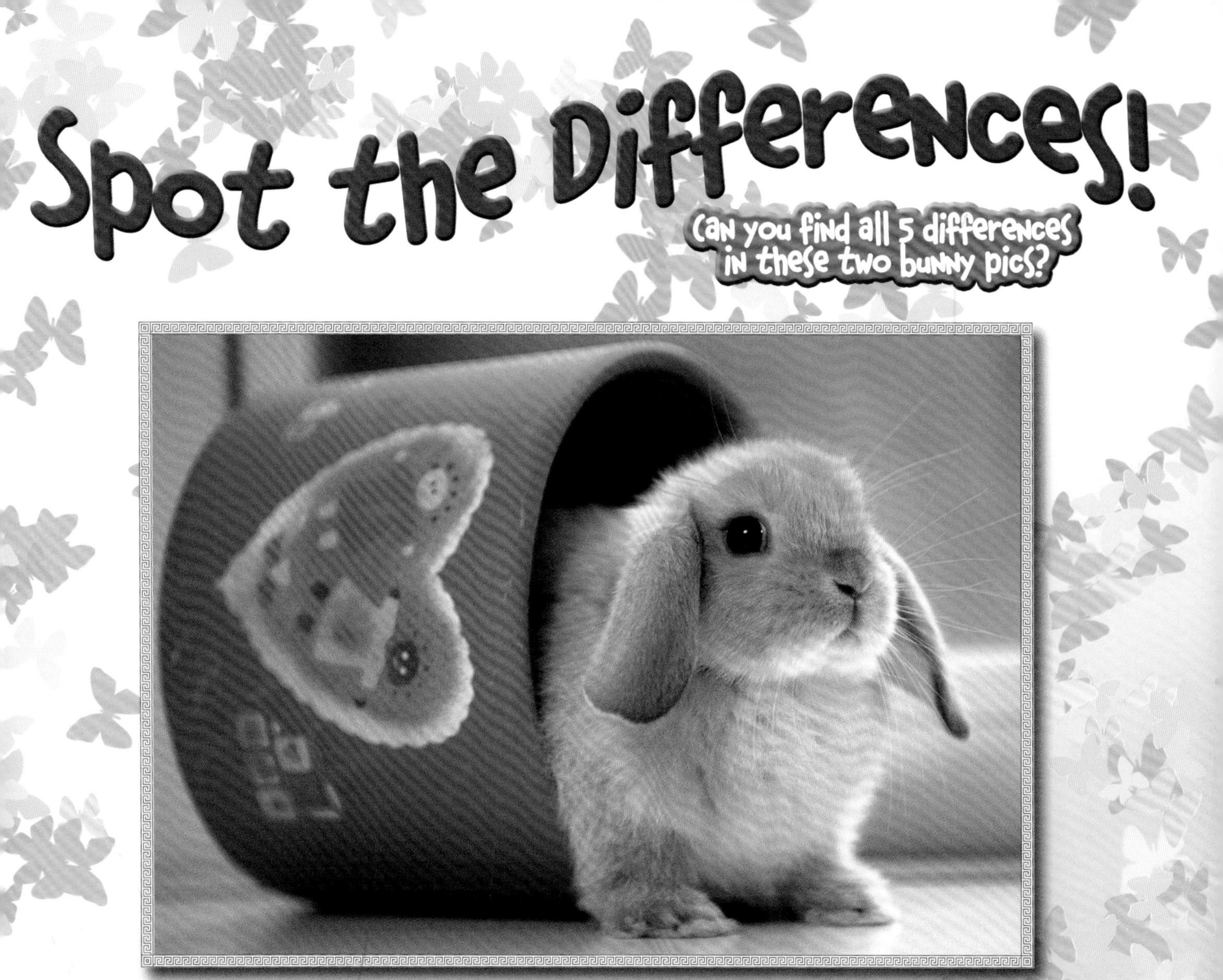

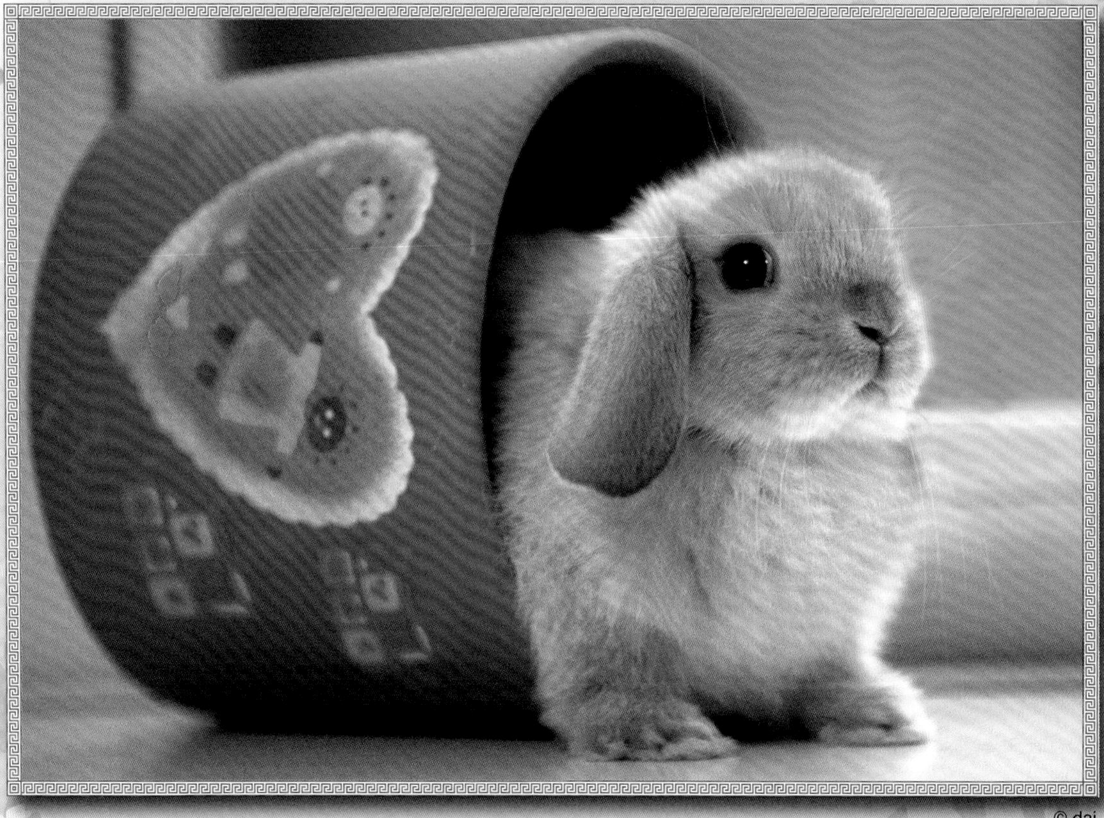

Answers:
1. Different eye colour. 2. Ear and whiskers are missing. 3. Different coloured hearts on pot (within big heart). 4. Missing squares on top of pot. 5. Extra squares on bottom of pot.

Safari Fun!

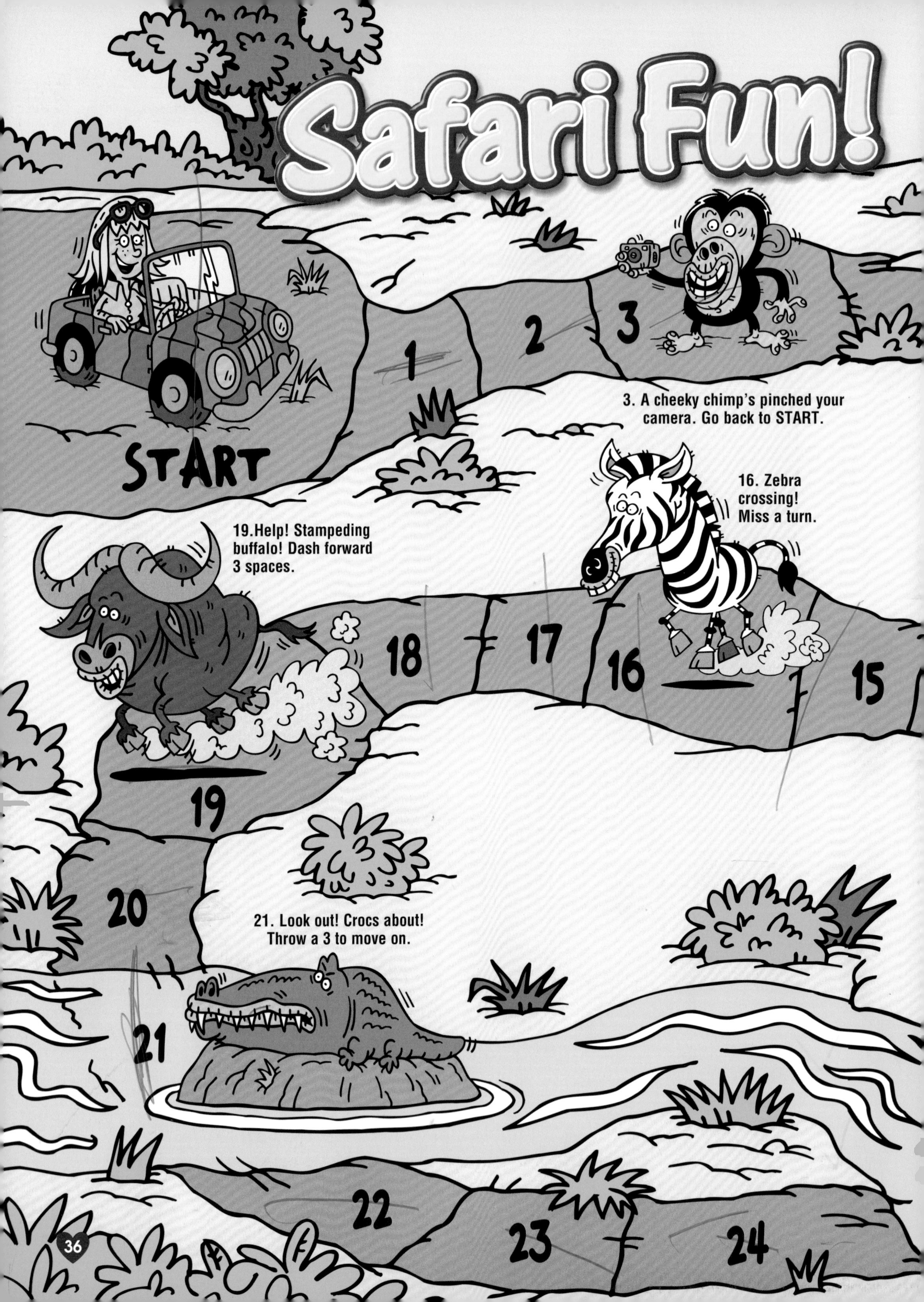
START
1
2
3
3. A cheeky chimp's pinched your camera. Go back to START.
16. Zebra crossing! Miss a turn.
19.Help! Stampeding buffalo! Dash forward 3 spaces.
18
17
16
15
19
20
21. Look out! Crocs about! Throw a 3 to move on.
21
22
23
24

Have fun on safari with our cool game! Trace the counters on to thin card if you don't want to cut the page. Throw a 1 on a dice to START then work your way round the board following the instructions. First to reach FINISH wins!

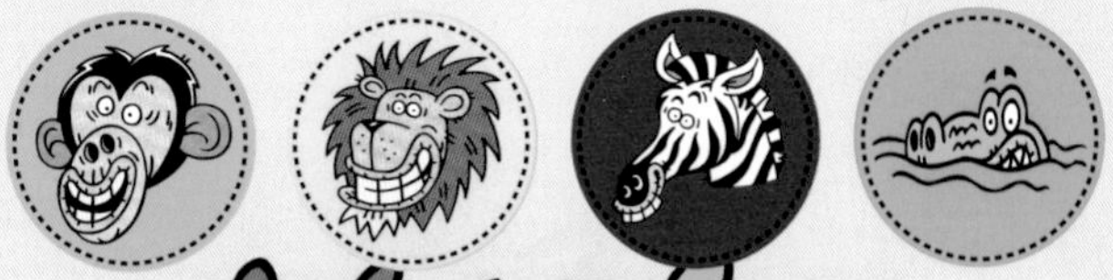

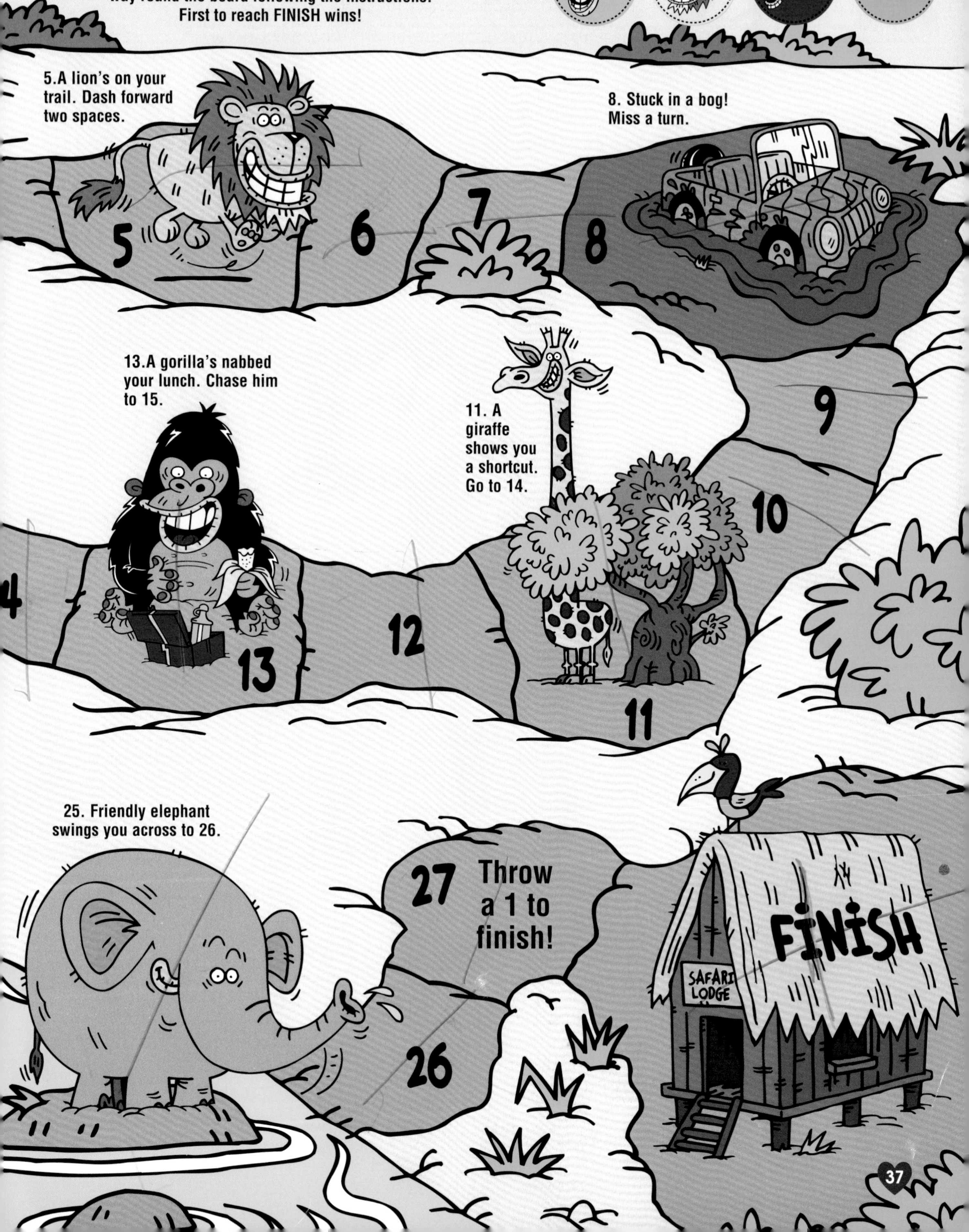
5.A lion's on your trail. Dash forward two spaces.
8. Stuck in a bog! Miss a turn.
5
6
7
8
9
10
11
12
13
4
13.A gorilla's nabbed your lunch. Chase him to 15.
11. A giraffe shows you a shortcut. Go to 14.
25. Friendly elephant swings you across to 26.
27
Throw a 1 to finish!
26
FINISH
SAFARI LODGE

ANIMALS UP TOP

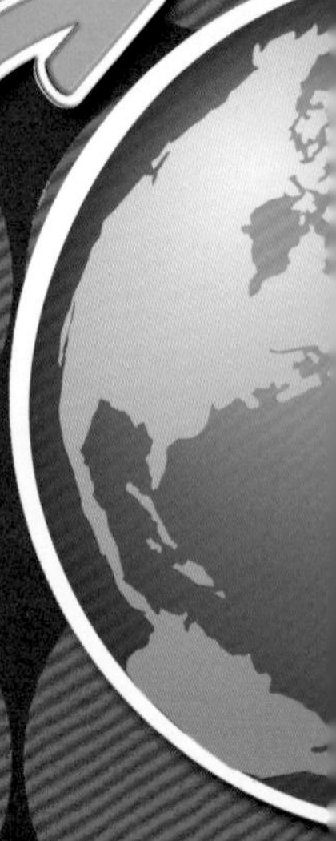

The Arctic and the Arctic Ocean are at the North Pole – that's as far north as you can go! Here are some of the hardy creatures that can survive the icy snow and freezing conditions –

polar bear

The world's largest bear spends much of its time swimming in the icy sea.

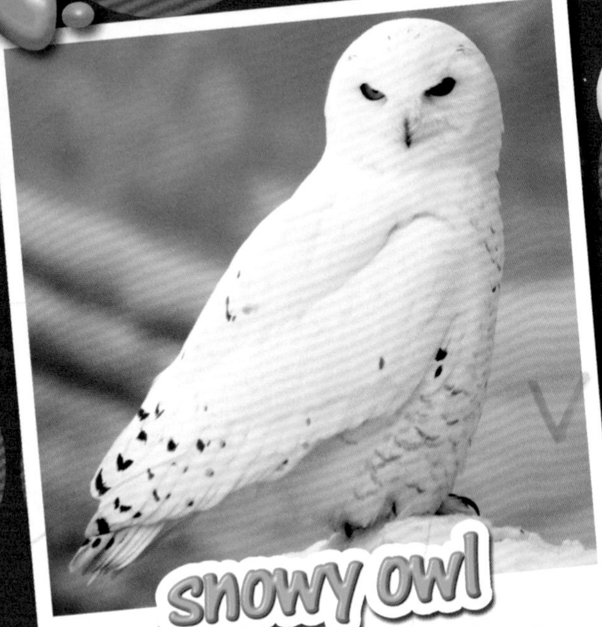

snowy owl

Unlike our owls, snowy owls are active during the day – not at night.

arctic hare

Grey-brown in the summer, this hare becomes white in the winter.

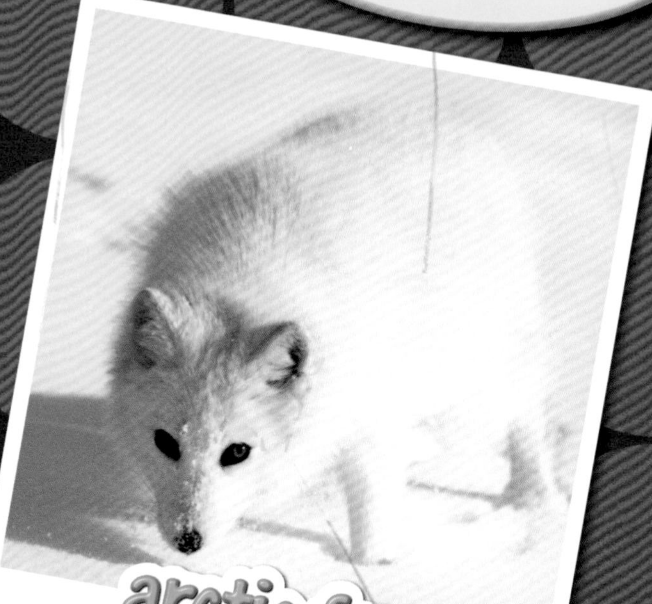

arctic fox

This small white fox lives farther north than any other land animal.

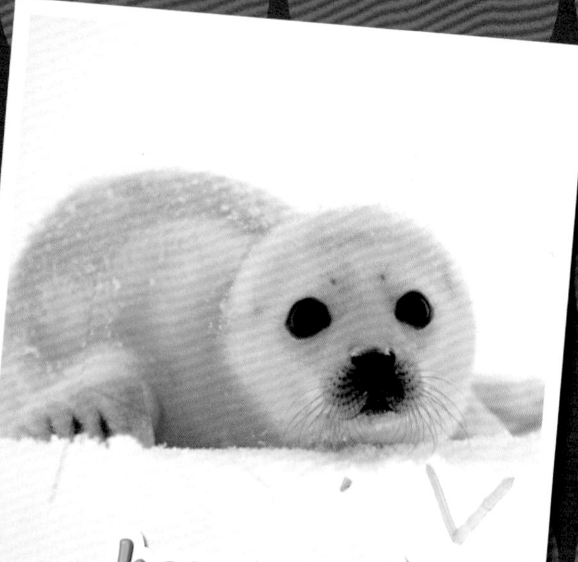

harp seal

Harp seal pups are pure white while their parents are grey.

arctic wolf

Wolves howl as a signal to other wolves, or howl just for fun!

ANIMALS DOWN UNDER

Down in Australia it's the high temperatures and lack of water that the animals have to survive. Lots of the animals are marsupials which means they have pouches for the babies to grow in.

emu
These large birds are very fast runners, but can't fly.

wombat
This big, burrowing mammal prefers to live alone.

koala
A koala rests or sleeps for up to 20 hours a day - *yawn!*

wallaby
Wallabies are small kangaroos, some as tiny as a rabbit.

duck-billed platypus
This mammal lives in water, lays eggs and uses its rubbery beak to dig out food.

kangaroo
Roos can jump over 9m in one hop!

© digital stock, photodisc & purestock © Jean Paul Ferrero, Masahiro Iijima /ardea.com

39

nice 'n' icy!

For some creatures it's cool to be in the cold and others think it's cooler to be in the sun!

ice is nice!

penguin

Penguins live on icefloes around Antarctica. They can't fly but are brilliant swimmers. The largest is the Emperor Penguin.

sun is fun!

fennec fox

These little African foxes are the smallest members of the dog family. Their huge ears keep them cool in the hot desert sun.

orca

The Killer Whale is another name for the Orca, but it's really a very big dolphin! Although they like icy waters, they can be found throughout the world.

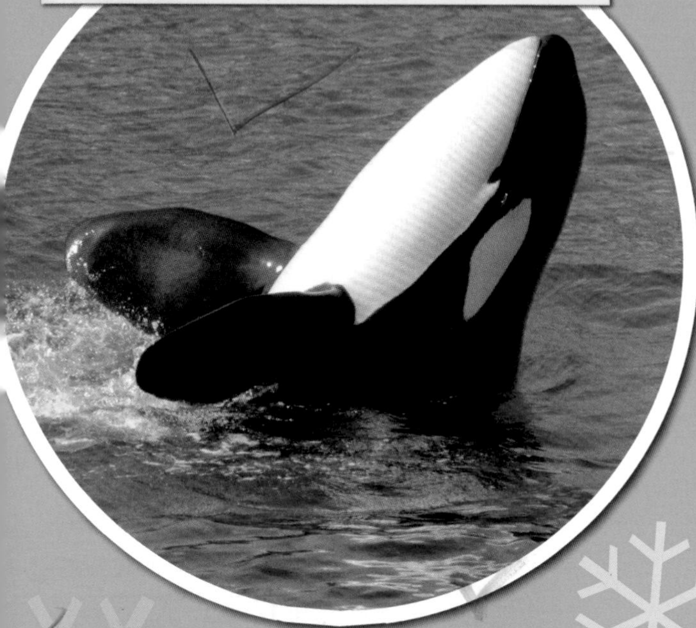

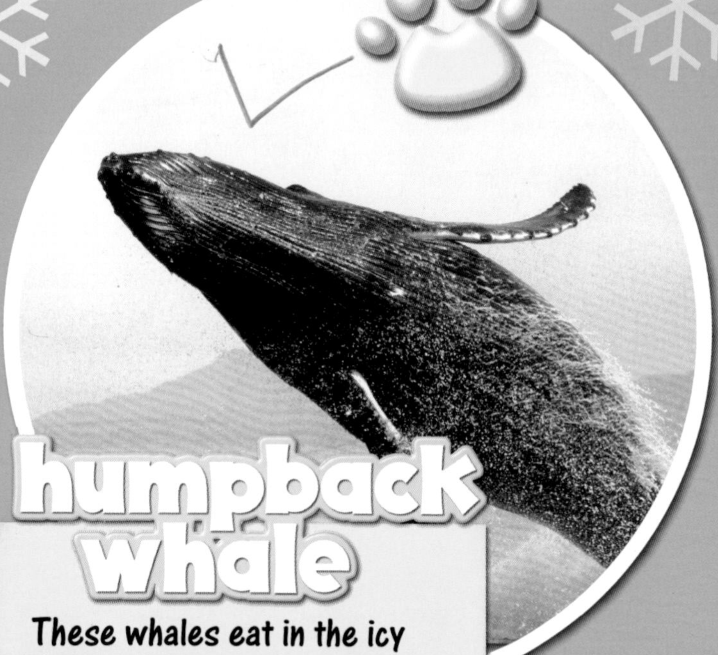

humpback whale

These whales eat in the icy oceans but move to warmer waters to have their calves. They're very noisy and well known for their 'songs'!

sand cat

This amazing cat doesn't need to drink and the extra thick fur on the soles of its feet stop it from sinking into the soft sand.

dromedary

These one-humped camels are able to go without food or water for 3-4 days and can close their nostrils if there's a sand storm!

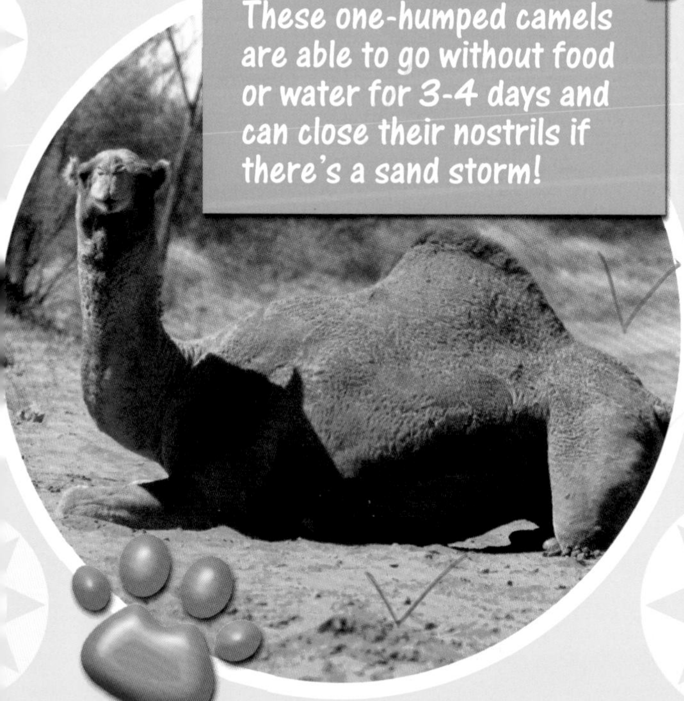

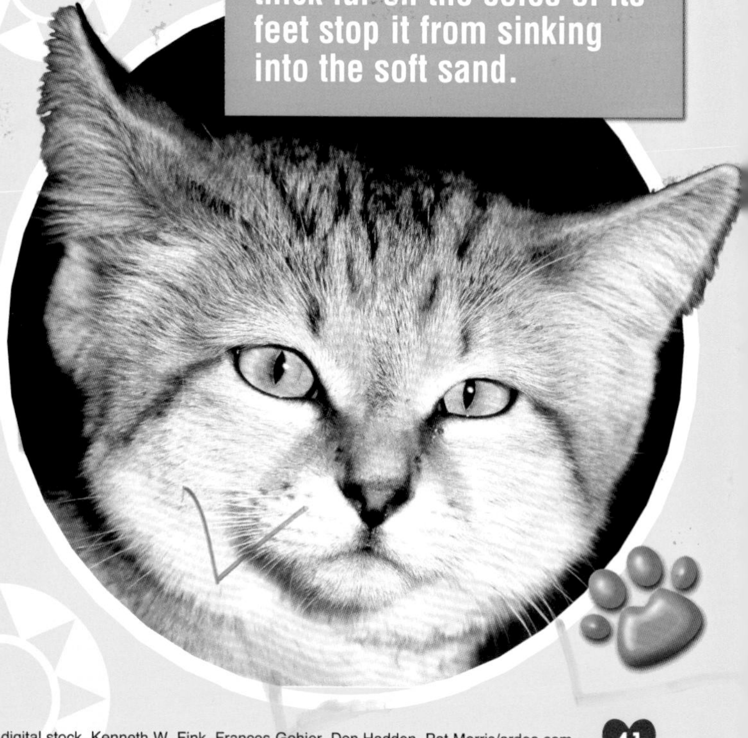

Keeper for a day!

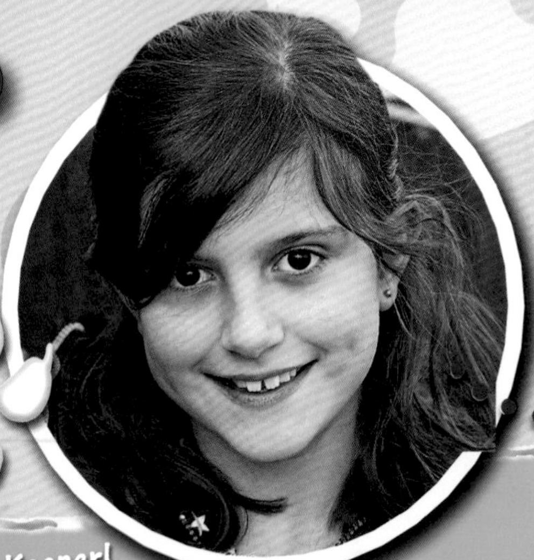

Hi, I'm Bella, and I've always wondered what it would be like to be a Zoo Keeper! Thanks to Animals and You I got to find out! I was taken to Chessington Zoo to try their Keeper for a Day scheme! Wanna see how it went?

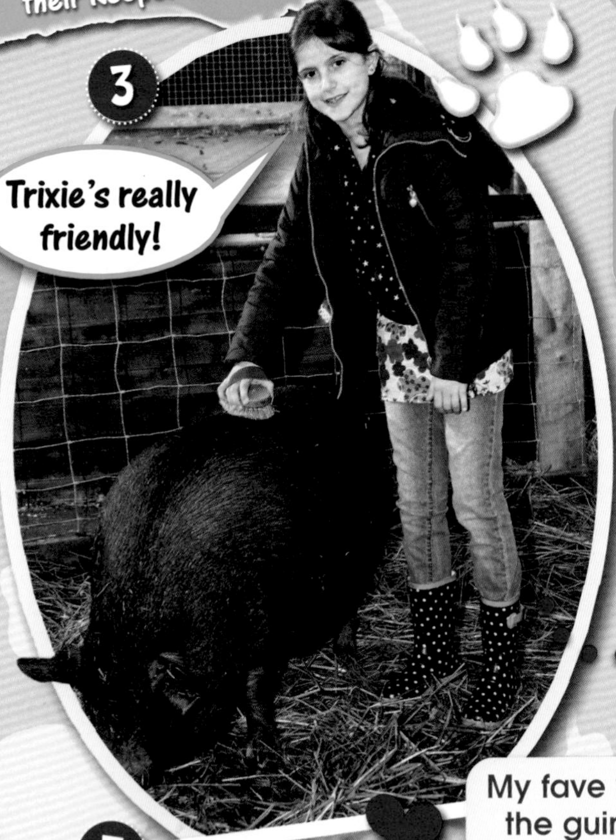

3
Trixie's really friendly!

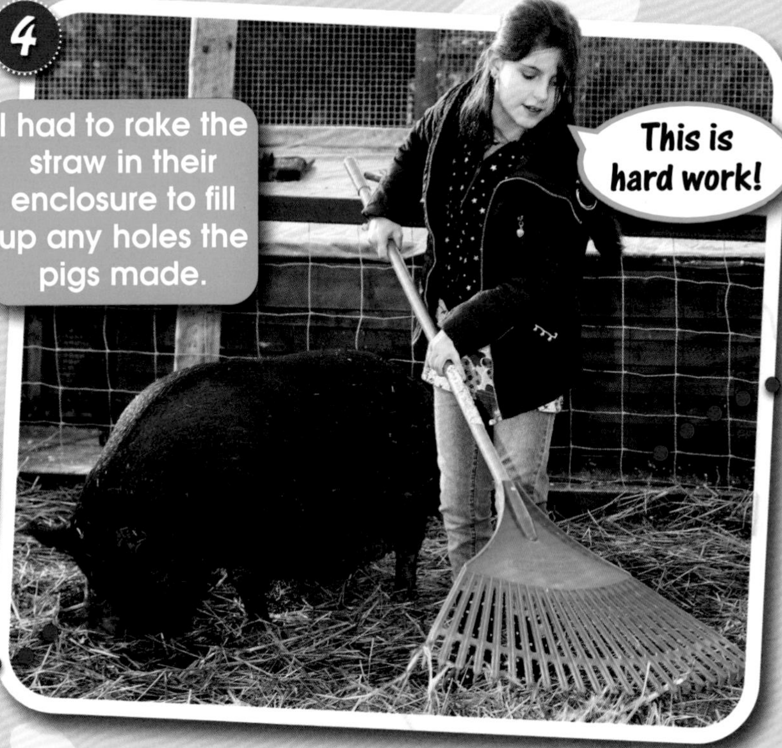

4
I had to rake the straw in their enclosure to fill up any holes the pigs made.
This is hard work!

My fave was Snuff the guinea pig. He was so sweet.

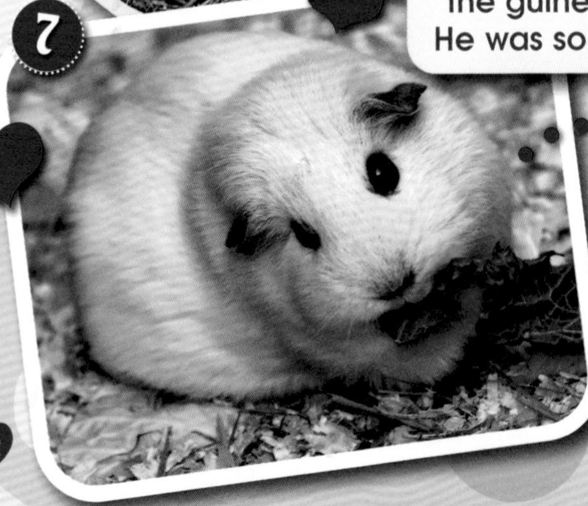

7

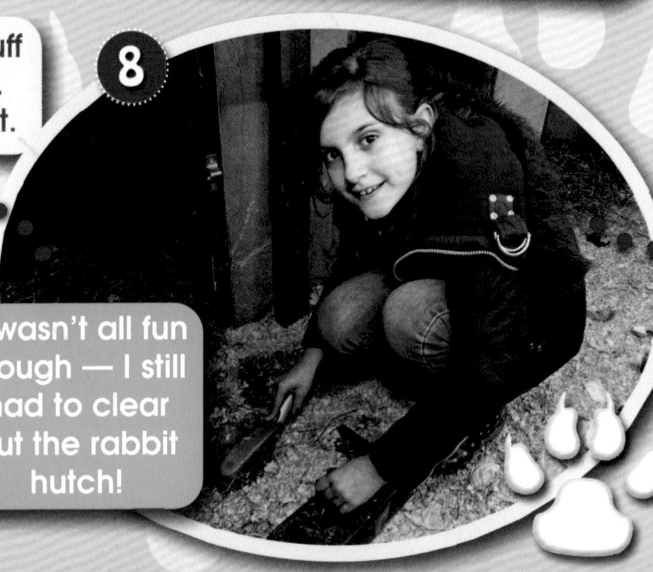

8
It wasn't all fun though — I still had to clear out the rabbit hutch!

1

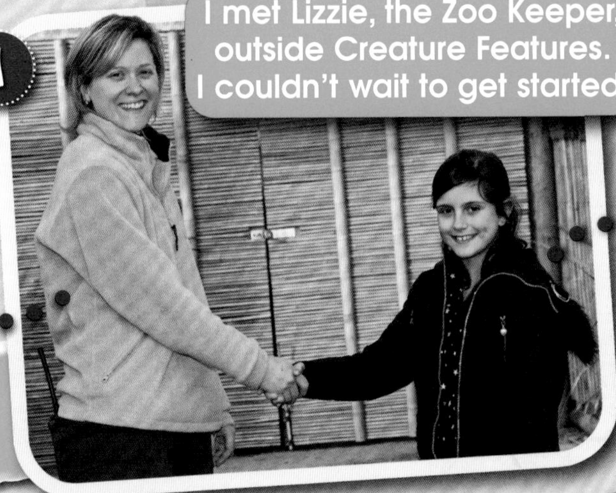

I met Lizzie, the Zoo Keeper, outside Creature Features. I couldn't wait to get started!

2

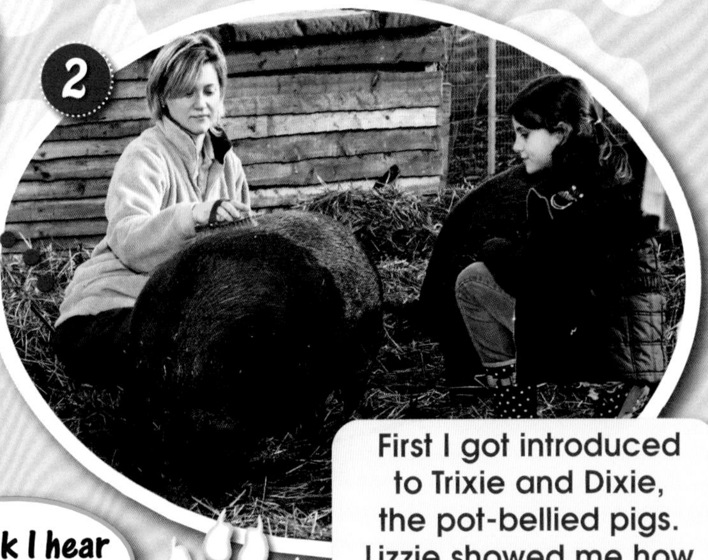

First I got introduced to Trixie and Dixie, the pot-bellied pigs. Lizzie showed me how to brush them. It helps them shed their coat.

5

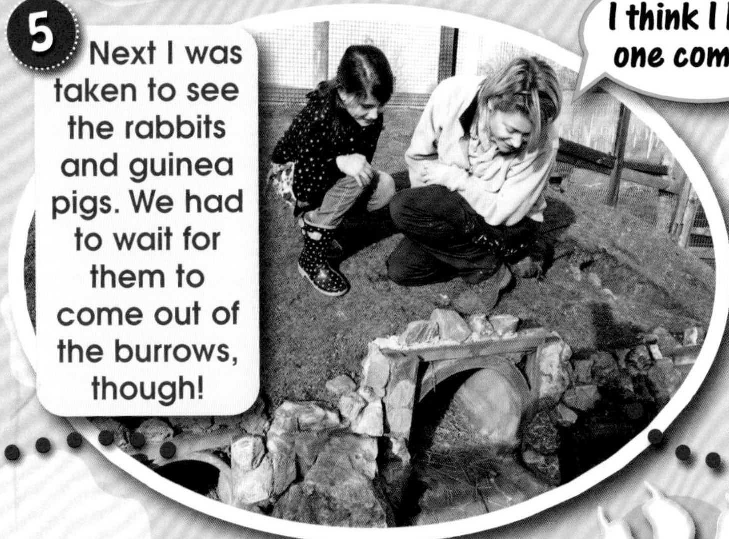
I think I hear one coming!

Next I was taken to see the rabbits and guinea pigs. We had to wait for them to come out of the burrows, though!

6

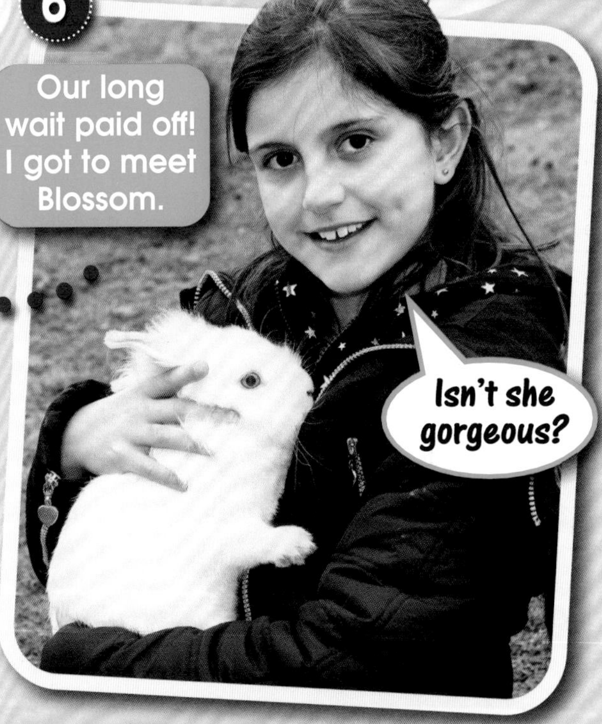
Isn't she gorgeous?

Our long wait paid off! I got to meet Blossom.

9

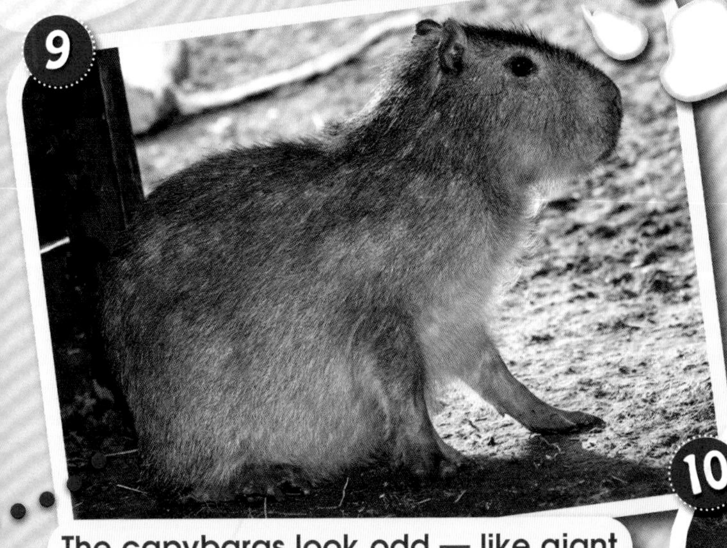

The capybaras look odd — like giant guinea pigs! What do you think?

10

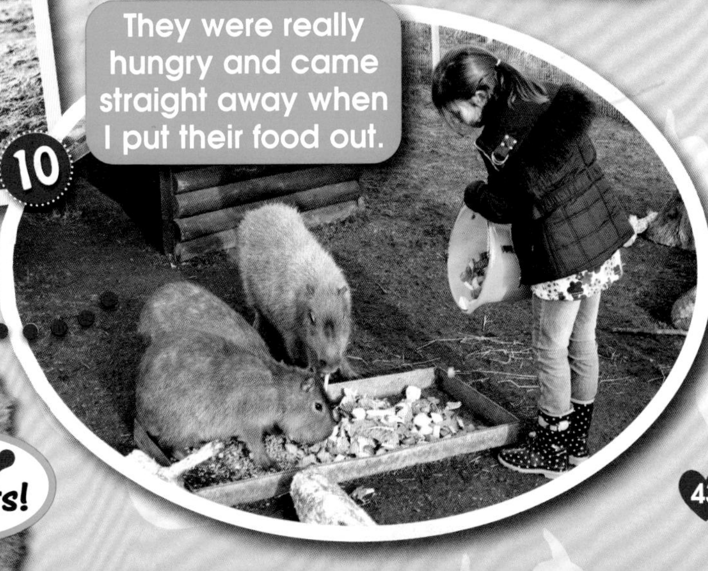

They were really hungry and came straight away when I put their food out.

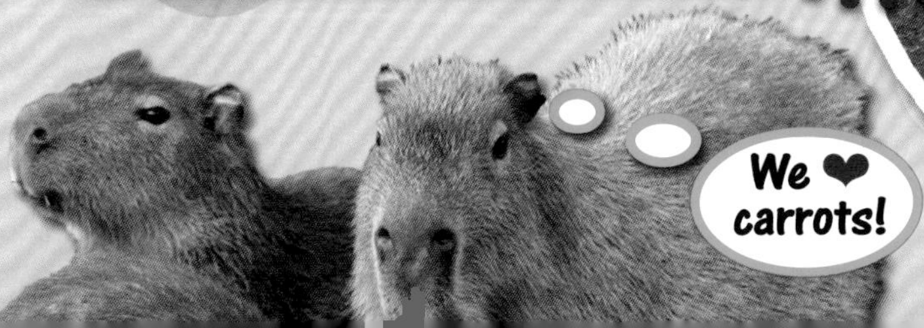
We ❤ carrots!

11

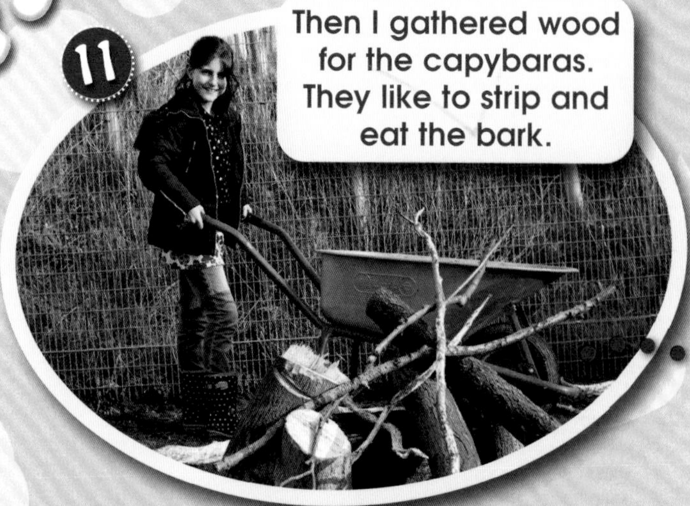

Then I gathered wood for the capybaras. They like to strip and eat the bark.

12

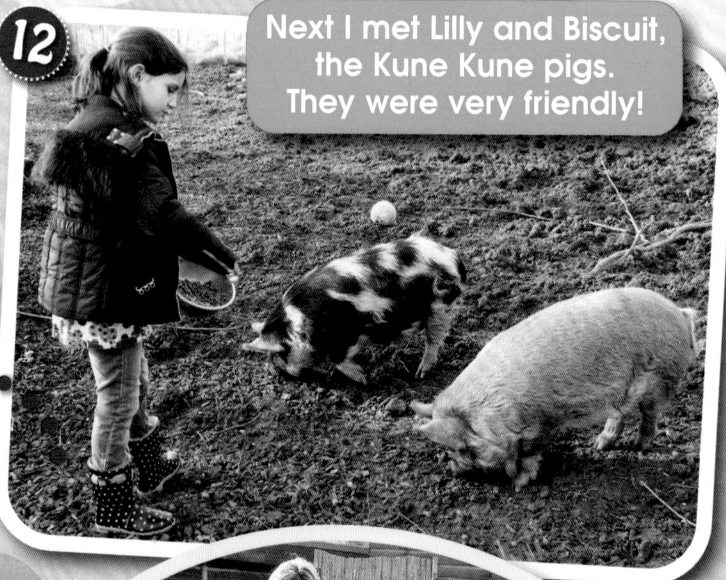

Next I met Lilly and Biscuit, the Kune Kune pigs. They were very friendly!

13

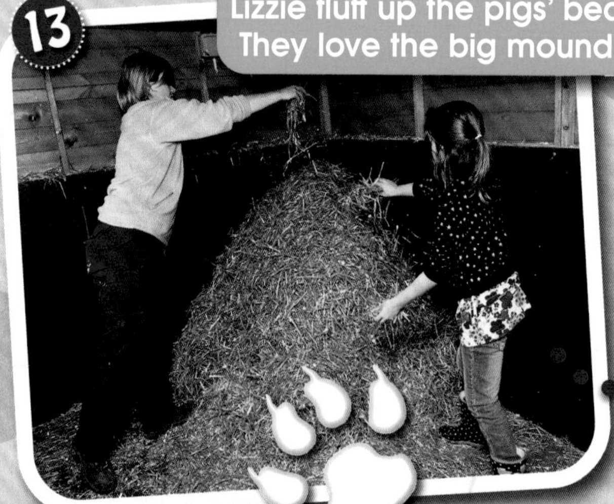

I had loads of fun helping Lizzie fluff up the pigs' bed. They love the big mound!

14

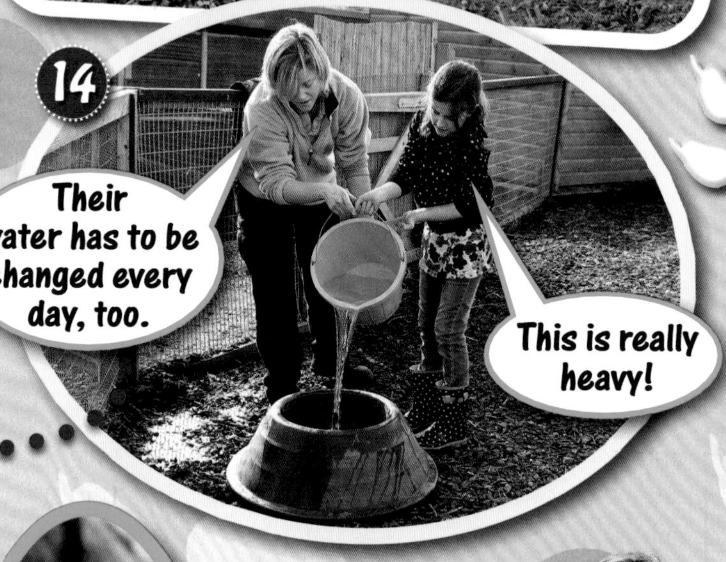
Their water has to be changed every day, too.
This is really heavy!

15

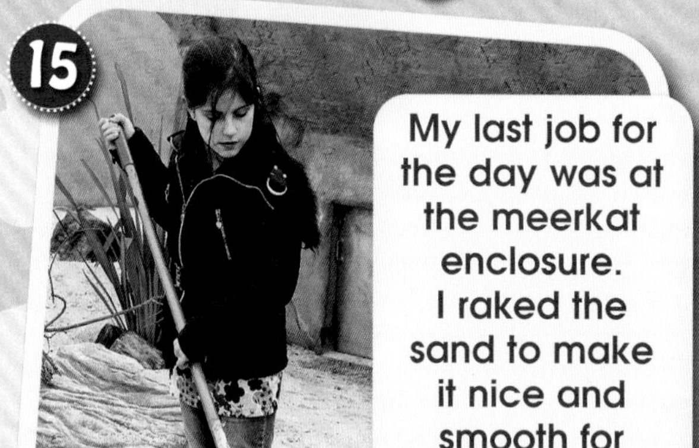

My last job for the day was at the meerkat enclosure. I raked the sand to make it nice and smooth for them — just the way they like it!

16

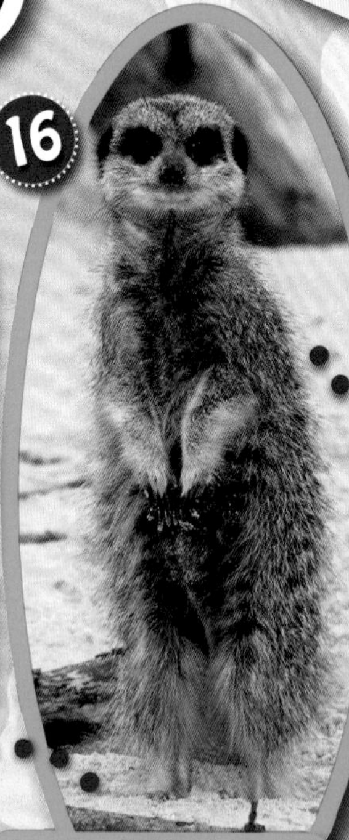

I loved watching the meerkats — they look so funny when they stand up!

17

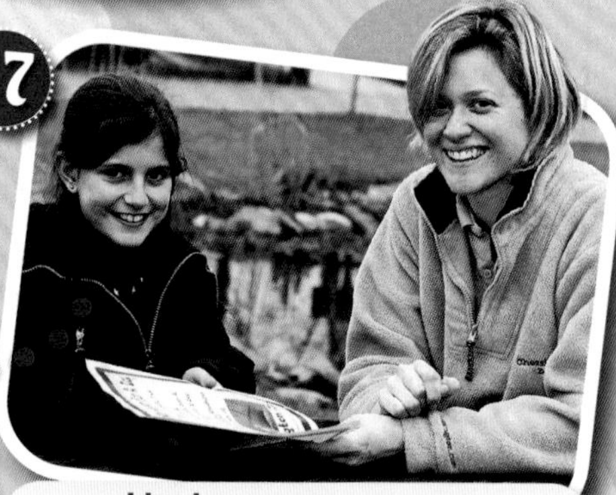

Lizzie gave me a certificate for taking part in the Keeper scheme! It's cool and I'll never forget my day as a Keeper!

18

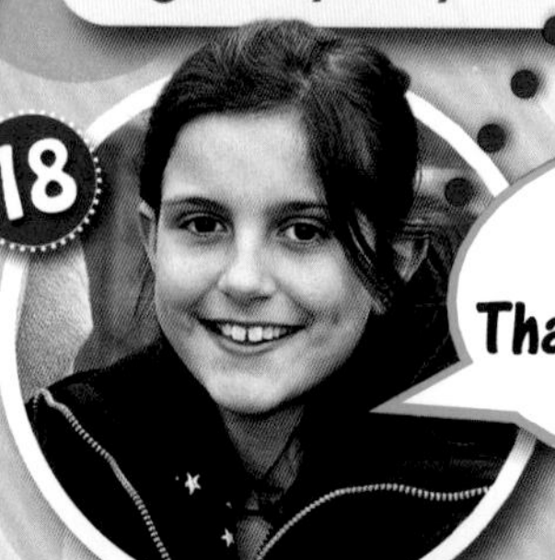
It was amazing! Thanks, Animals and You!

If you'd like more info on the Keeper for a Day scheme, visit www.chessington.co.uk.

RESCUED!

Ruby, the little Shetland pony was orphaned when she was only eight weeks old. Her owner struggled to cope and asked the horse charity, Redwings, for help with the tiny foal.

Redwings took Ruby in and the staff became her mum! She was hand fed day and night for six weeks and she got lots of cuddles too - aaw! With all that tender loving care, Ruby got steadily stronger.

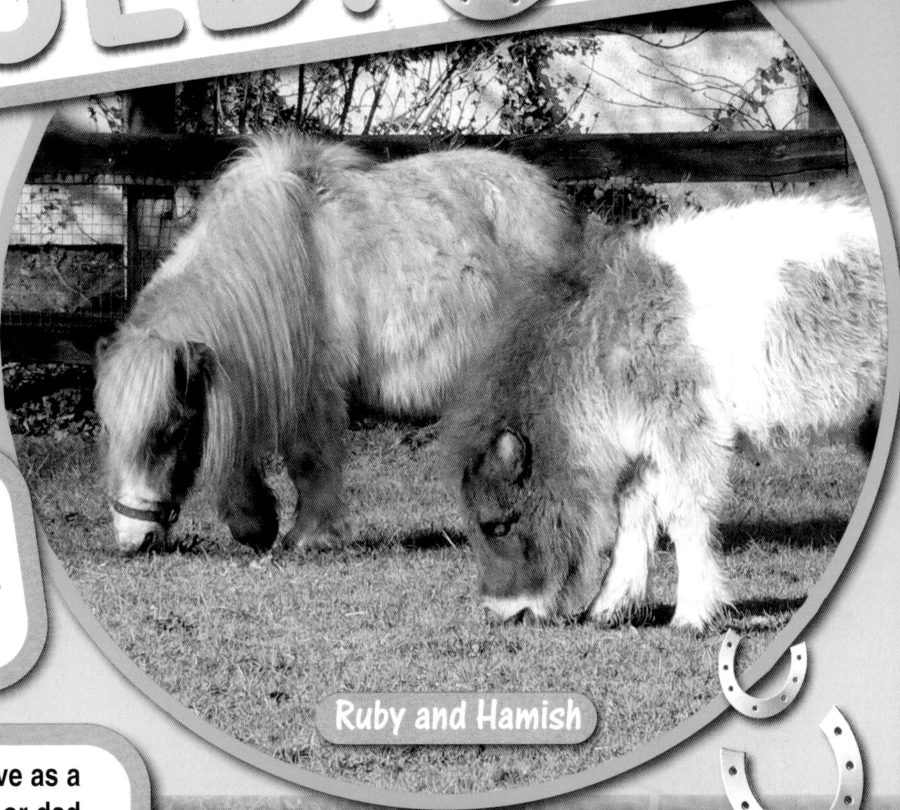

Ruby and Hamish

Ruby then needed to learn how to behave as a pony which was difficult without a mum or dad. That's when Hamish, an 11-year-old Shetland, was brought in. The two little ponies bonded right away and with Hamish's help, Ruby was soon doing all kinds of pony things! Now Ruby and Hamish are always seen together - the best of friends.

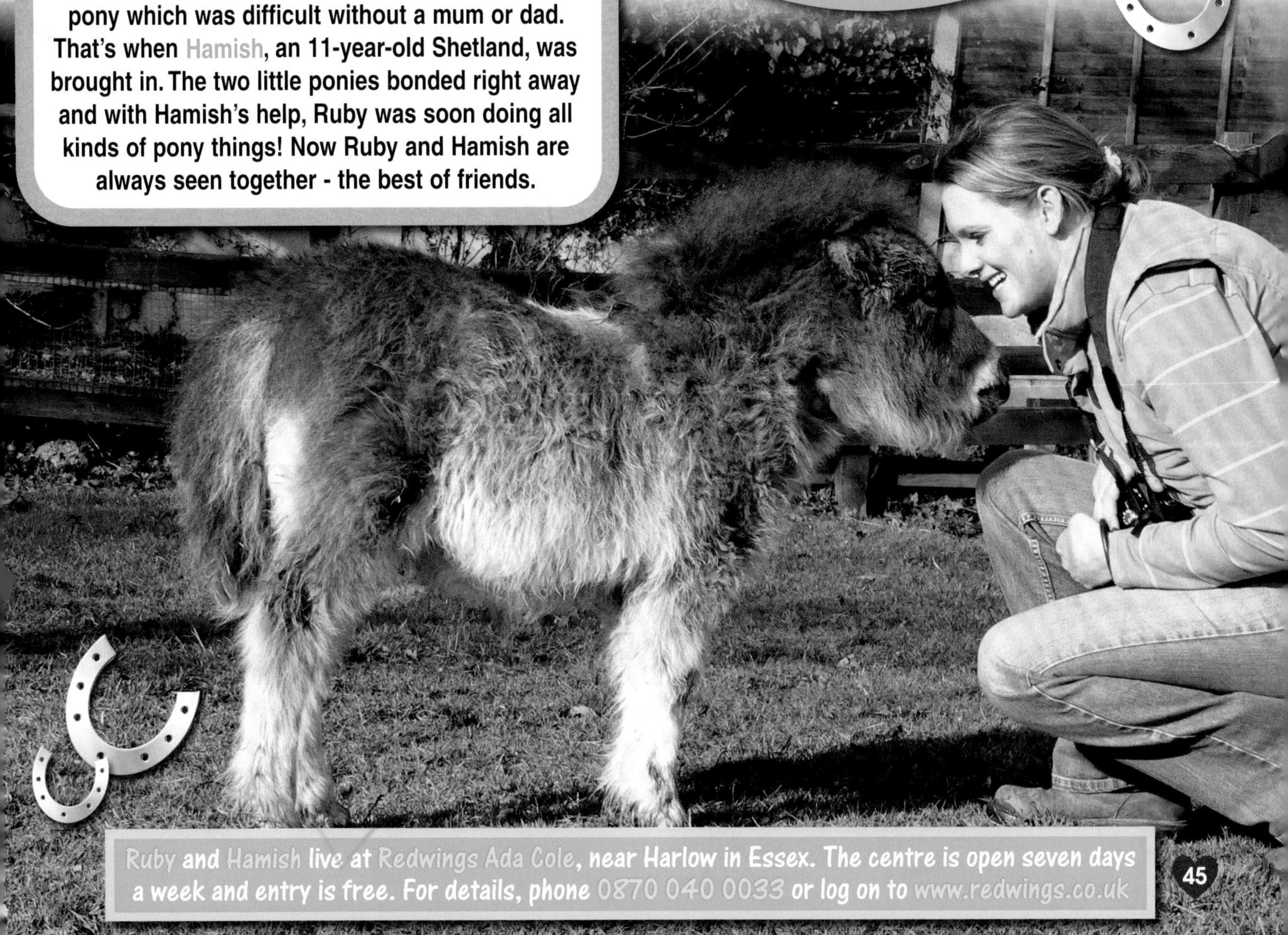

Ruby and Hamish live at Redwings Ada Cole, near Harlow in Essex. The centre is open seven days a week and entry is free. For details, phone 0870 040 0033 or log on to www.redwings.co.uk

dolphin babies

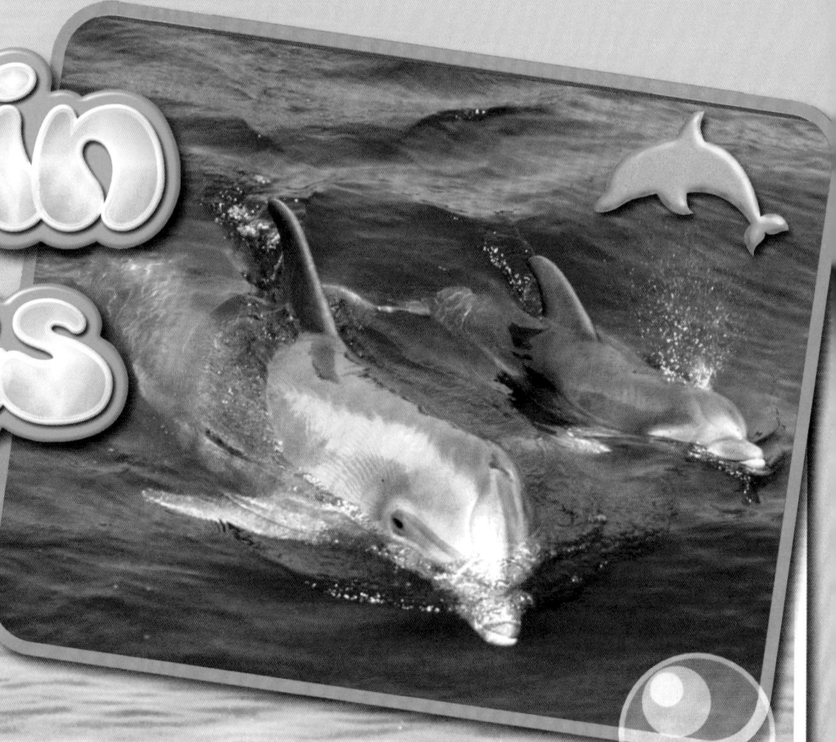

A baby dolphin is called a calf and, even though dolphins breathe air, their babies are born underwater!

Mum immediately pushes her calf to the surface to let it breathe then floats on her side to let it drink her rich milk.

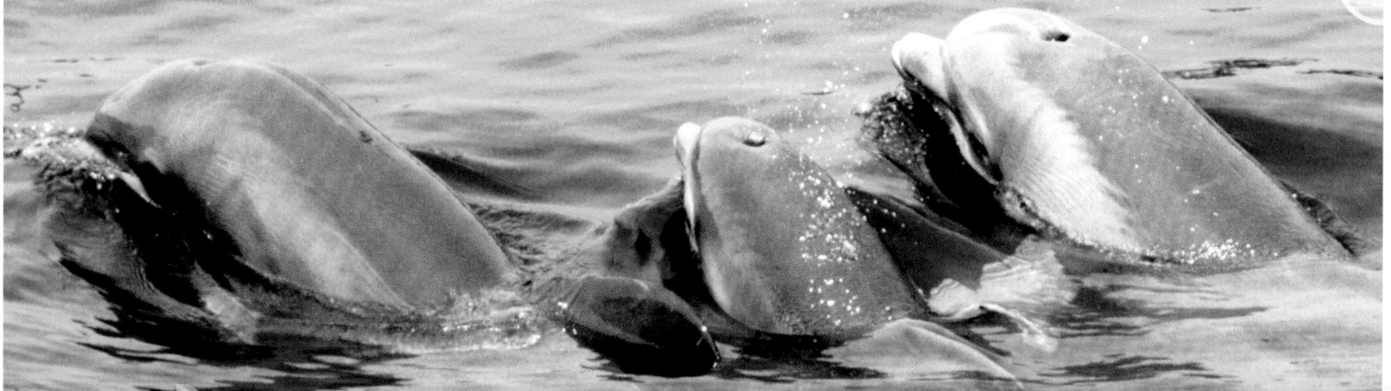

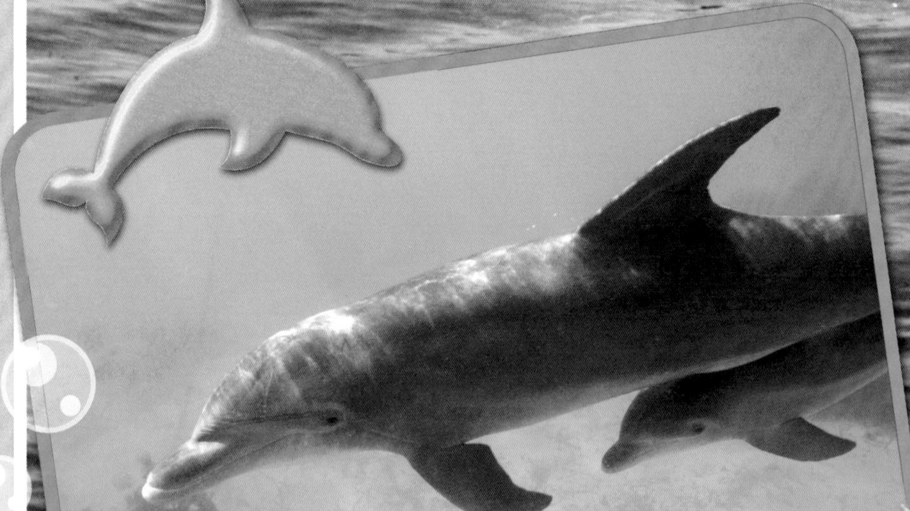

Dolphins are so protective of their young that they will fight off menacing sharks by crashing into them over and over again, using their snouts as battering rams.

Playing and feeding together are very important bonding times for dolphins.

Bottlenose dolphins have only one calf every 2-3 years.

The calf will drink Mum's milk for up to 18 months before feeding on fish.

Their favourite game is bow-riding which is swimming alongside ships, leaping out of the water and doing somersaults!

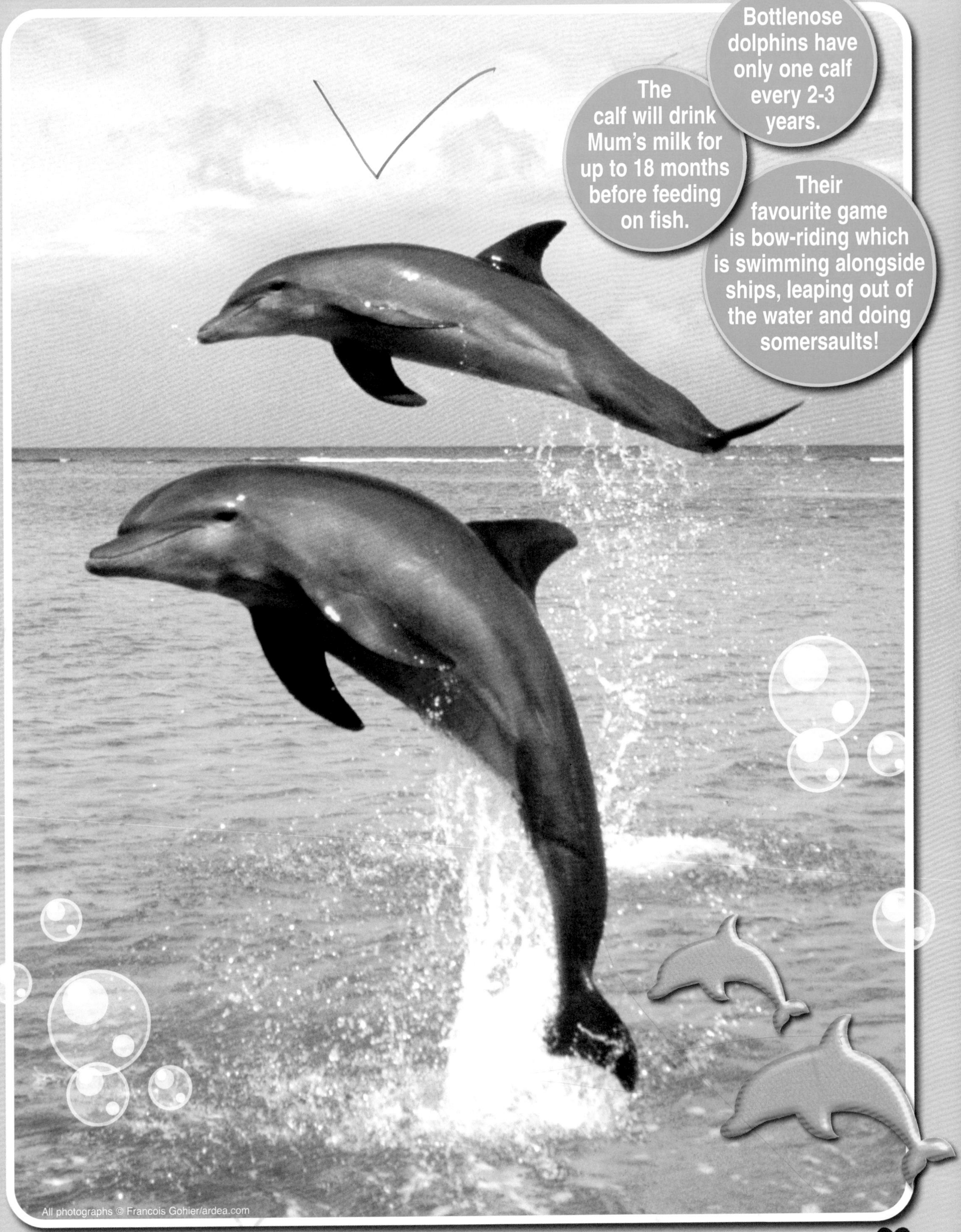

Dizzy's Amazing Dog Facts

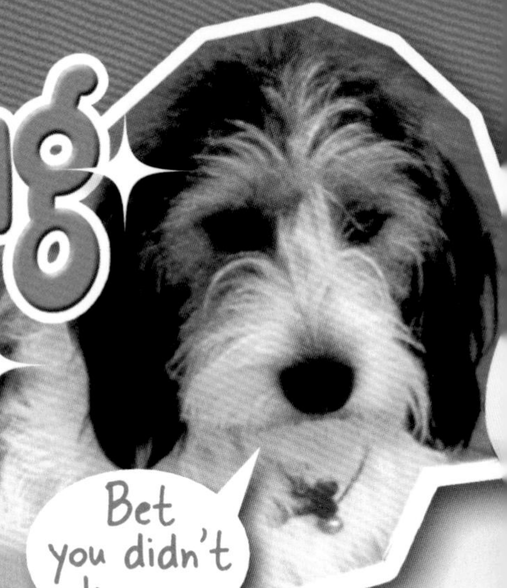
Bet you didn't know...

Three dogs survived the sinking of the Titanic - a Newfoundland, a Pomeranian and a Pekingese.

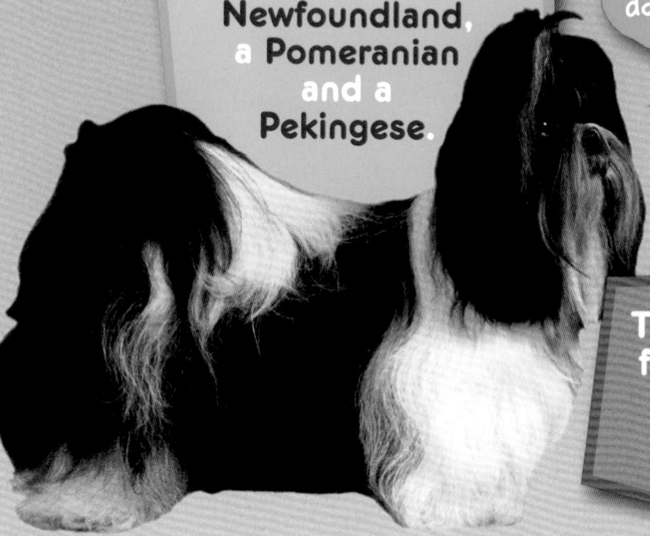
I swam doggy-paddle!

Hollywood's first doggy superstar, Rin Tin Tin signed all his movie contracts with a paw print!

Tigger, a bloodhound from Illinois, has the longest doggie ears... more than 34 cm long!

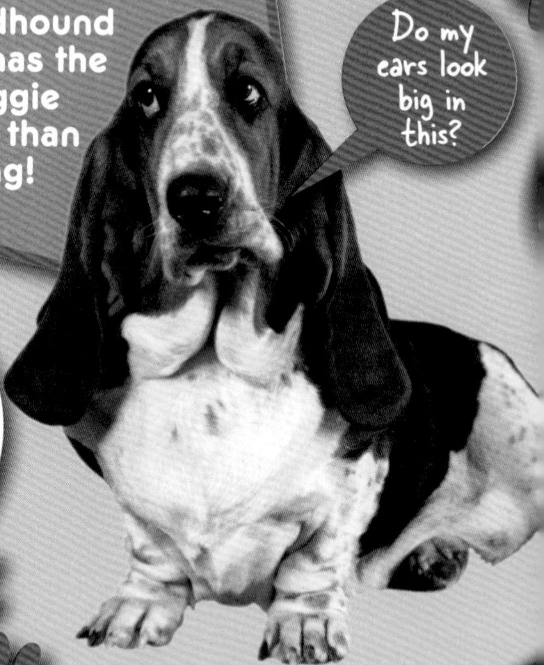
Do my ears look big in this?

Dogs' only sweat glands are between their paw pads.

Dogs' nose prints are as unique as human fingerprints and can be used to identify them.

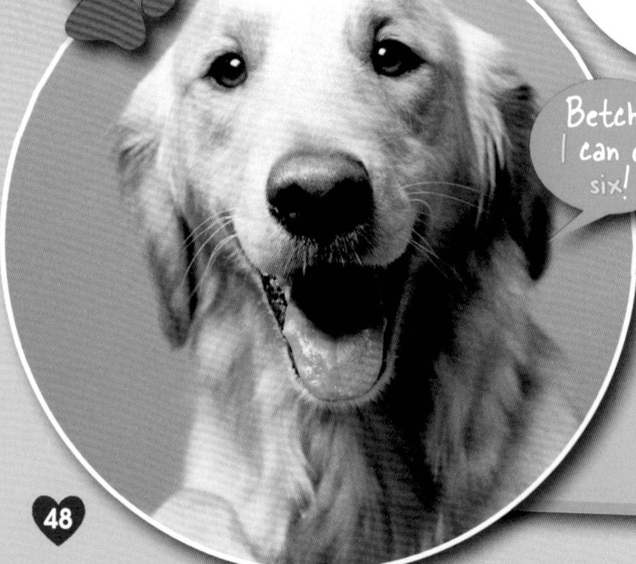
Betcha I can do six!

A Golden Retriever called Augie holds the world record for keeping the most tennis balls in his mouth. He managed five! Big mouth!

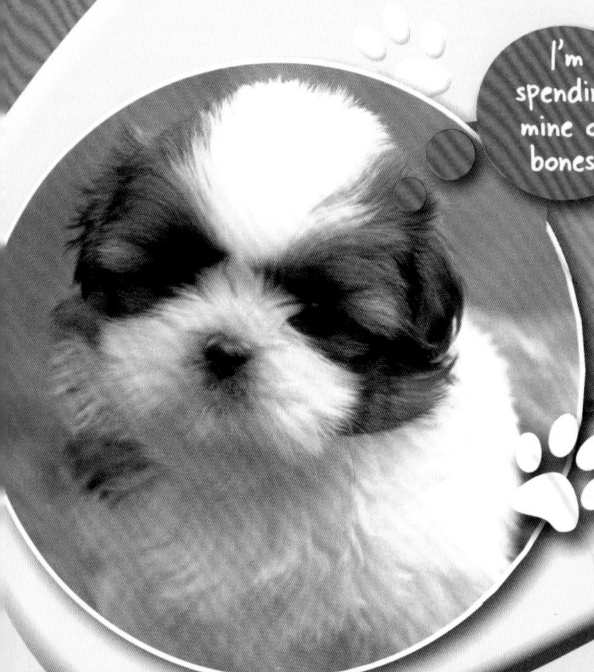
I'm spending mine on bones!

It's thought over a million dogs in the USA have inherited most of their owners' money in their wills! Minted mutts!

A third of American dog owners talk to their pooches on the phone and leave answering machine messages for them!

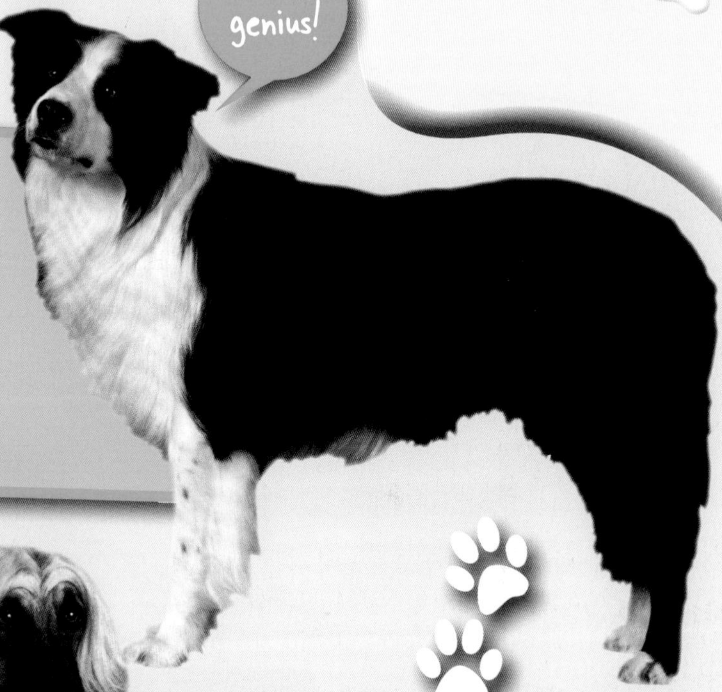
I'm a genius!

The Lundehune breed has six toes and can close its ears...handy when parents are being annoying??!

The world's smartest dogs are thought to be 1) the border collie, 2) the poodle and 3) the golden retriever...

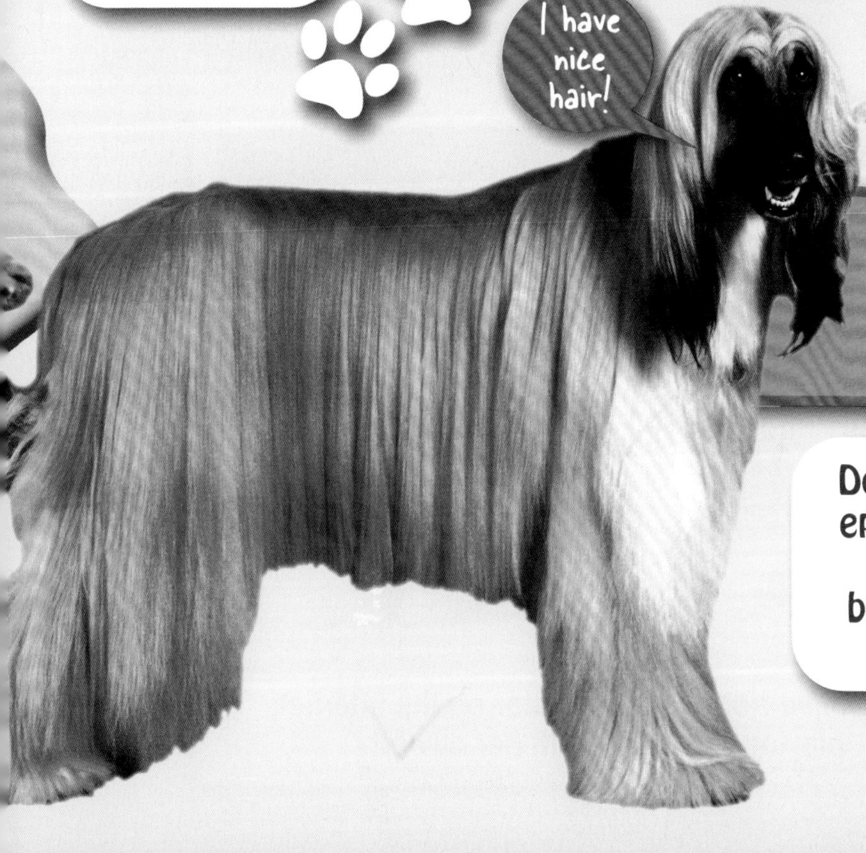
I have nice hair!

...Afghans are believed to be the dumbest! (But who needs brains when you're that beautiful?!).

Dogs can be trained to detect epileptic fits (where a person suffering from epilepsy becomes ill) - before they've actually happened!

Clever Kitties!

Cats are amazing creatures! Here's why...

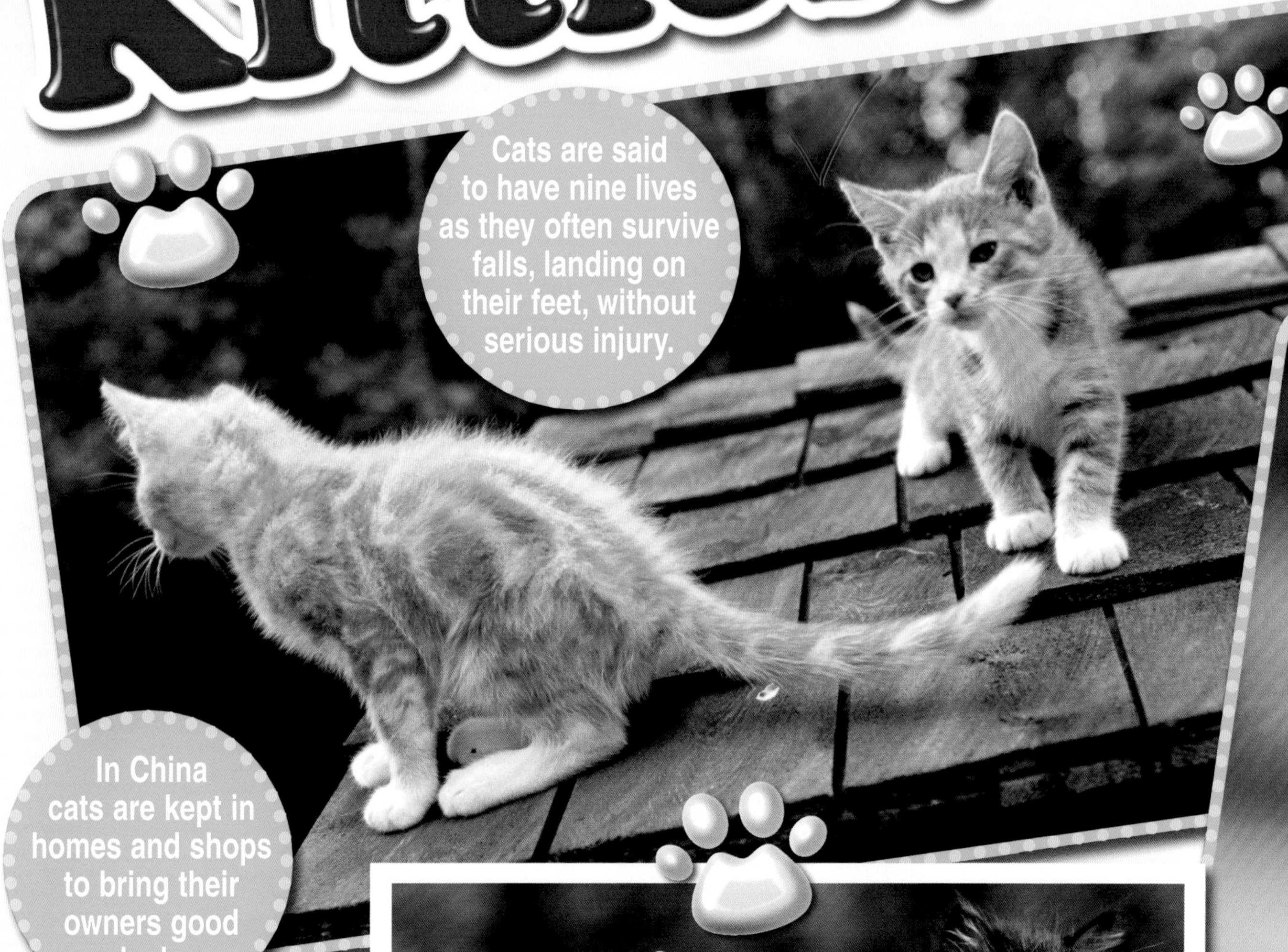

Cats are said to have nine lives as they often survive falls, landing on their feet, without serious injury.

In China cats are kept in homes and shops to bring their owners good luck.

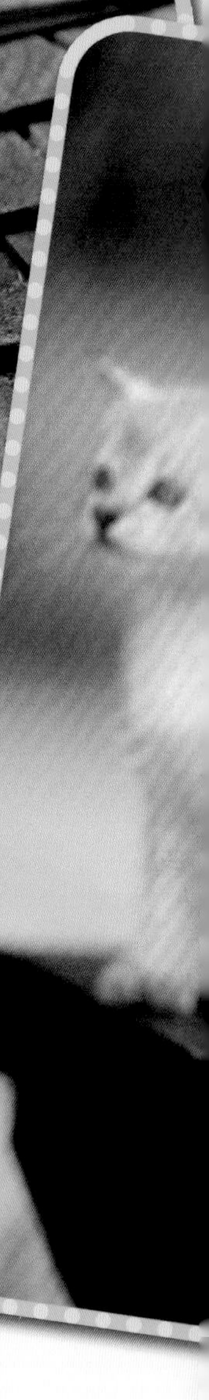

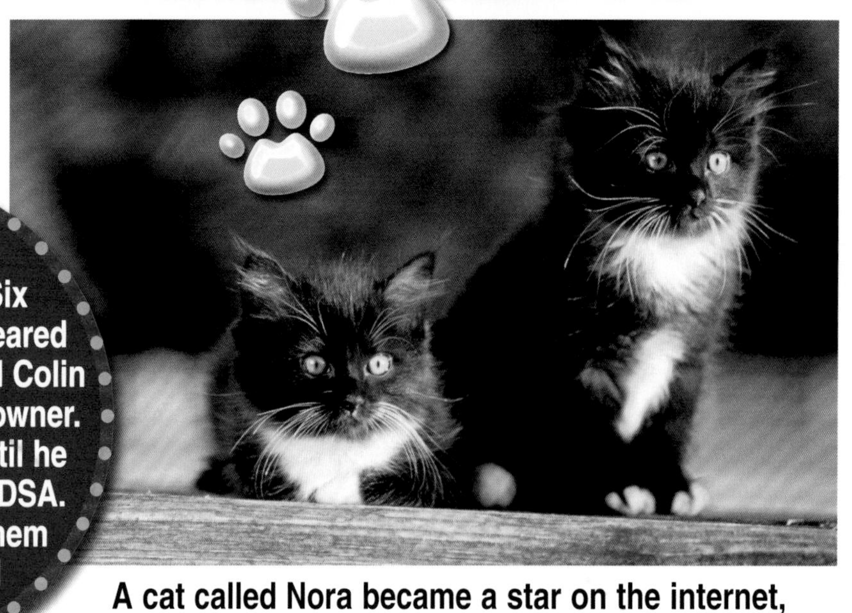

Cats sometimes go missing for ages. Six years after he disappeared from home, a cat called Colin was reunited with his owner. He lived as a stray until he was rescued by the PDSA. His microchip told them who he belonged to.

A cat called Nora became a star on the internet, playing the piano with her owner!

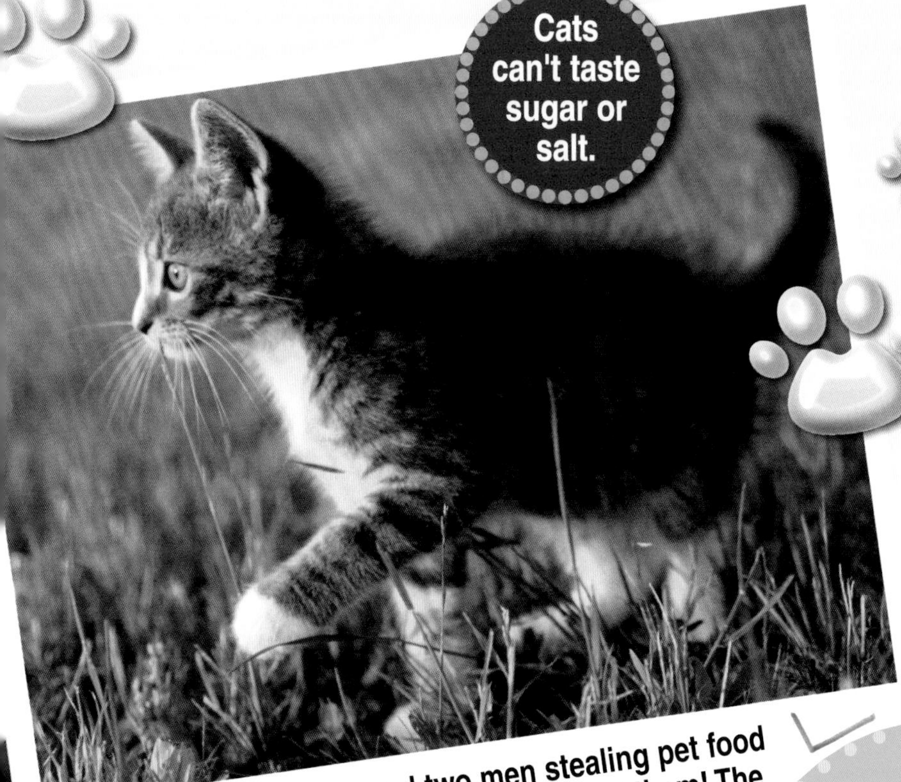

Cats can't taste sugar or salt.

When Bonnie the cat found two men stealing pet food from her owner's warehouse, she attacked them! The thieves were scared off by the angry moggy!

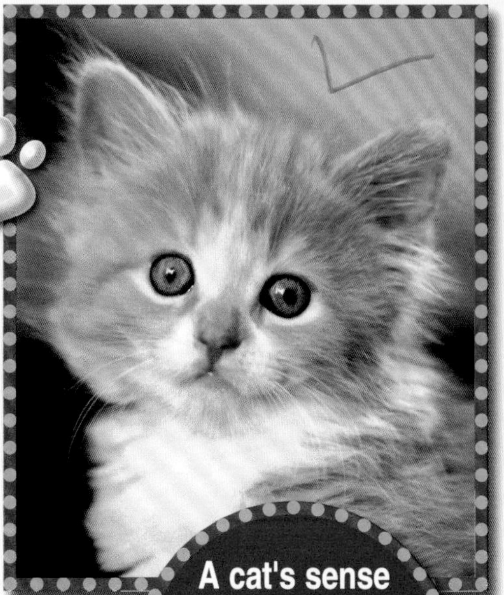

A cat's sense of smell is so strong it can detect another cat up to 100 metres away.

A Canadian cat that hitched a lift on a truck ended up 600 miles from home. The truck driver managed to track down his owners and later flew him back home!

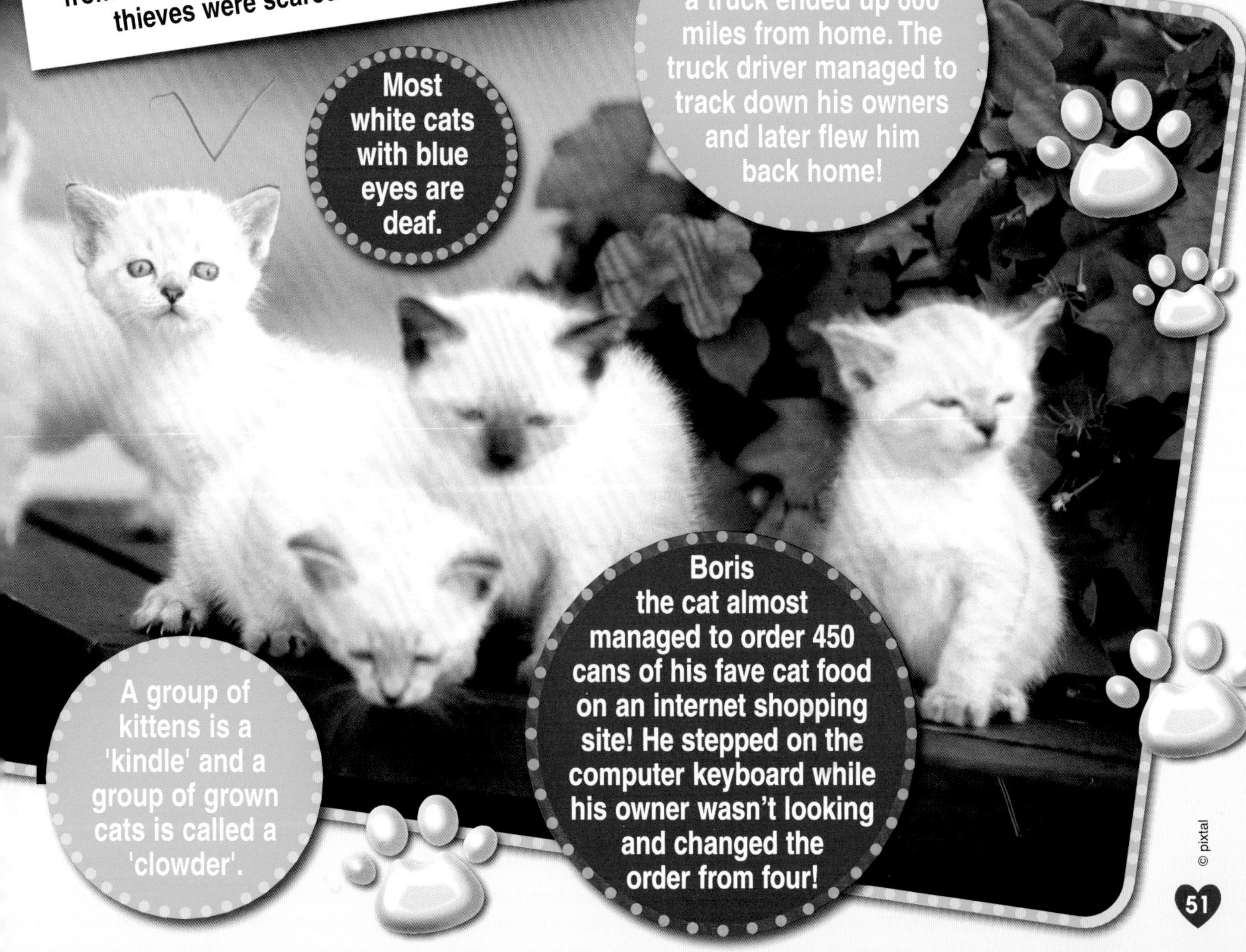

Most white cats with blue eyes are deaf.

Boris the cat almost managed to order 450 cans of his fave cat food on an internet shopping site! He stepped on the computer keyboard while his owner wasn't looking and changed the order from four!

A group of kittens is a 'kindle' and a group of grown cats is called a 'clowder'.

Christmas Kisses!

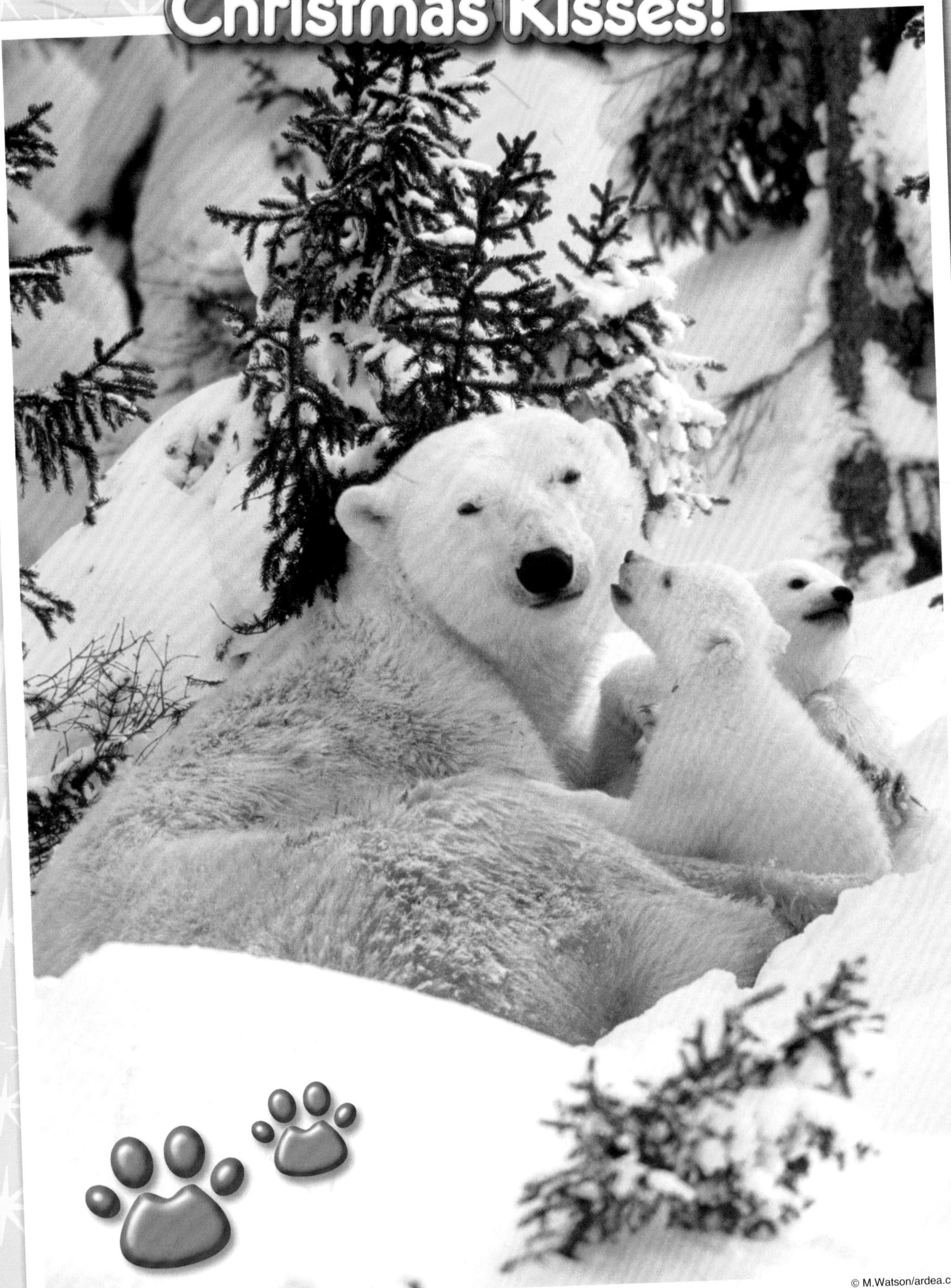

how to draw... a polar bear

Get your pencils at the ready because we're about to show you an easy peasy step by step way to draw this cute furry critter.

1

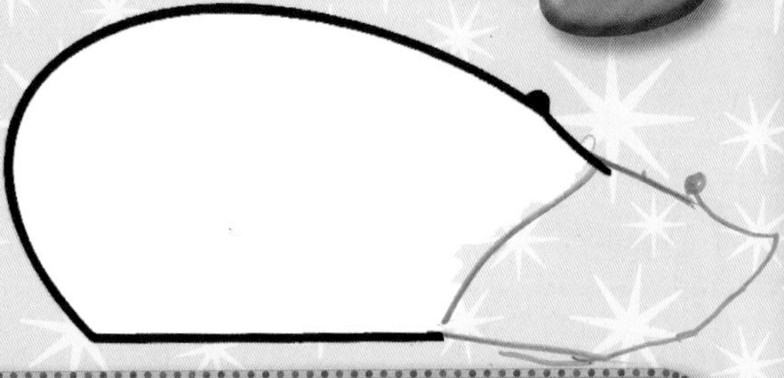

Using a pencil, draw a line that looks like the shape of a mouse with a little ear.

2

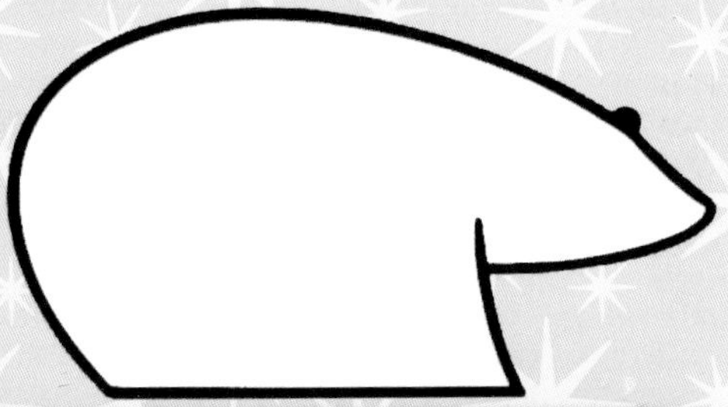

Draw the front leg by adding a line and then draw the head by joining the body to the front leg like this.

3

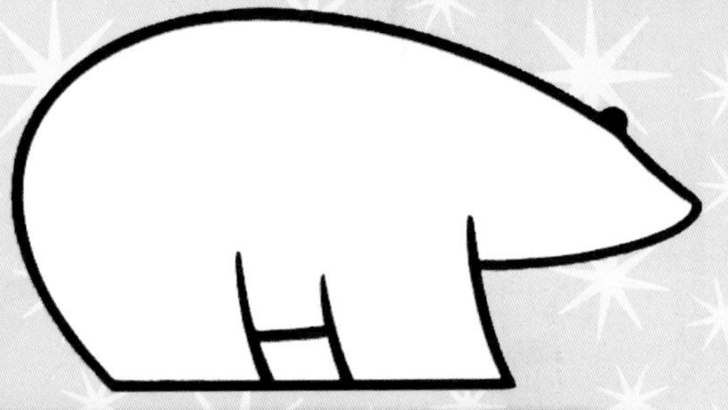

Draw in the rest of his legs and his tummy with 3 lines just like these.

4

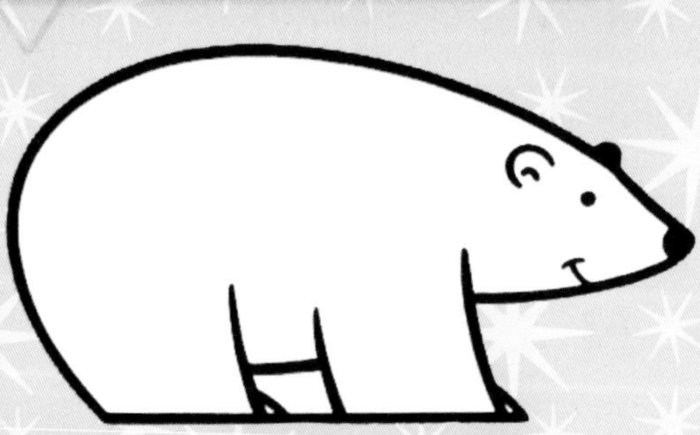

Draw in his nose, other ear, eye, smiley face and his toes.

5

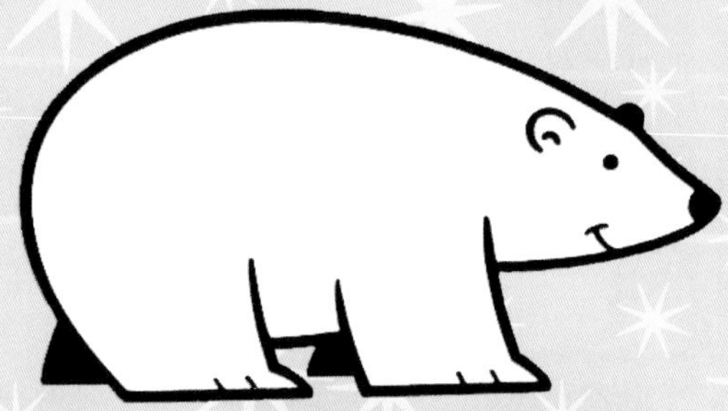

Now draw in his back legs and rub out the pencil lines that join his toes to his legs. Finally, draw in his individual toes.

6

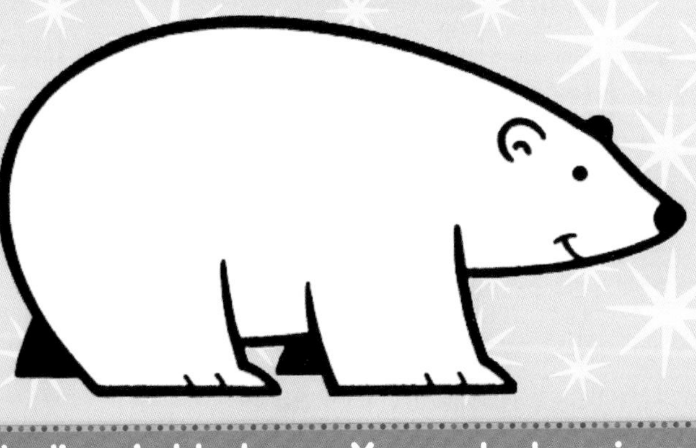

Go over the lines in black pen. Your polar bear is complete!

Which Snowy Cre

Go with the snow flow and do this fun quiz to find your snowy animal mate.

START

Are you a bit of a tomboy? (Y / N)

Dogs first, cats second? (Y / N)

Is winter the best season? (Y / N)

Do you like wrapping up warmly? (Y / N)

Skis over sledge? (Y / N)

Have you only one or two close friends? (Y / N)

Do you like long walks? (Y / N)

Are you part of a big crowd? (Y / N)

Do you like playing with babies? (Y / N)

Do you enjoy dressing up? (Y / N)

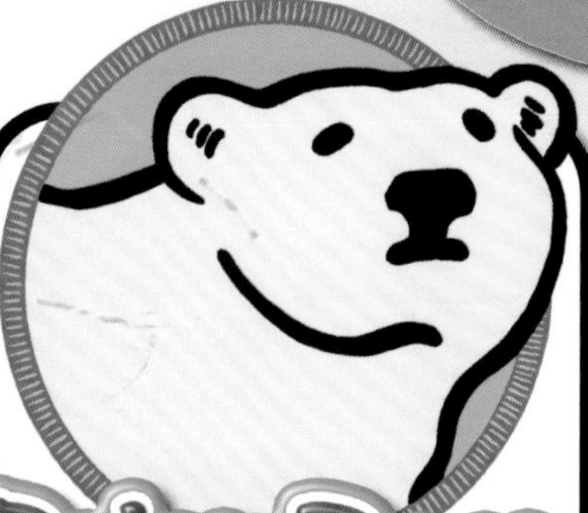

Polar Bear

You're the leader of the pack! All your friends look up to you and admire you cos you always know what's best.

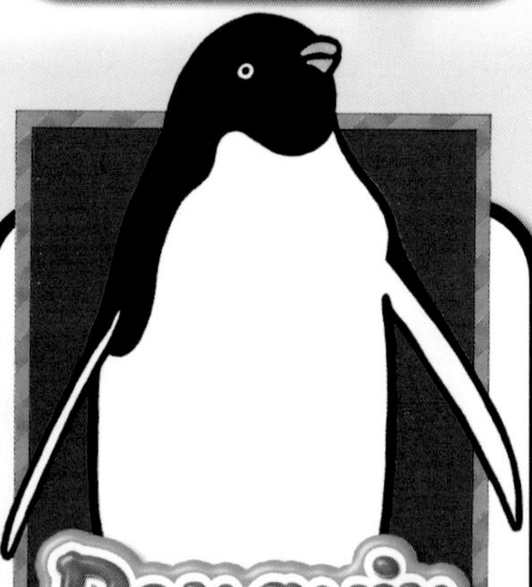

Penguin

Caring for others is what you do best. You have lots of mates and they all know they can rely on you to keep secrets.

Is travelling fun?

Do you work hard at school? — Y

Do you like having 'me time'? — Y

Are you a party lover? — N

N (from travelling fun)

Y (from travelling fun → me time)

N (from work hard → pets)

N (from me time)

Pets always come first?

Are you happy just chillin' out? — N / Y

Do you cry easily? — N

Y

Ice lolly over hot choc?

N

Is swimming your fave sport? — Y

Do you mind getting wet? — Y / N

Y

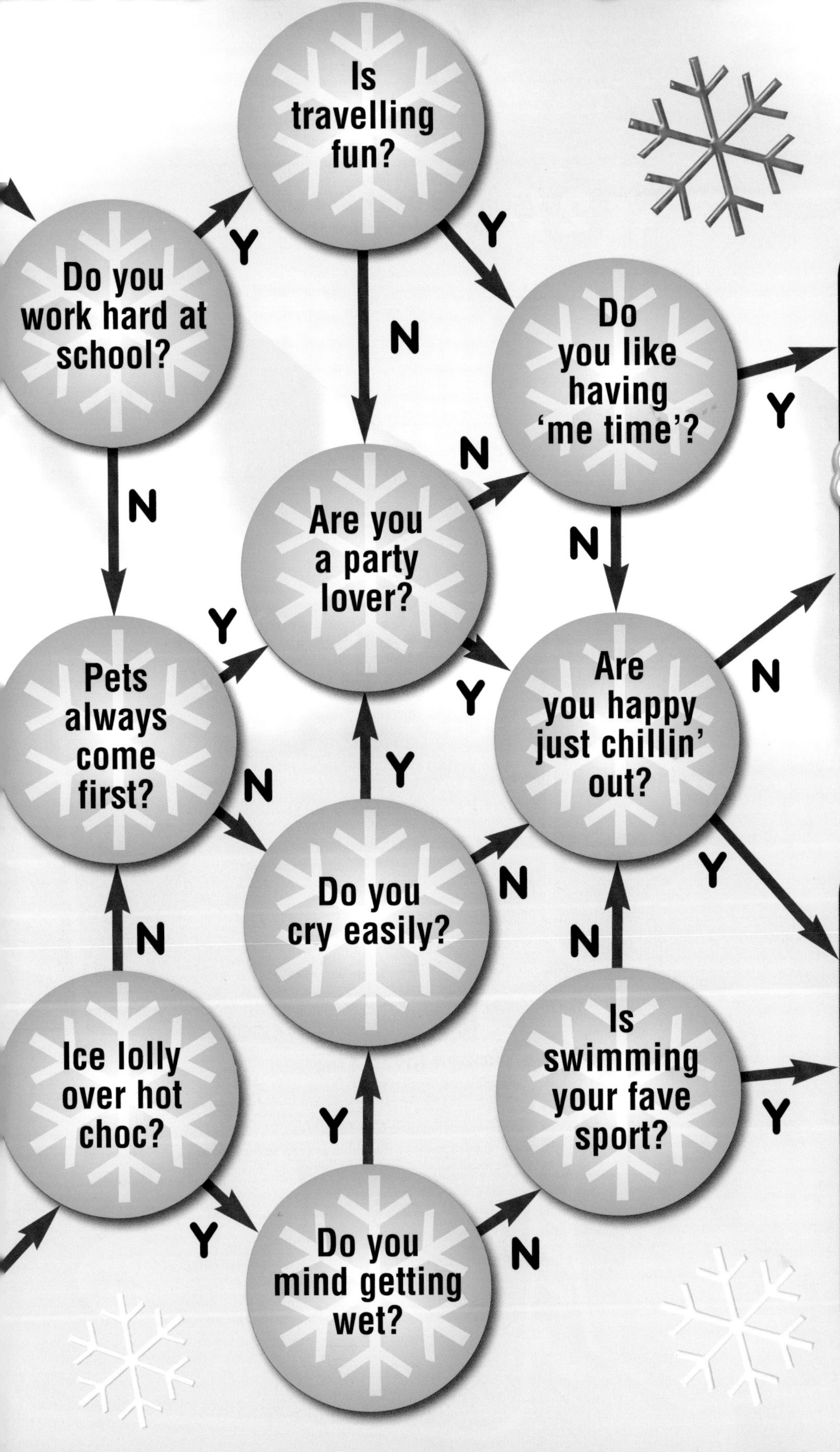

Snowy Owl

You're the daydreamer of the class. Your mind is full of ideas and many of these will come true if you set your mind to it.

Seal

You're either busy or lazy – there's no in between with you! Fun is your middle name and you're first up dancing at any party.

walking

**The only reindeer in Britain can be four
Animals and You readers, Amber**

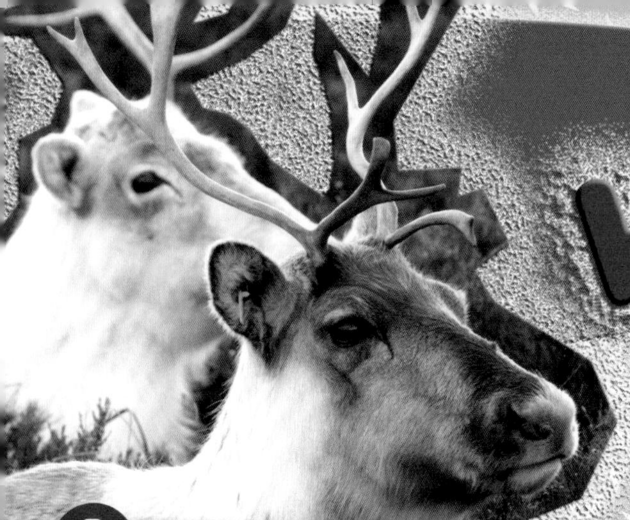

1

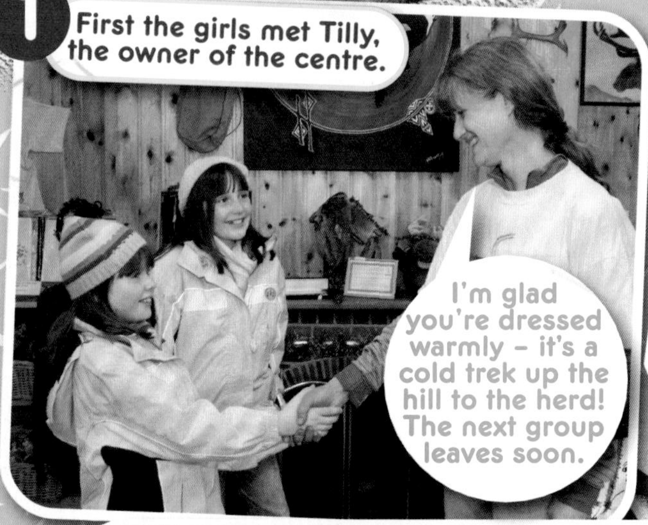
First the girls met Tilly, the owner of the centre.
I'm glad you're dressed warmly – it's a cold trek up the hill to the herd! The next group leaves soon.

2

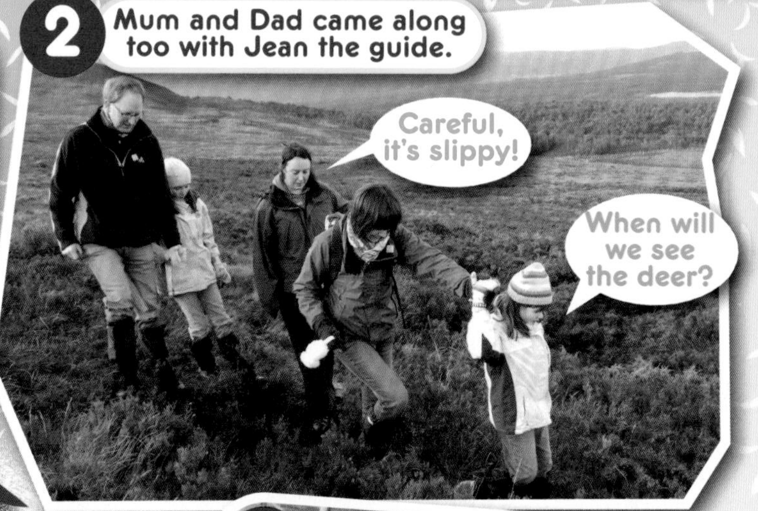
Mum and Dad came along too with Jean the guide.
Careful, it's slippy!
When will we see the deer?

5

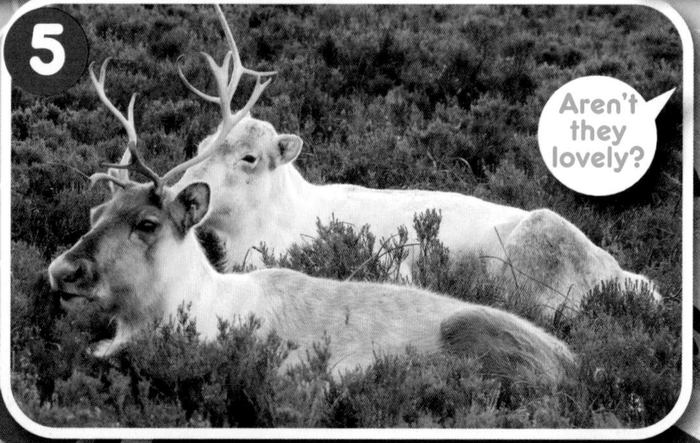
Aren't they lovely?

6

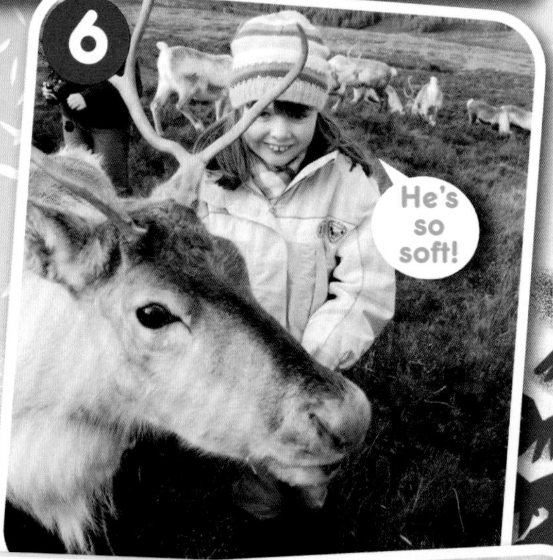
He's so soft!

9

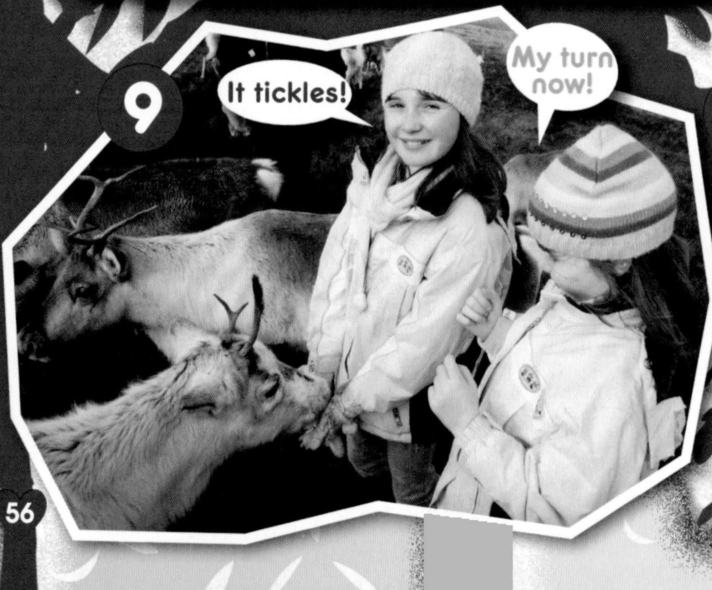
It tickles!
My turn now!

10

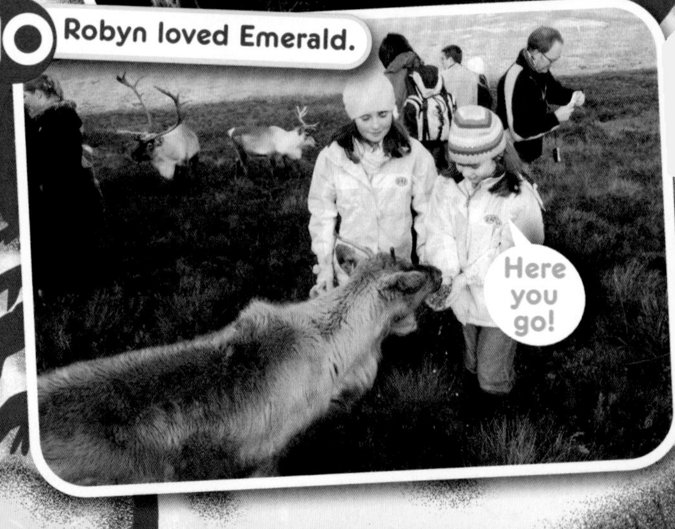
Robyn loved Emerald.
Here you go!

with Reindeer

n the Cairngorms in Scotland! We took
Robyn, along to meet the herd.

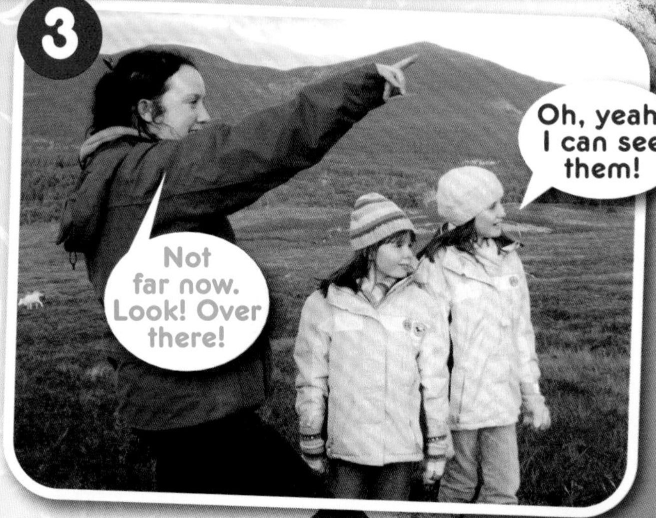
3
Not far now. Look! Over there!
Oh, yeah! I can see them!

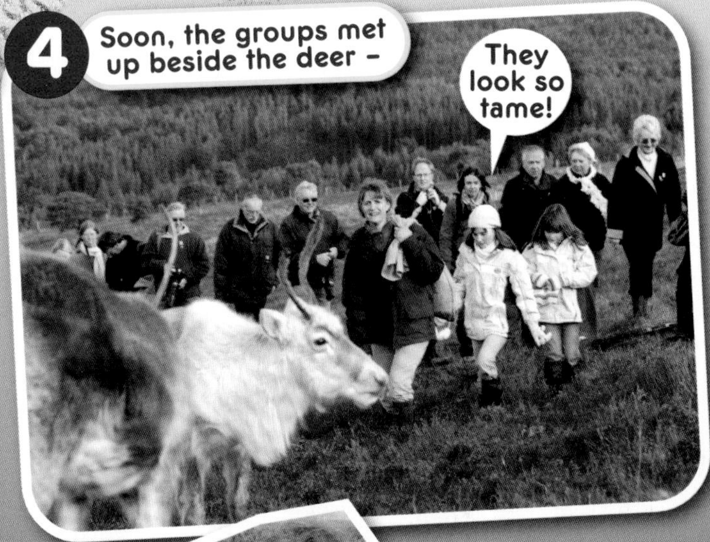
4
Soon, the groups met up beside the deer –
They look so tame!

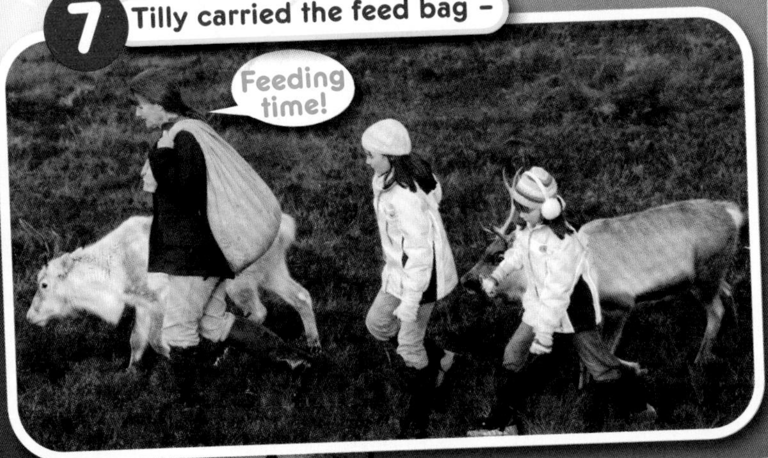
7
Tilly carried the feed bag –
Feeding time!

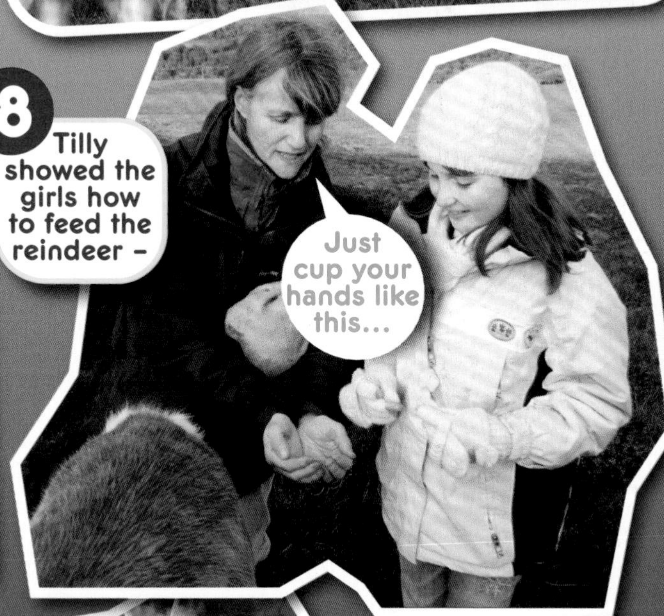
8
Tilly showed the girls how to feed the reindeer –
Just cup your hands like this...

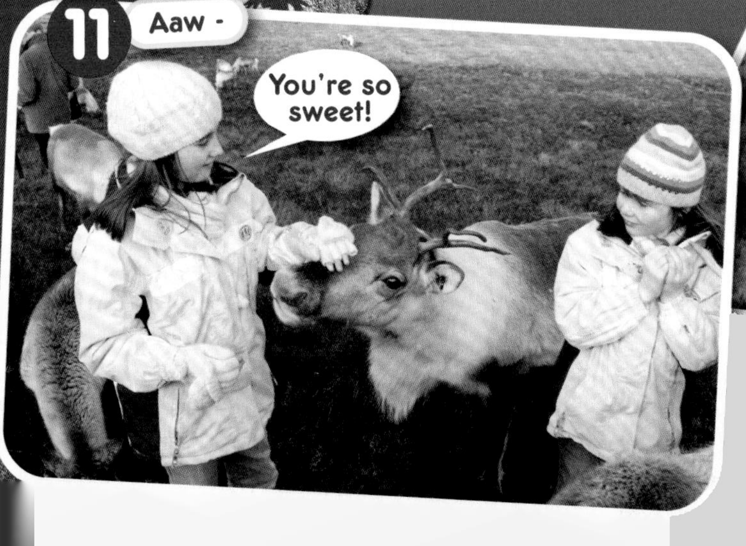
11
Aaw –
You're so sweet!

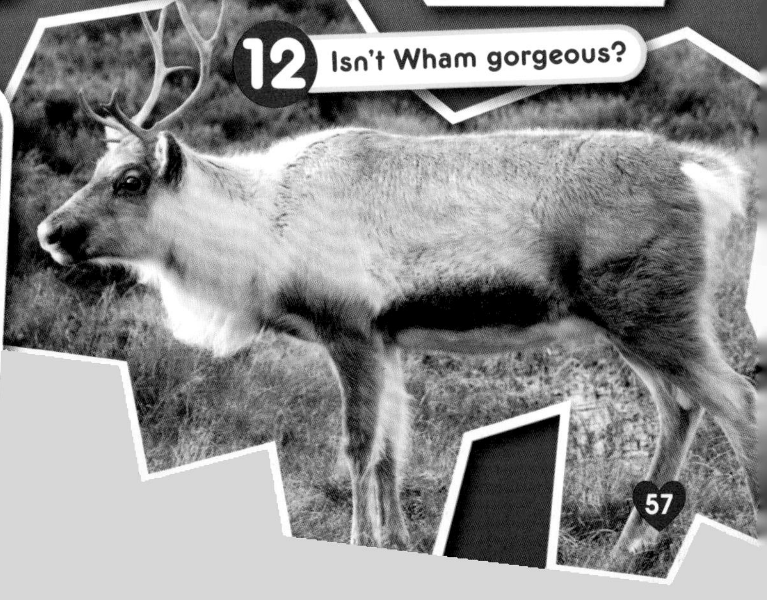
12
Isn't Wham gorgeous?

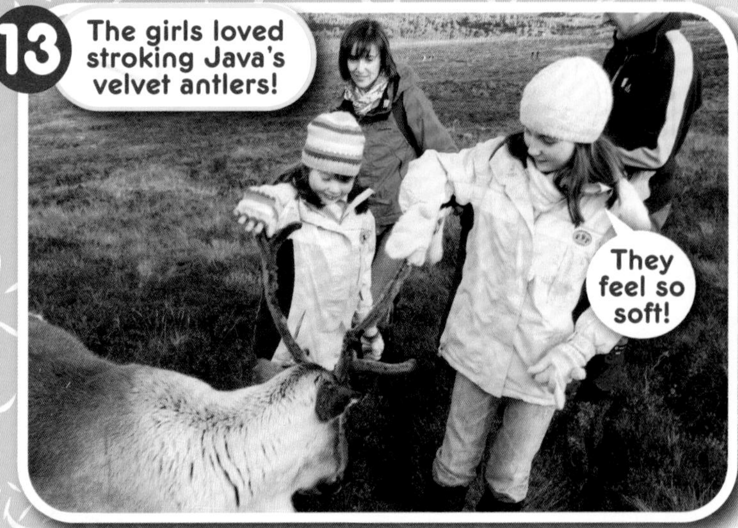
13
The girls loved stroking Java's velvet antlers!
They feel so soft!

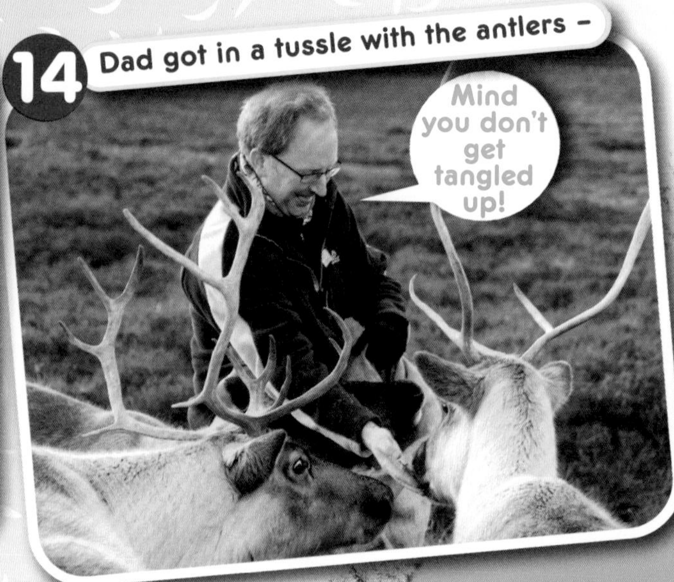
14
Dad got in a tussle with the antlers –
Mind you don't get tangled up!

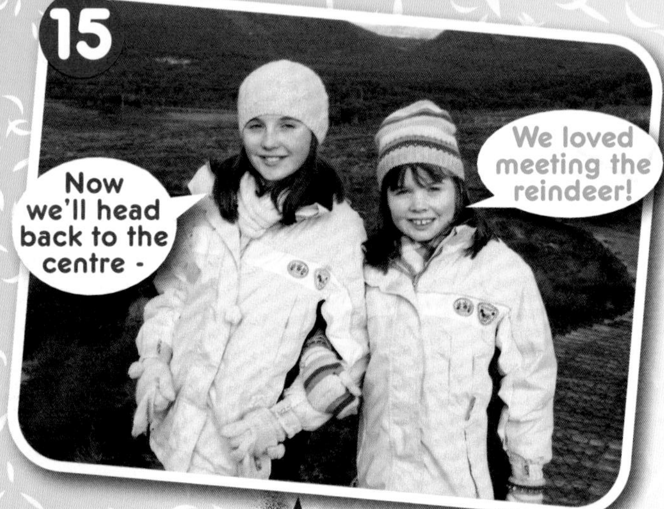
15
Now we'll head back to the centre –
We loved meeting the reindeer!

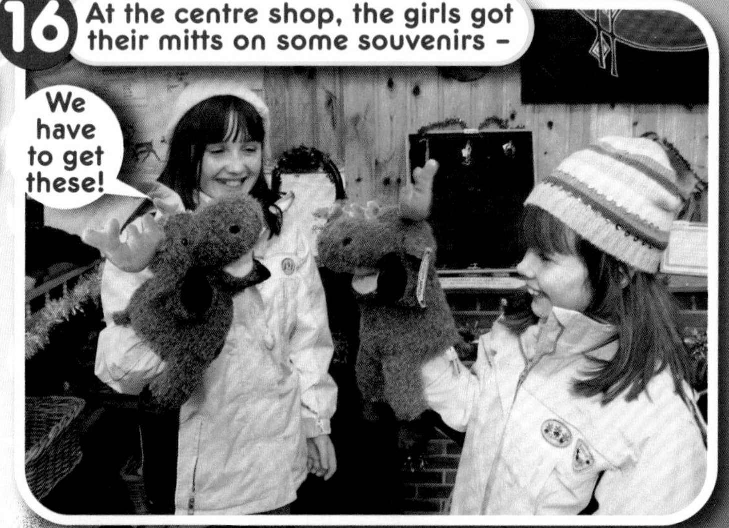
16
At the centre shop, the girls got their mitts on some souvenirs –
We have to get these!

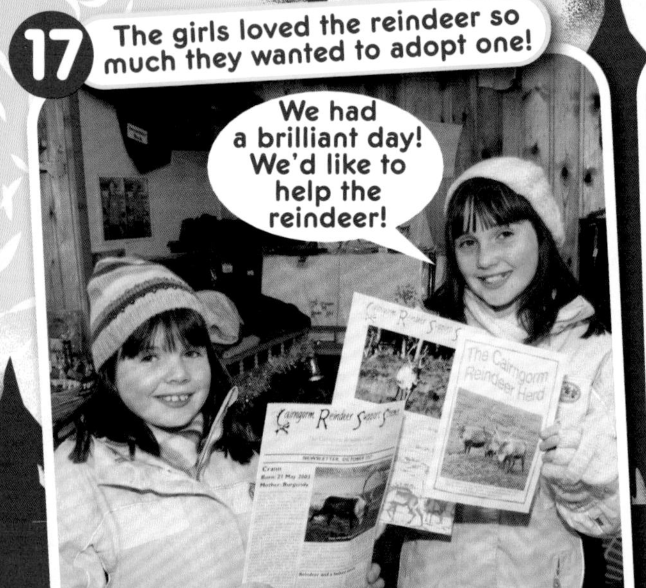
17
The girls loved the reindeer so much they wanted to adopt one!
We had a brilliant day! We'd like to help the reindeer!

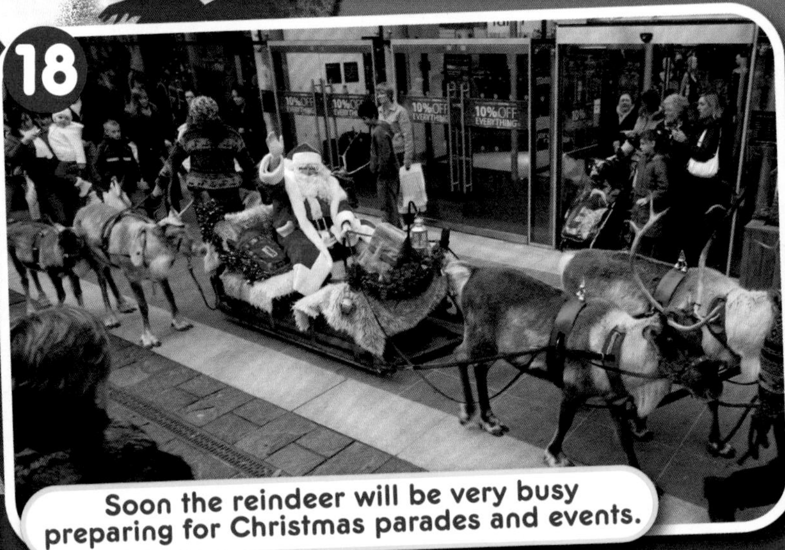
18
10% OFF EVERYTHING
Soon the reindeer will be very busy preparing for Christmas parades and events.

For more info or to adopt a reindeer visit www.reindeer-company.demon.co.uk or call 01479 861228.

Cairngorm Reindeer Support Scheme

Dish Delish!

While we're tucking into Christmas dinners, these birds and animals will be munching on what they like best -

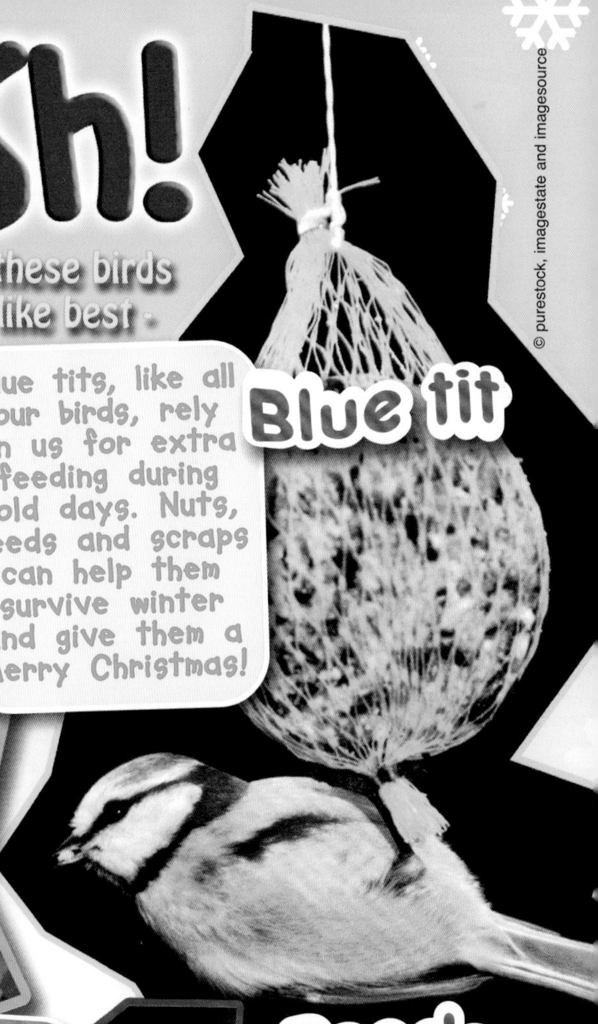

Blue tit

Blue tits, like all our birds, rely on us for extra feeding during cold days. Nuts, seeds and scraps can help them survive winter and give them a Merry Christmas!

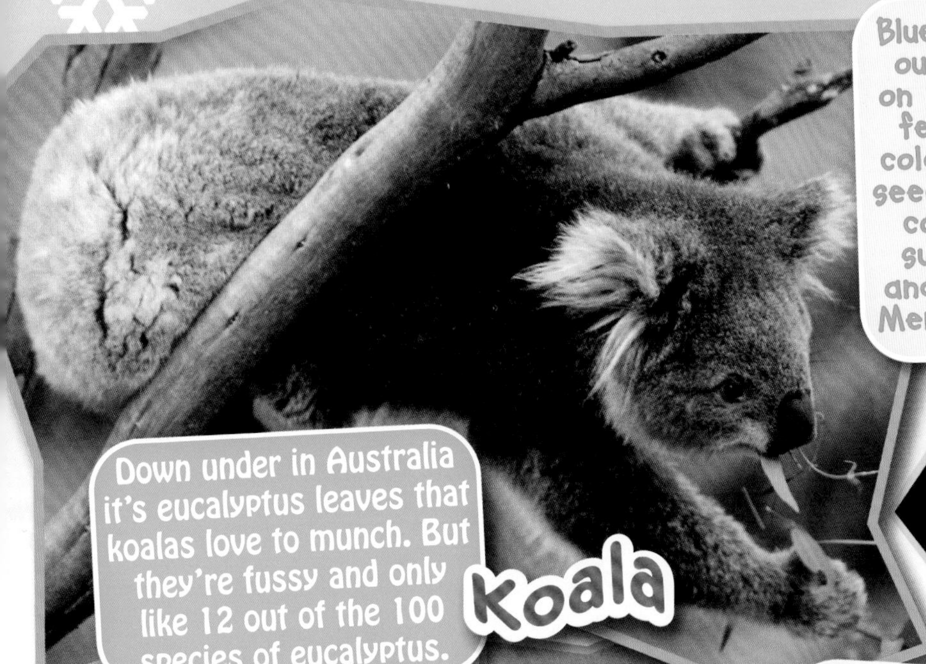

Koala

Down under in Australia it's eucalyptus leaves that koalas love to munch. But they're fussy and only like 12 out of the 100 species of eucalyptus.

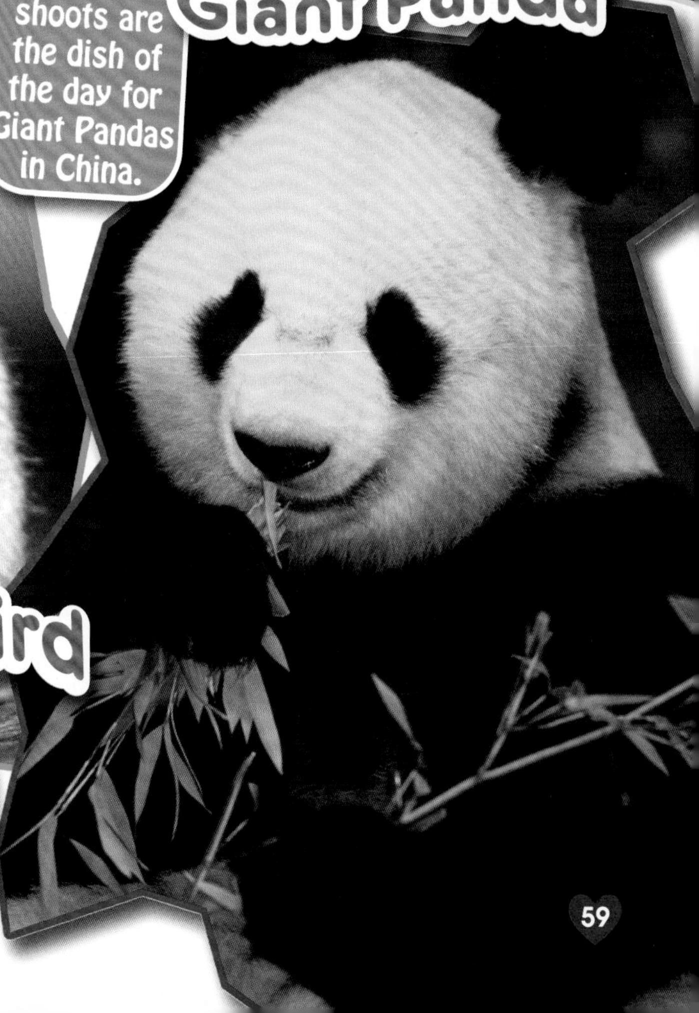

Giant Panda

Bamboo shoots are the dish of the day for Giant Pandas in China.

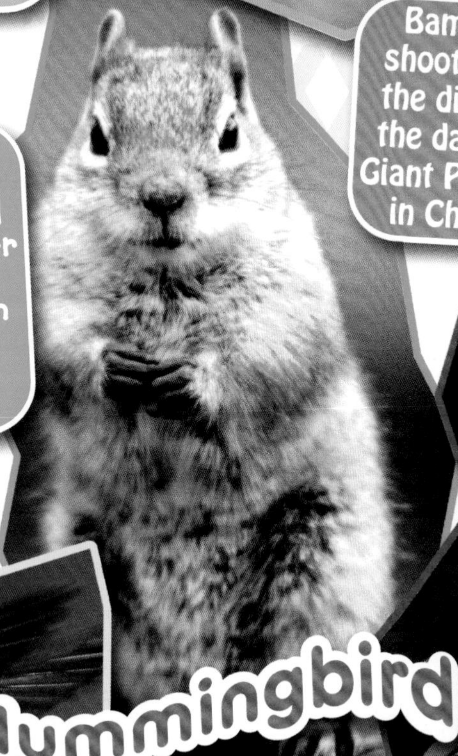

Squirrel

Squirrels are not real hibernators and on warmer winter days can be seen feeding on pine cones and nuts they have stashed away.

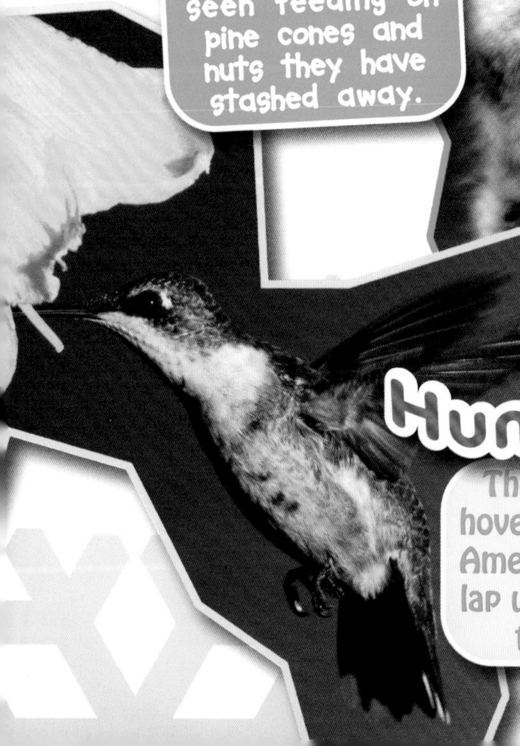

Hummingbird

These clever birds hover by exotic South American flowers and lap up the nectar with their tongues.

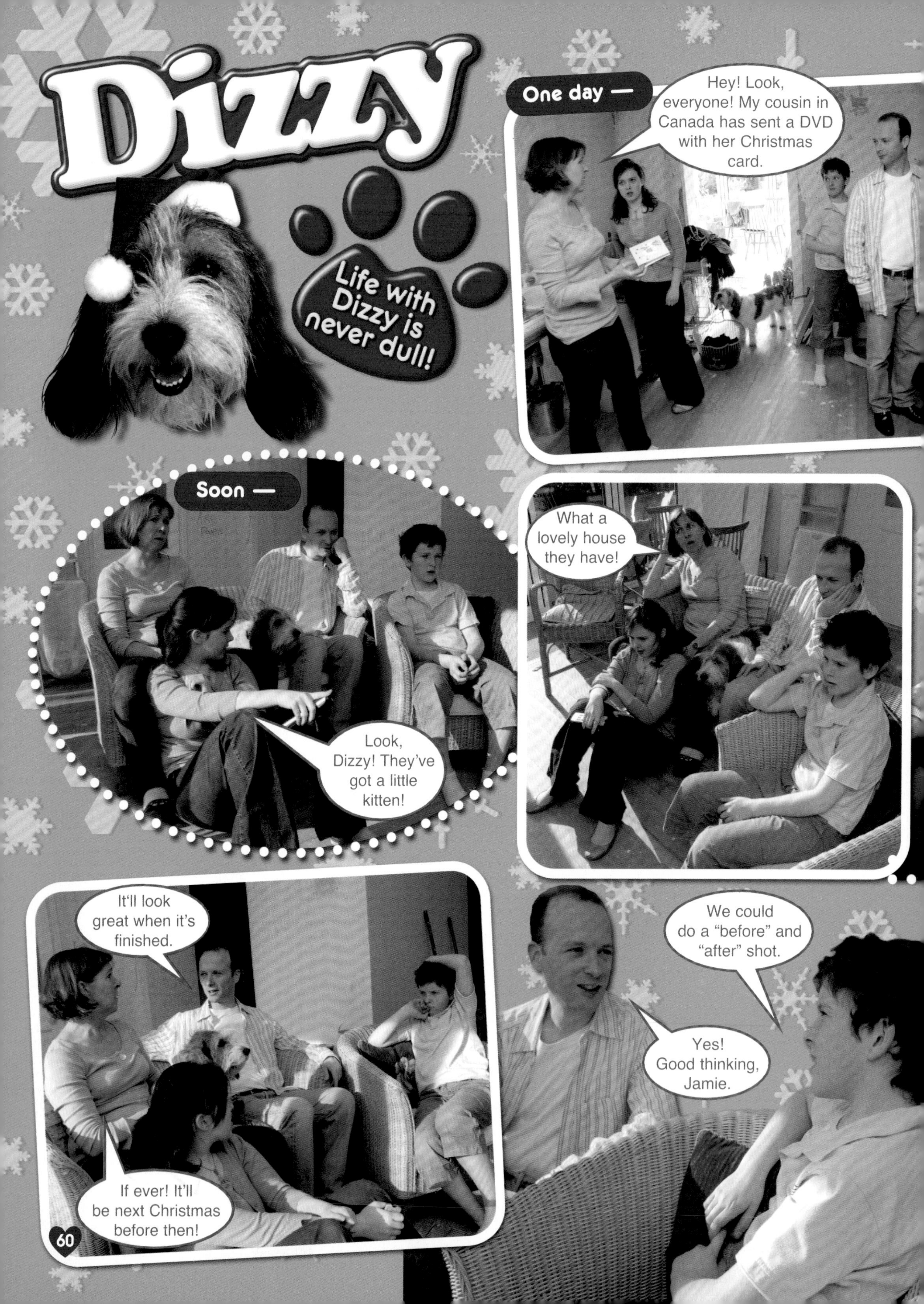
Dizzy
Life with Dizzy is never dull!
One day —
Hey! Look, everyone! My cousin in Canada has sent a DVD with her Christmas card.
Soon —
Look, Dizzy! They've got a little kitten!
What a lovely house they have!
It'll look great when it's finished.
If ever! It'll be next Christmas before then!
We could do a "before" and "after" shot.
Yes! Good thinking, Jamie.

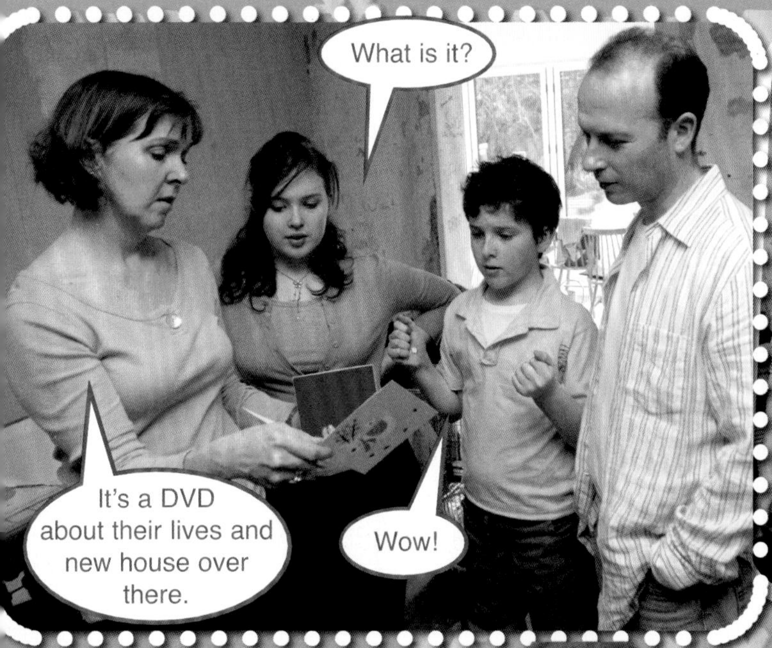
What is it?
It's a DVD about their lives and new house over there.
Wow!

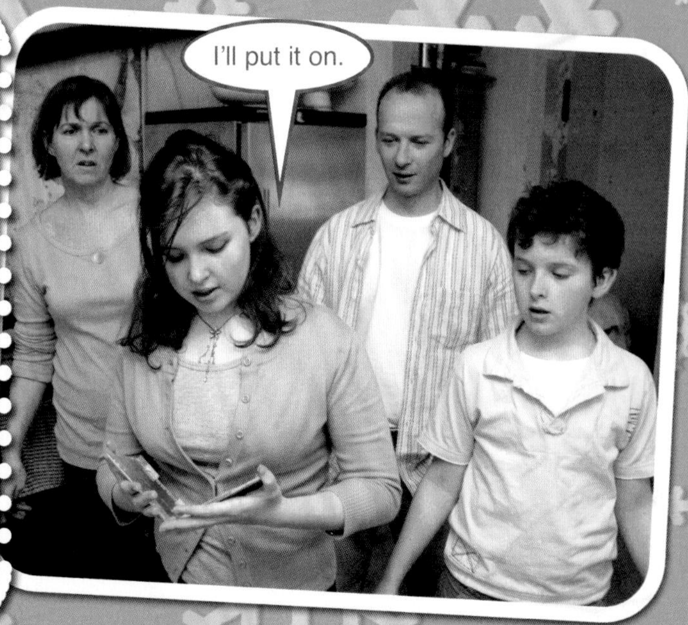
I'll put it on.

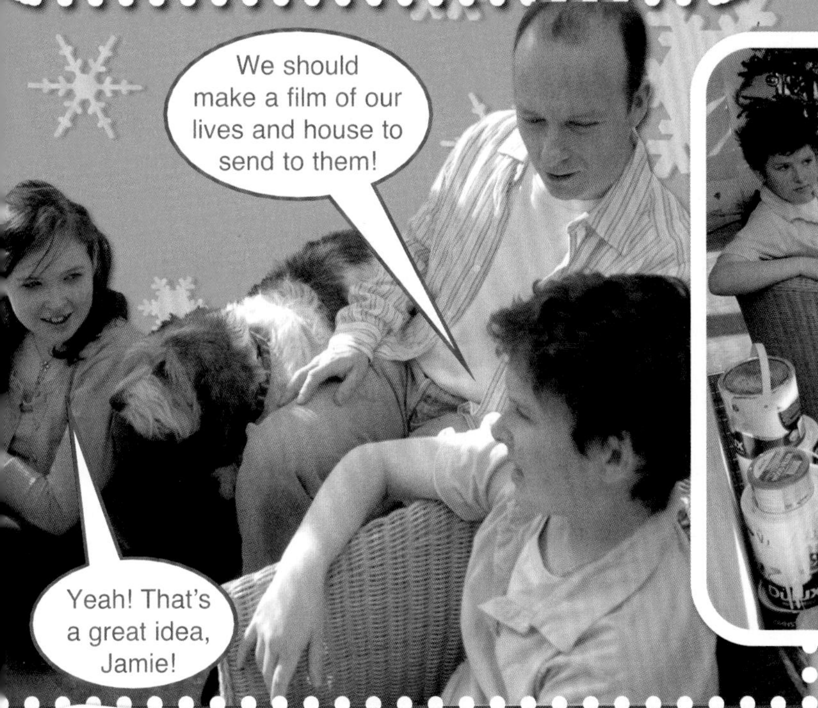
We should make a film of our lives and house to send to them!
Yeah! That's a great idea, Jamie!

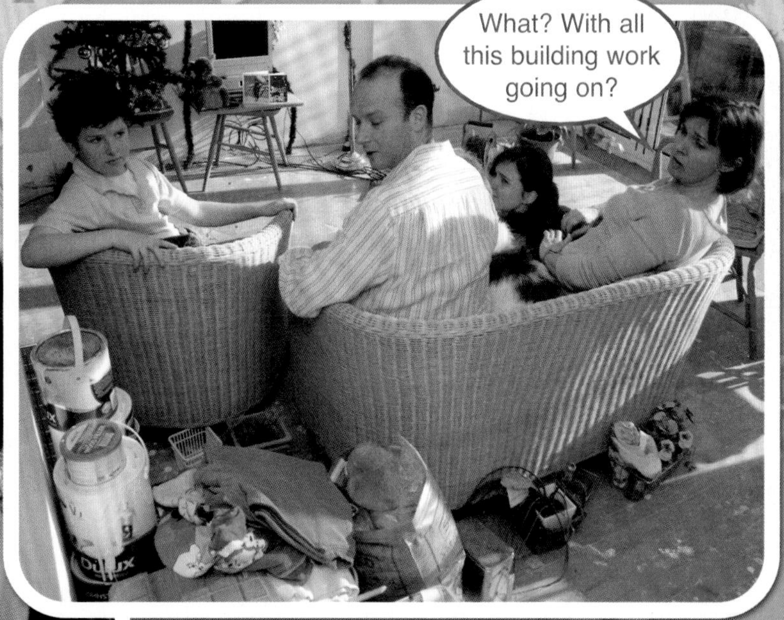
What? With all this building work going on?

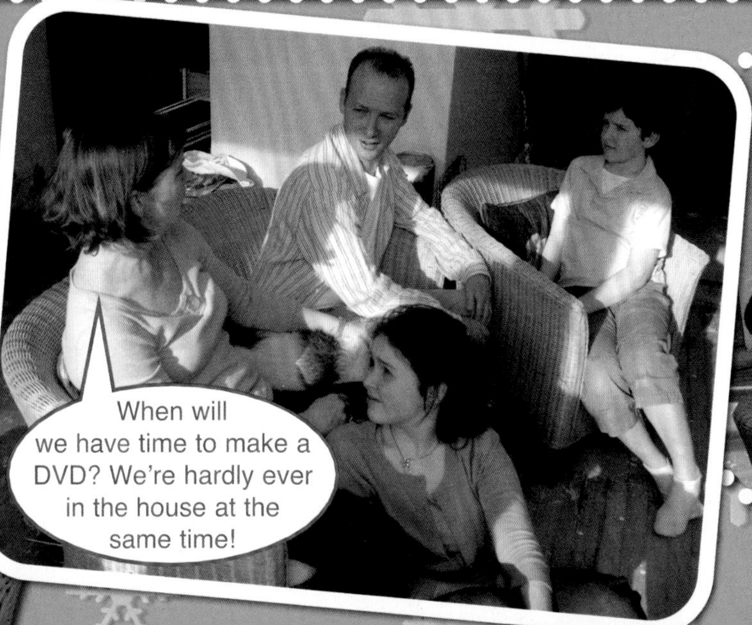
When will we have time to make a DVD? We're hardly ever in the house at the same time!

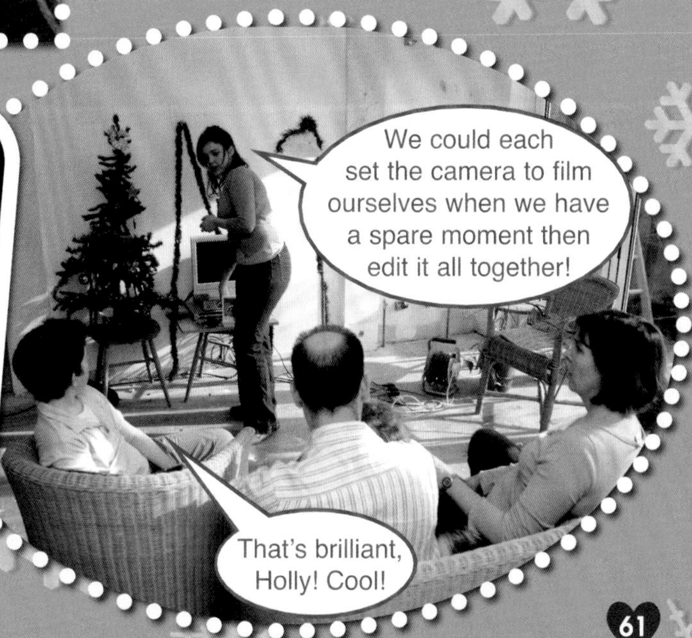
We could each set the camera to film ourselves when we have a spare moment then edit it all together!
That's brilliant, Holly! Cool!

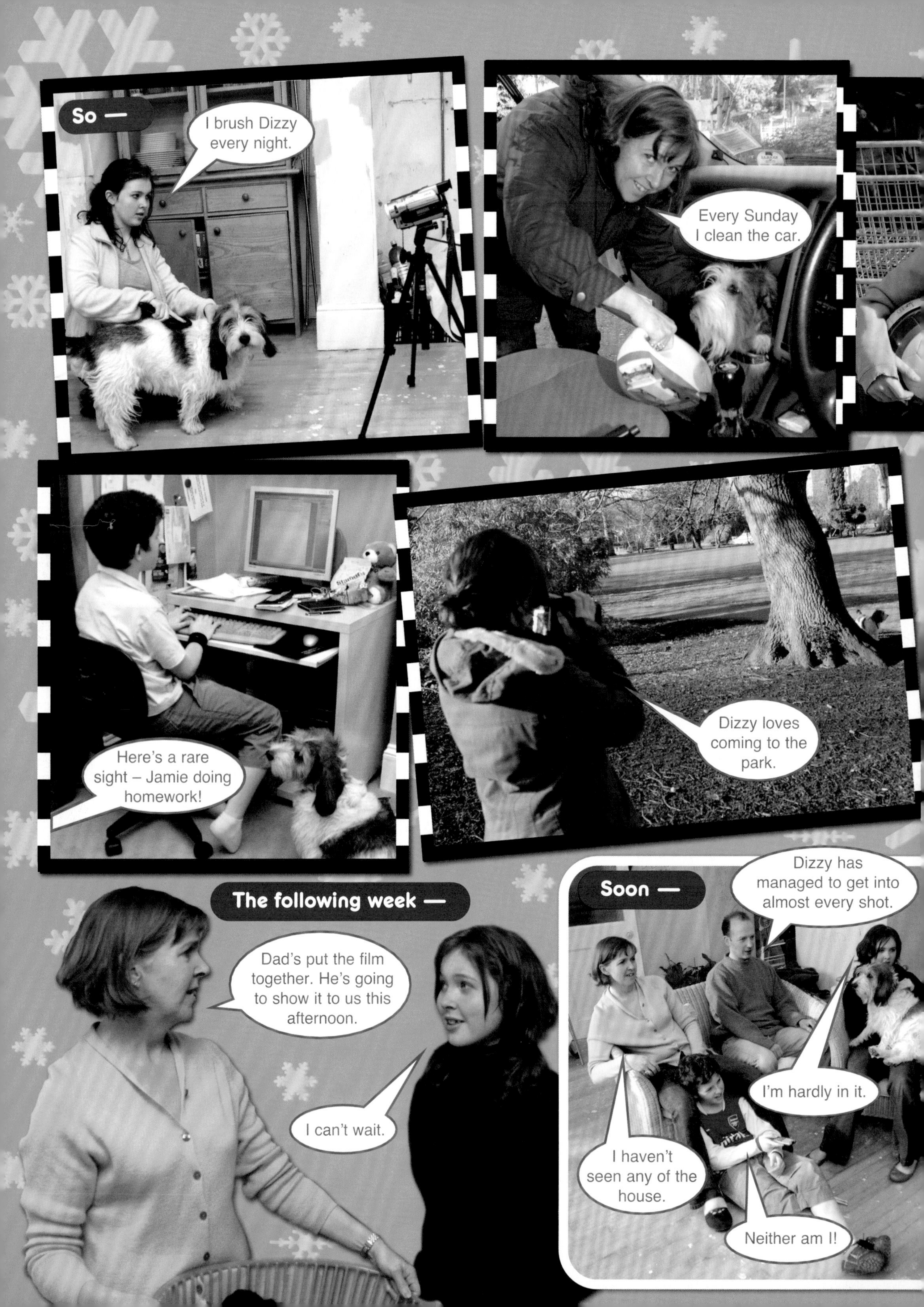

So —
I brush Dizzy every night.
Every Sunday I clean the car.
Here's a rare sight – Jamie doing homework!
Dizzy loves coming to the park.
The following week —
Dad's put the film together. He's going to show it to us this afternoon.
I can't wait.
Soon —
Dizzy has managed to get into almost every shot.
I'm hardly in it.
I haven't seen any of the house.
Neither am I!

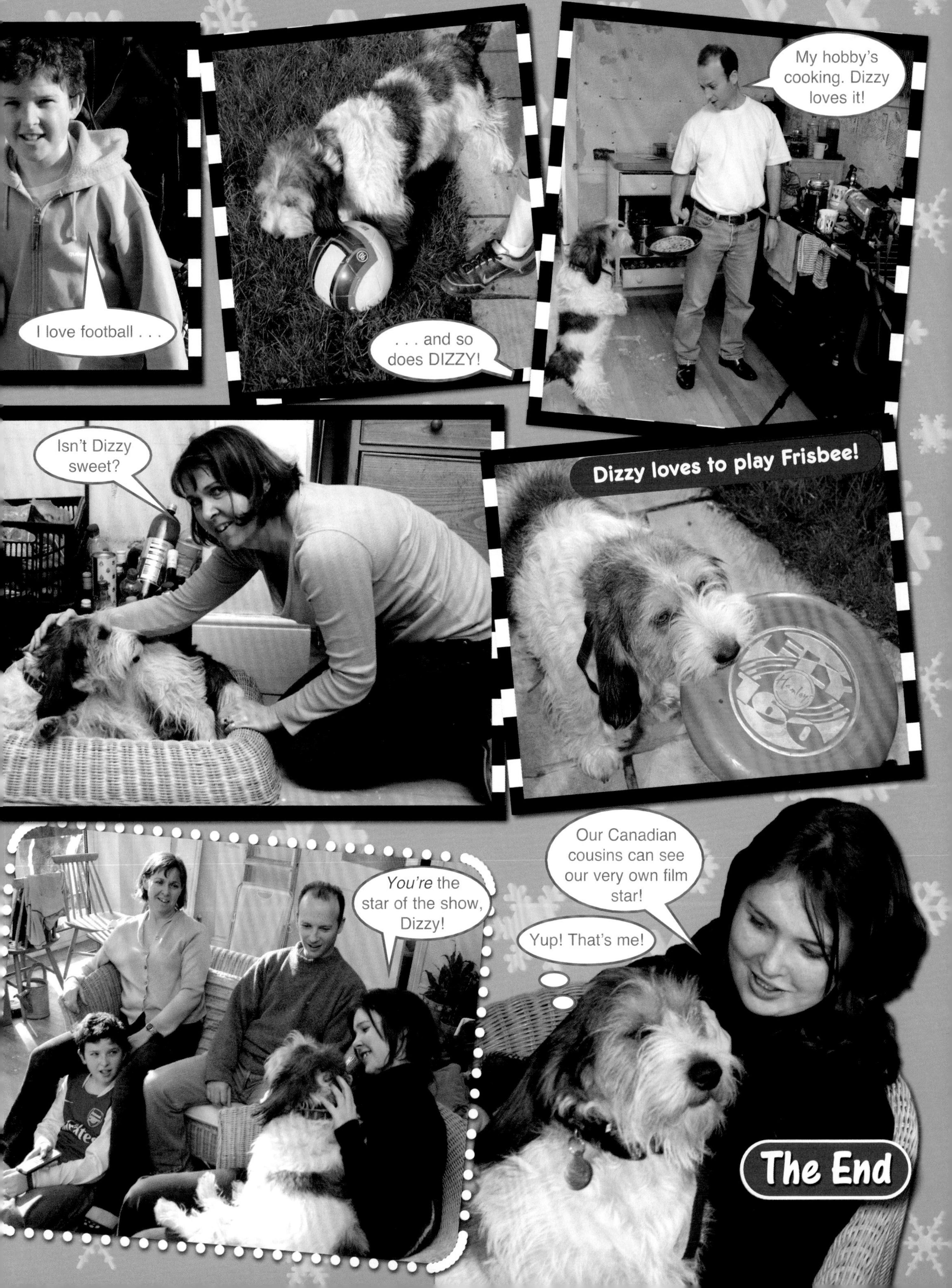
I love football . . .
. . . and so does DIZZY!
My hobby's cooking. Dizzy loves it!
Isn't Dizzy sweet?
Dizzy loves to play Frisbee!
You're the star of the show, Dizzy!
Our Canadian cousins can see our very own film star!
Yup! That's me!
The End

Make it

Box-er Chocolates!

Make these doggy-licious choccies for your furry friend!

These sweets are the perfect pressie for your faithful friend — he'll love you even more! If you don't have moulds for making chocolates, use an ice-cube tray instead. The recipe makes 15-25 chocolates and takes about 15 minutes.

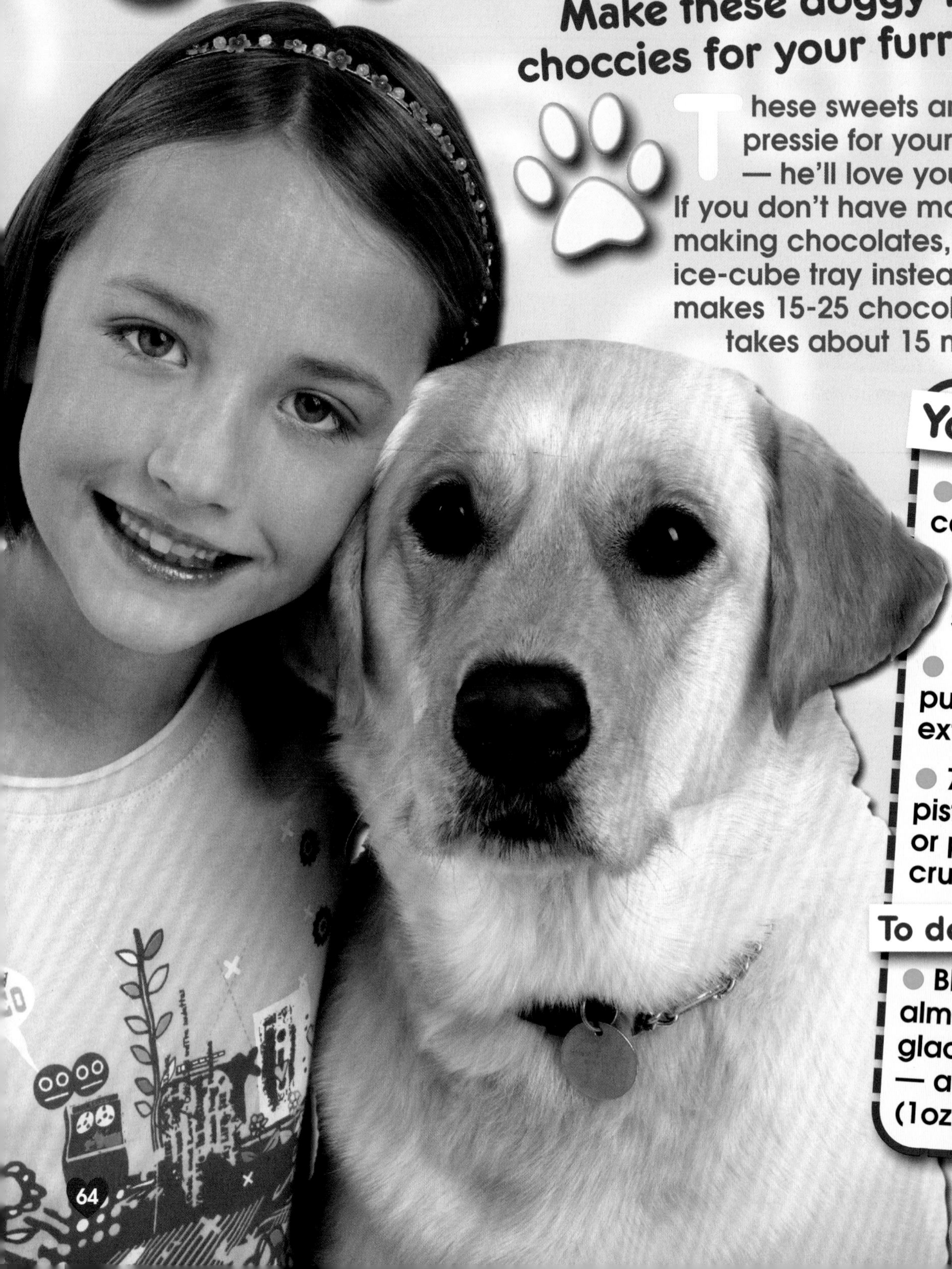

You'll need

- 250g (8oz) carob chips or carob bar broken into small pieces
- 1 tablespoon pure vanilla extract
- 75g (3oz) pistachio nuts or peanuts, crushed

To decorate:

- Blanched almonds and glace cherries — about 25g (1oz) of each

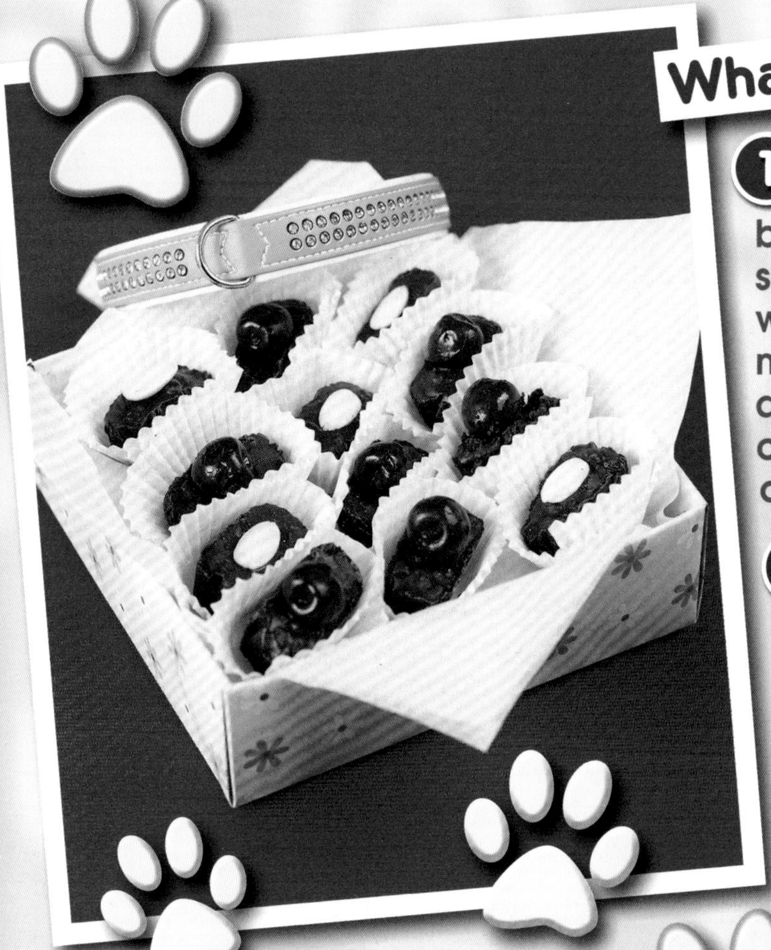

What to do

Ask an adult to help you with this part.

1. Place the carob in a heatproof glass bowl. Set the bowl over a saucepan of lightly simmering water and heat till the carob has melted. Stir in the vanilla extract and crushed nuts. Pour into the chocolate moulds or ice-cube trays and transfer to the fridge until set.

2. Carefully press the chocolates out of the mould or tray. Decorate each with an almond or glace cherry. Transfer to truffle or mini cake cases and place in a small, decorated box. Cover with cling film, add a bow and you've got a cool box of canine choccies!

The chocolates will only keep for 5-7 days as they are made from natural ingredients.
- **Never substitute chocolate or cocoa powder for the carob as they are poisonous to dogs.**

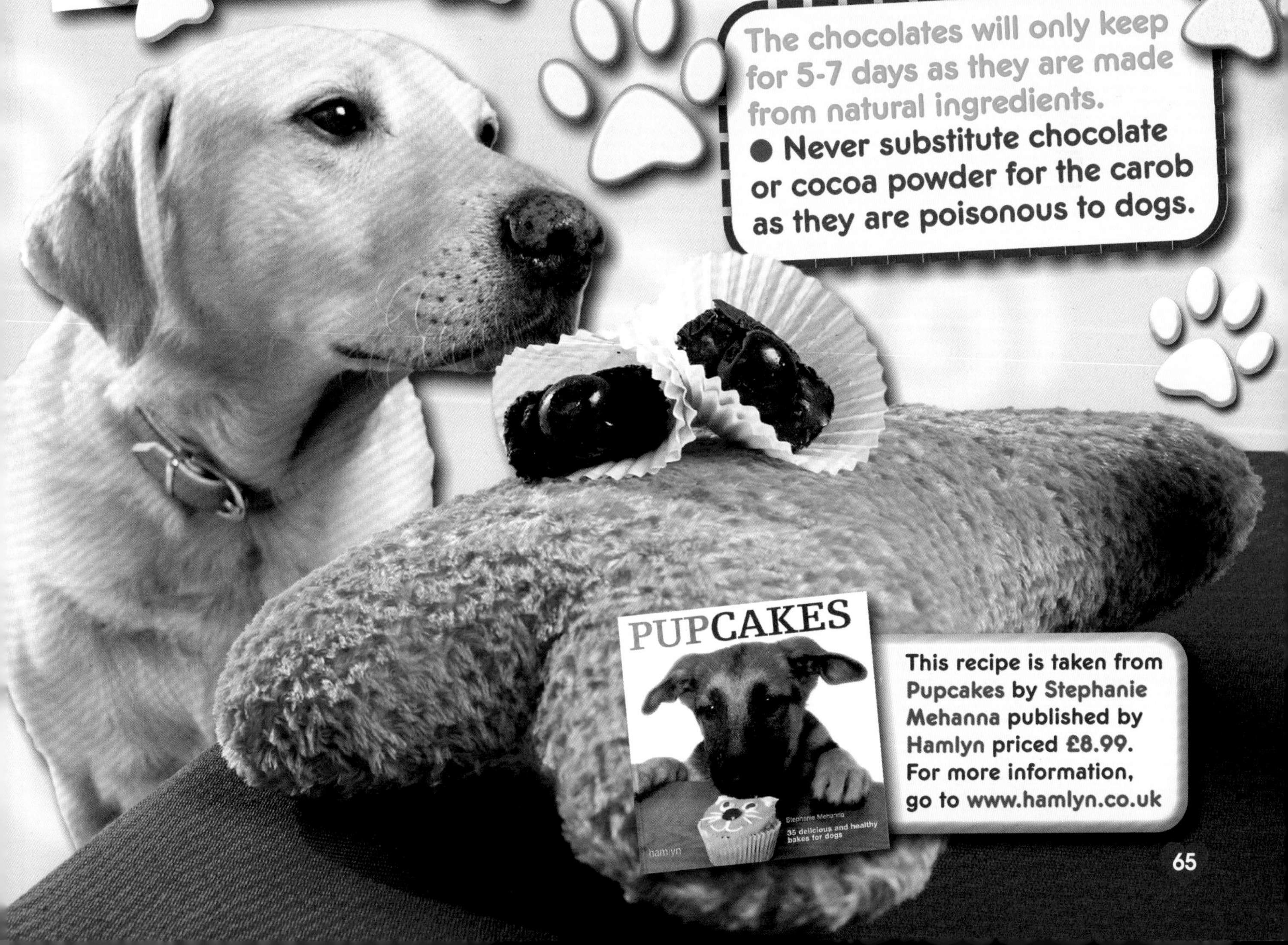
PUPCAKES
Stephanie Mehanna
35 delicious and healthy bakes for dogs
hamlyn

This recipe is taken from Pupcakes by Stephanie Mehanna published by Hamlyn priced £8.99. For more information, go to www.hamlyn.co.uk

ABC animals

Continued from page 7

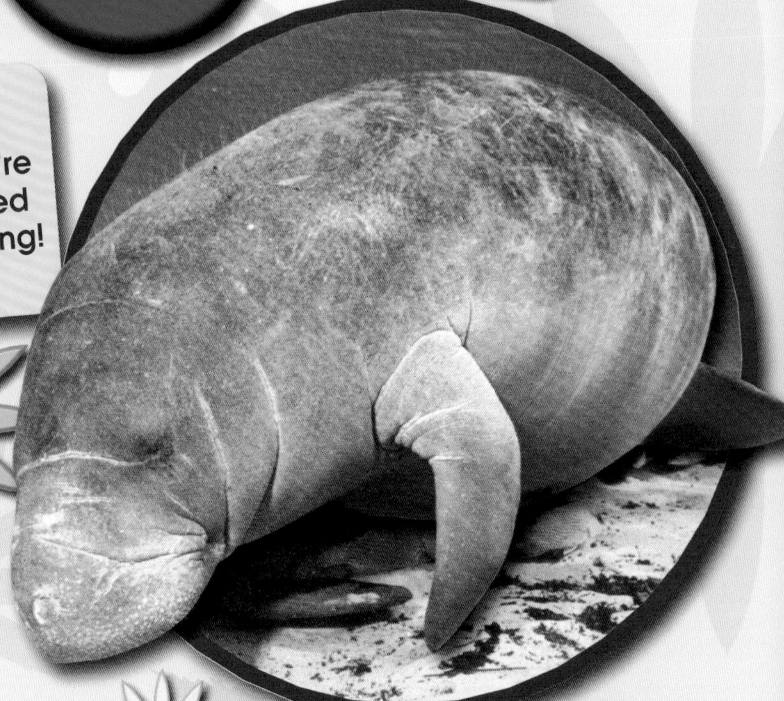

Manatee

Manatees are related to elephants. They're gentle and playful and have been spotted playing follow-the-leader and body surfing!

Meerkat, Mole, Moose

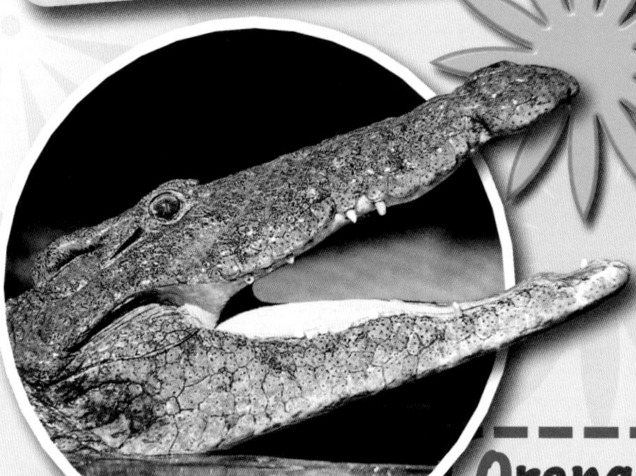

Nile Crocodile

Watch out, even if this animal's smiling! It's the length of a large limo and the biggest croc in the world! Crocs might look clumsy, but they can run as fast as a human!

Narwhal, Nyala

Orangutan

These colourful cuties have arms which reach all the way down to their ankles! Their loud cries can be heard up to a kilometre away! Orangutans are endangered — only 10% of their natural habitat remains.

Otter, Okapi, Octopus

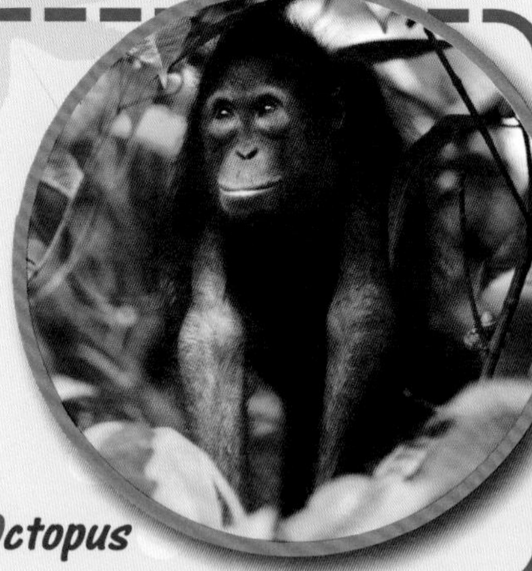

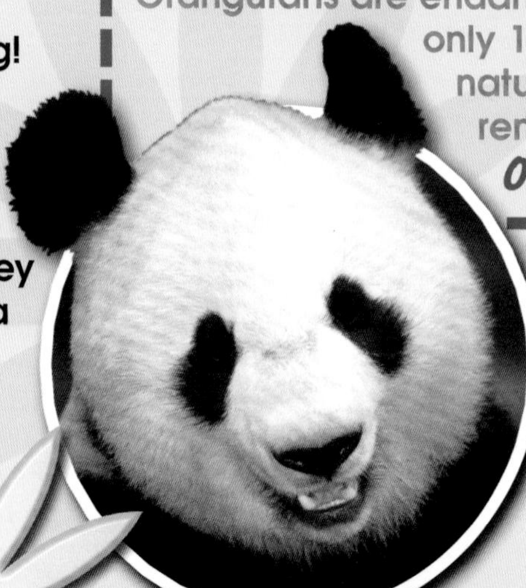

Panda

Giant pandas have to munch bamboo for 14 hours a day to get enough nutrients to survive! There are only about 1000 of these furry cuties left in the wild.

Polar Bear, Puffin, Porcupine

Quetzal

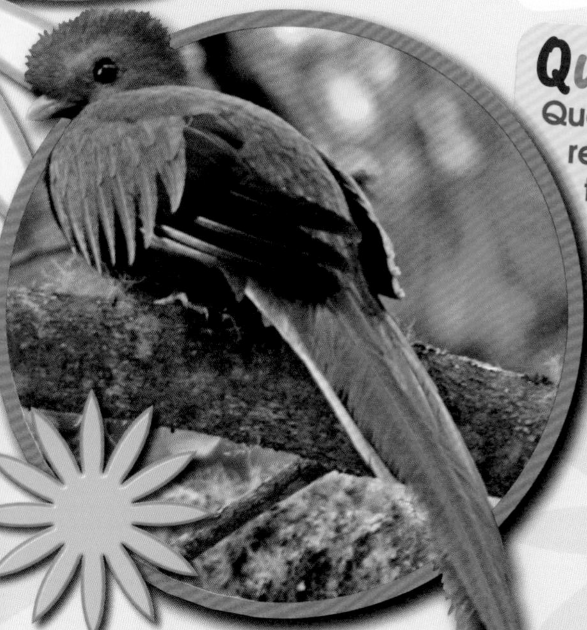

Quetzals are birds with shimmering green, gold and red feathers which grow to almost a metre long in the breeding season. Quetzals appear on flags, coins and stamps in Guatemala.

Quaker Moth

Rhinoceros

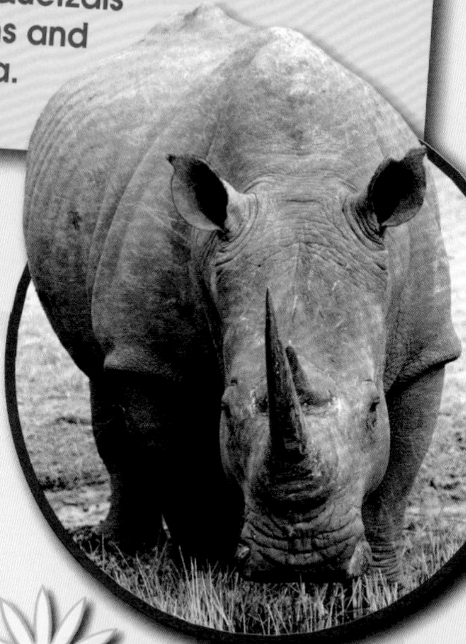

Their tough horns are made from the same stuff as human hair and nails. Rhinos mark their territory with huge piles of dung up to a metre high — poo-ee!

Rattlesnake, Raccoon, Reindeer

Shark

Great white sharks have up to 3,000 teeth! Sharks have a good sense of smell, keen eyesight and can leap out of the water to catch their prey. Scary!

Stoat, Sloth, Seahorse

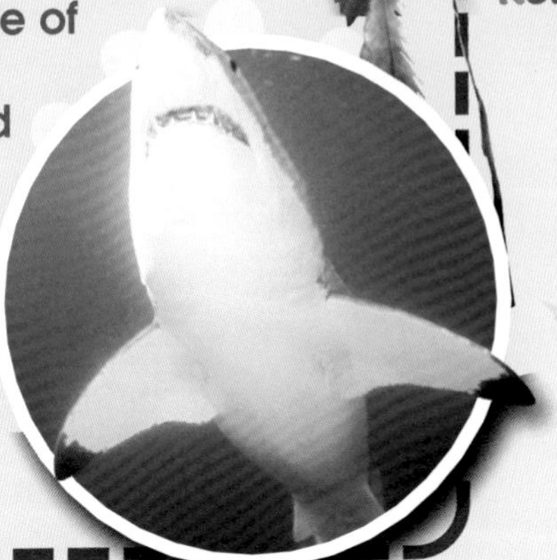

Tiger

No two tigers have the same stripy markings. Unfortunately, they're hunted for their fur and only 6,000 of these magnificent big cats are left in the wild.

Tapir, Toucan, Tasmanian Devil

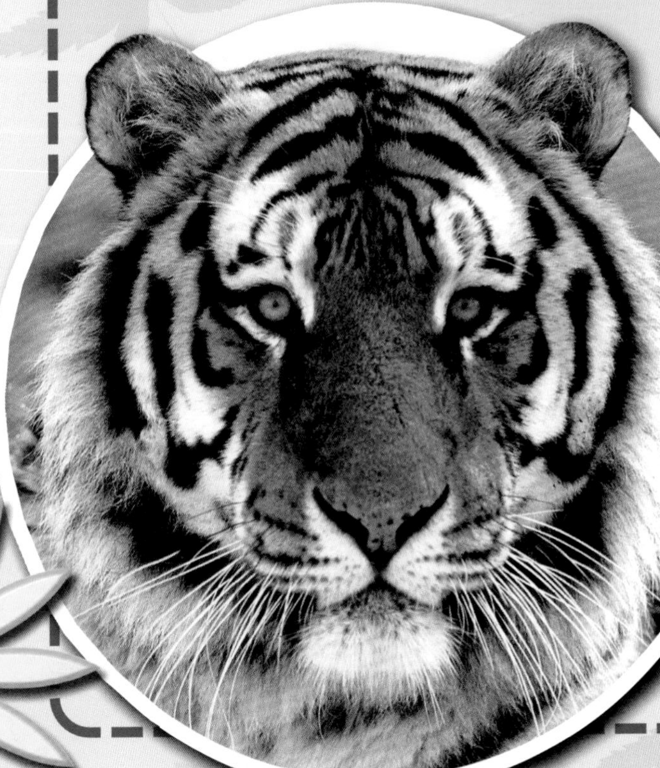

Uakari Monkey

Uakaris are amazingly good at jumping! They can leap up to 30m from one tree to another through the Amazon rainforests where they live. Their jaws are strong enough to crack Brazil nuts!

Unau

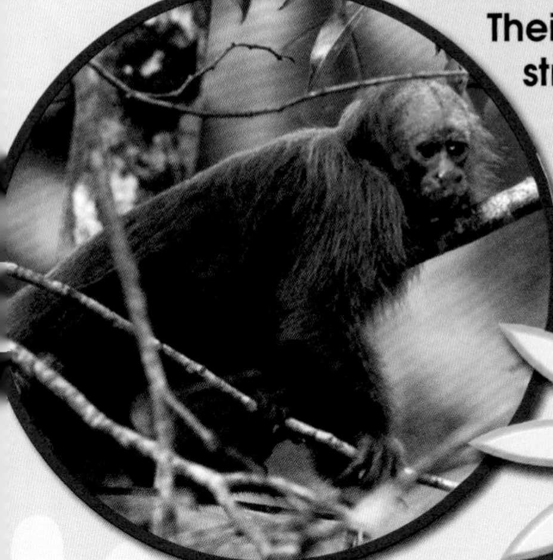

Vole

Voles are teeny rodents like mice but with plumper bodies and hairy tails! They live in woodland areas in Europe and Asia.

Vampire Bat, Vulture, Vicuna

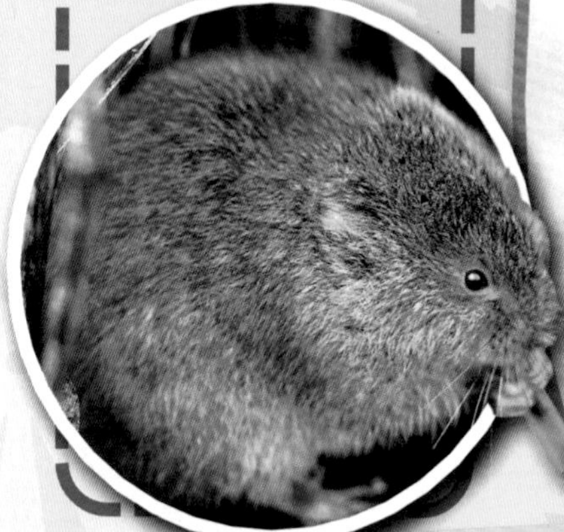

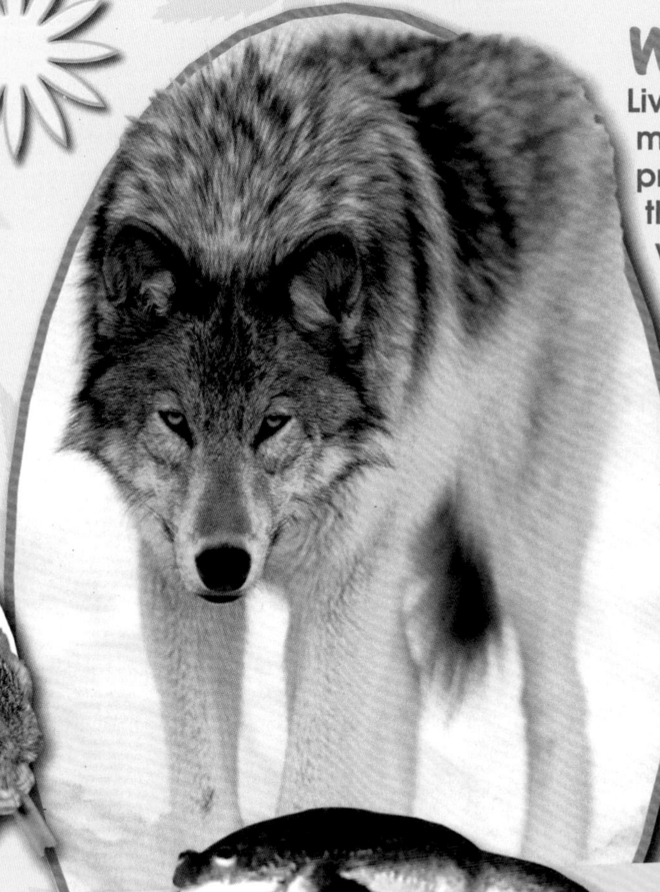

Wolf

Living in large packs means wolves can hunt prey that's much bigger than them. A howling wolf is either trying to find its pack, warning off other packs or helping its pack to bond (like having a sing-along with friends!).

Walrus, Wombat, Woodpecker

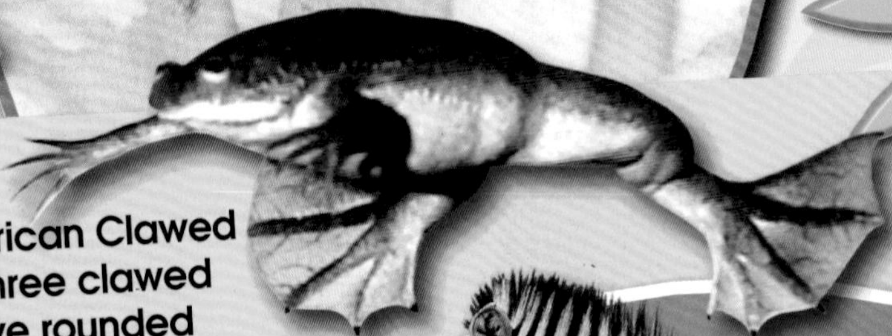

Xenopus

These are also known as African Clawed Frogs because they have three clawed toes on each foot. They have rounded snouts and golden eyes but don't have eyelids or a tongue! Xenopus means 'strange foot'!

X-ray Fish

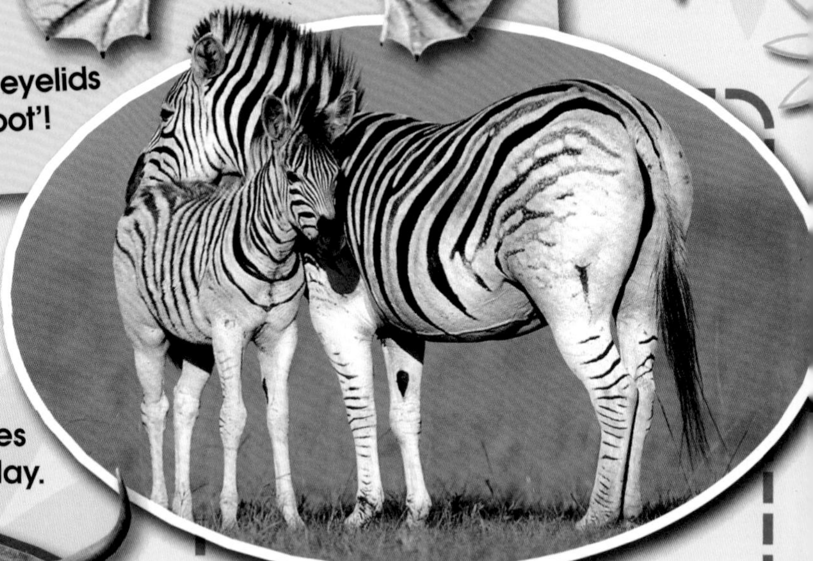

Yak

Yaks live higher up mountains than any other animals and eat snow in winter when they can't find water to drink. Romans used Yak tails to swat flies and yaks are still kept for their milk today.

Yapock

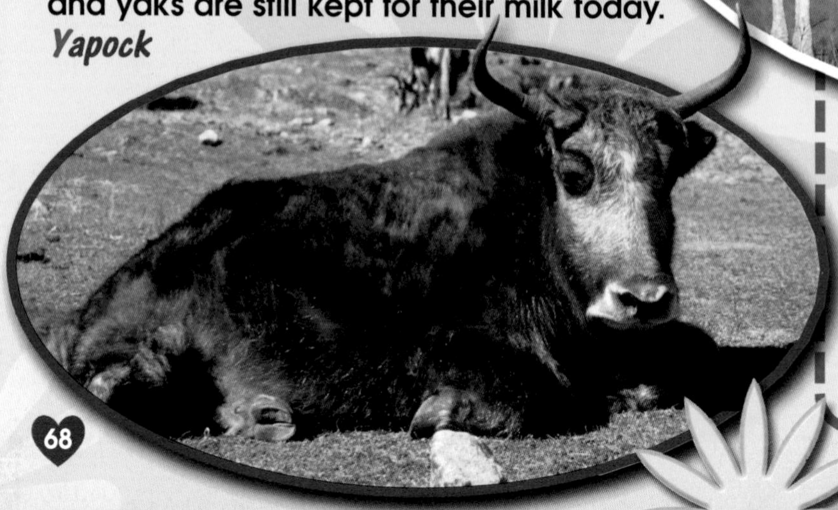

Zebra

Zebras communicate by moving their ears and tails, as well as by squealing and braying. They can rotate their ears without moving their bodies to listen out for danger!

Zorilla

Sun Or Moon?

Some of these animals prefer to work and play during the day and some at night. Can you work out which is which and tick the sun or moon boxes?

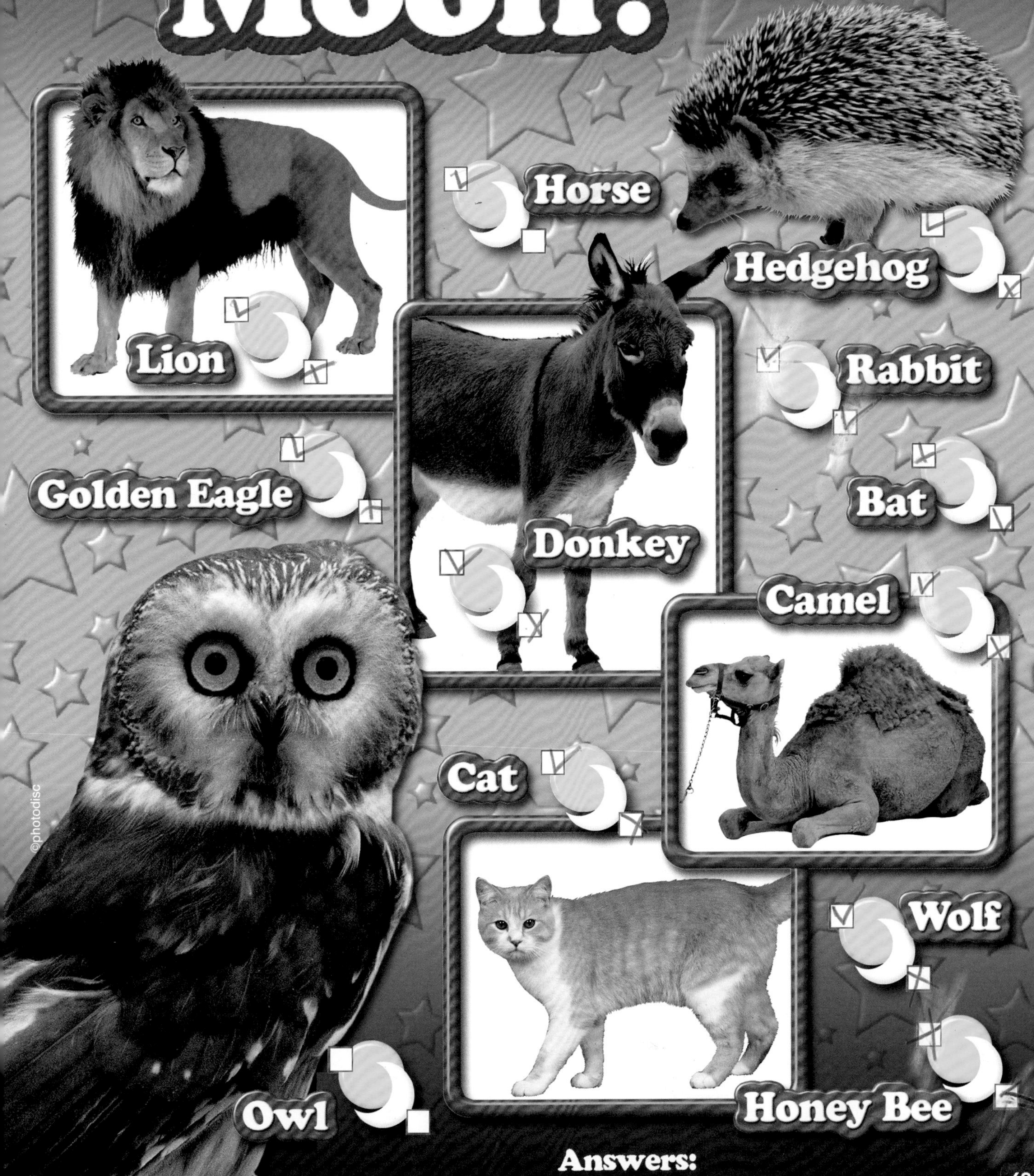
Horse
Hedgehog
Lion
Rabbit
Golden Eagle
Bat
Donkey
Camel
Cat
Wolf
Owl
Honey Bee
©photodisc

Answers:

Moon: Bat, Owl, Cat, Wolf, Hedgehog, Lion Sun: Honey Bee, Camel, Donkey, Rabbit, Golden Eagle

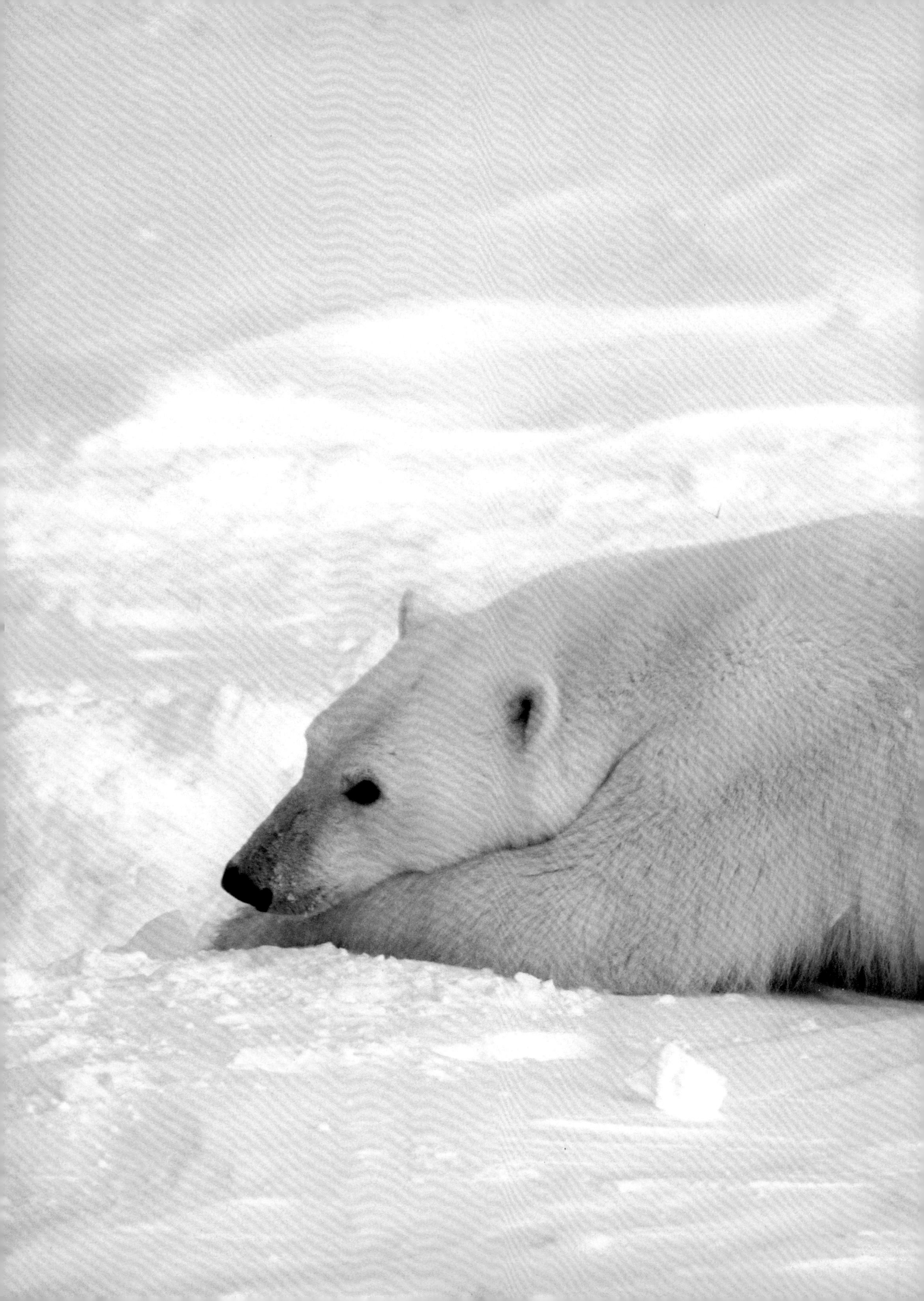